AM I BOVVERED?

THE CATHERINE TATE SHOW SCRIPTS

SERIES 1 & 2

FOURTH ESTATE • LONDON

First published in Great Britain in 2006 by Fourth Estate
An imprint of HarperCollinsPublishers
77-85 Fulham Palace Road, London W6 8JB
www.4thestate.co.uk

The Catherine Tate Show Series 1
A Tiger Aspect production for the BBC
© BBC MMIV

The Catherine Tate Show Series 2
A Tiger Aspect production for the BBC
© Tiger Aspect Productions MMV

1

Book authors: Tiger Aspect & Catherine Tate. Script authors: Catherine Tate, Derrin Litten, Aschlin Ditta, Mathew Horne, Arthur Mathews, Jenny Lecoat, Gordon Anderson and the Cast. The moral rights of the authors to be identified has been asserted by them in accordance with the Copyright, Designs and Patents Act 1988

A catalogue record for this book is available from the British Library

ISBN-13 978-0-00-724218-4
ISBN-10 0-00-724218-2

Photographs © BBC 2004 and © Tiger Aspect 2005
BBC Logo is a trademark of the British Broadcasting Corporation and is used under licence, © BBC 1996.

Typeset in Futura by EstuaryEnglish
Printed in Great Britain by Butler and Tanner Ltd, Frome

HOW VERY DARE YOU...

CONTENTS
SERIES 1

1

2

SERIES 2

THE CATHERINE TATE SHOW

SCRIPTS

SERIES 1

1

SERIES 1   EPISODE 1

OPENING TITLES / THEME MUSIC

FRIGHTENED WOMAN CEREAL

MARGARET AND MICHAEL ARE EATING BREAKFAST IN THE KITCHEN.
MICHAEL TURNS A PAGE OF HIS NEWSPAPER.

MARGARET	(SCREAMS)
	SHE COMPOSES HERSELF. MICHAEL PUTS HIS COFFEE CUP INTO ITS SAUCER.
MARGARET	(SCREAMS)
	SHE COMPOSES HERSELF AGAIN. MICHAEL TAKES A BITE OF TOAST.
MARGARET	(SCREAMS) Jesus Christ! It's like Piccadilly Circus in here.
	MARGARET POURS MILK ONTO HER RICE KRISPIES. THEY MAKE A SLIGHT POPPING SOUND.
MARGARET	(SCREAMS)

NOT DRUNK ENOUGH

CLAIRE AND JAMES ARE WALKING HOME AFTER A NIGHT OUT.

CLAIRE	Well, here we are then.
JAMES	Well, thanks for a lovely evening.
CLAIRE	No, no, thank you ... Well, goodnight.
JAMES	Night.
	JAMES GOES TO KISS CLAIRE. SHE TURNS HER FACE AWAY AND HE CAN ONLY KISS HER CHEEK. SHE HEADS FOR HER FRONT DOOR.
JAMES	Claire?
CLAIRE	Yes?
JAMES	You know, I don't ... I don't really feel like going home now. Is ... is there any chance of another drink ...
CLAIRE	James.
JAMES	... or cup of coffee?

13

CLAIRE	James, I know you want to come in and I know you probably want more than just a drink or a cup of coffee, it's just that I'm not drunk enough.
JAMES	What's wrong, Claire, don't ... don't you like me?
CLAIRE	Of course I like you, I'm just not drunk enough to find you attractive.
JAMES	Oh.
CLAIRE	I really want to be drunk enough.
JAMES	Well why aren't you drunk now?
CLAIRE	I am drunk now. I can hardly stand up. I'm just not drunk enough.
JAMES	Is there anything I can do?
CLAIRE	No. Because you're just not attractive.
JAMES	But I took you to the Munich Beer Festival.
CLAIRE	I know. I thought that would be it, and I tried. I drank my own body weight in German beer ... I was completely out of my tree the whole time we were there. I got arrested ... twice ... but it still wasn't enough.
JAMES	Maybe, maybe you'll never be drunk enough.
CLAIRE	Oh James, I do like you. If only I could get so spectacularly pissed I just wasn't aware of what you looked like.
JAMES	Hang on, there's ... there's an operation you can have which allows more alcohol into your bloodstream.
CLAIRE	James, no. My liver's wrecked as it is. I've drunk so much to try and find you attractive, the doctors say I may be dead within a year ... Goodnight, James.
	SHE TURNS TO GO.
JAMES	Claire ...
	HE FUMBLES IN HIS POCKET AND BRINGS OUT A CAN OF SPECIAL BREW, WHICH HE PRESENTS TO CLAIRE.
	... Give me a call.

LAUREN BING BING

LAUREN AND HER FRIENDS ARE ON A TRAIN.

LAUREN	Did you see Beyoncé last night on the television?
RYAN	Yeah, man. She is well fit.
LAUREN	That's a well nice song.
RYAN	Yeah, she's fit as well.
LIESE	She's better now she's left Destiny's, don't you think?
RYAN	Much better. But the other two were fit, man.
LIESE	Yeah, I love that tune.
LAUREN	Yeah right, she's well bing bing.
RYAN	What?
LAUREN	I said Beyoncé is well bing bing.
LIESE	What is she, mate?
LAUREN	She's bing bing.
RYAN	It's bling bling, mate, bling bling.
LAUREN	What?
LIESE	Bling bling.
RYAN	Bing bing! That is bad.
LAUREN	Am I bovvered?
RYAN	That is funny, man.
LAUREN	Am I bovvered though?
RYAN	Take the shame, man.
LAUREN	No, 'cos I ain't bovvered.
RYAN	You've shown yourself up there though, innit?
LAUREN	No I ain't because I ain't bovvered.
RYAN	Because that is funny though, innit?
LAUREN	No it ain't actually.
RYAN	Well look, just relax, all right.
LAUREN	Don't tell me what to do.
RYAN	Come on, relax about it.
LAUREN	Are you telling me what to do?

RYAN	No, I'm just saying don't worry about it.
LAUREN	Are you disrespecting me?
RYAN	No I'm not, I'm just ...
LAUREN	Are you disrespecting me, though?
RYAN	No I'm not disrespecting you, I just ...
LAUREN	You're disrespecting me.
RYAN	No, wait a minute, I'm ...
LAUREN	No, because you're disrespecting me.
RYAN	I'm not disrespecting you, just chill out, man.
LIESE	It was funny though.
LAUREN	Are you stupid?
LIESE	No, I'm just saying that ...
LAUREN	Are you stupid though?
LIESE	I'm just laughing.
LAUREN	Are you stupid or something?
LIESE	Look, I'm just laughing.
LAUREN	Why don't you shut up though?
LIESE	I'm not laughing at you or nothing.
LAUREN	Why don't you shut up though?
LIESE	Because it's just funny, ain't it?
LAUREN	Did I ask you to shut up?
LIESE	Yeah I know, but ...
LAUREN	Well shut up then.
LIESE	Well yeah, but ...
LAUREN	But I don't care though.
RYAN	Come on, man.
LAUREN	But do I care though?
RYAN	Yeah, but you can't ...
LAUREN	But I don't care.
RYAN	But I'm not saying ...
LAUREN	I don't care.

RYAN	But wait ...
LAUREN	I ain't bovvered.
RYAN	But we ...
LAUREN	I'm not bovvered.
RYAN	Come on.
LAUREN	I don't care.
RYAN	Well it's ...
LAUREN	I don't care, mate.

LAUREN AND RYAN TALKING OVER EACH OTHER:

RYAN	It's just that ... That's not...
LAUREN	I don't give ... care ... bovvered ... give ...
RYAN	You can't ... When I ... You can't ... The thing is ...
LAUREN	Mate. I ain't bovvered.

LAUREN'S PHONE RINGS.

RYAN	I think I can hear your phone binging, mate.

BOTOX BABE

WE'RE ON THE SET OF AN AMERICAN COURTROOM DRAMA.

BOTOX BABE	Are they gonna put Bobby on the stand?
BRANDON	Hard to say, he's a kid, it's a gamble. Sometimes it pays off.
BOTOX BABE	He's just a little boy.
BRANDON	He's the only eyewitness the prosecution have.
BOTOX BABE	I don't want to put him through that.
BRANDON	Well then you'd better start telling me the truth.
BOTOX BABE	I am telling you the truth.
BRANDON	No you're not. In fact you haven't given me a straight answer since this trial began. Now if you want your ass to rot in jail for the rest of your life, that's fine, because that's just where you're headed ... Erin, until you start telling me what really happened, I can't defend you one way or the other. Did you kill your husband?

ARE THEY GONNA PU

BOBBY ON THE STAND?

BOTOX BABE	No ... But I tried to. And at the time I meant it.
	CLAPPERBOARD IS VISIBLE.
DIRECTOR	(OUT OF VIEW) Okay, guys, that's a wrap. Same set-up tomorrow.
VOICES OFF	No problem.
	CLAPPERBOARD IS VISIBLE AS ACTION RESUMES THE FOLLOWING DAY.
CLAPPERMAN	(OUT OF VIEW) 171 take 1.
DIRECTOR	(OUT OF VIEW) And action.
BRANDON	Did you kill your husband?
BOTOX BABE	No ... But I tried to. And at the time I meant it.
	ACTRESS TURNS TO CAMERA. SINCE THE LAST SHOOT SHE HAS OBVIOUSLY HAD COSMETIC SURGERY AND NOW HAS HUGE PUFFY LIPS.
BRANDON	Why?
BOTOX BABE	You know why.
BRANDON	Don't say that.
BOTOX BABE	I can't live like this any more.
BRANDON	Erin, this wasn't the way to do this, this is wrong.
BOTOX BABE	Don't tell me what I'm feeling is wrong.
BRANDON	Erin, don't.
BOTOX BABE	Look at me and tell me you don't feel it too.
BRANDON	(HE LOOKS DIRECTLY AT HER AND APPEARS SLIGHTLY DISORIENTATED. HE STANDS UP AND ASKS THE DIRECTOR) You know what, is this working? Is this ... is this right, it ... it seemed different yesterday? Er, was yesterday different? It felt different yesterday. Er, is it just me? It's me. It's fine, it's me ... Yeah, okay, I'm sorry, let's ... let's go again. Um ...
BRANDON	Erin, this wasn't the way to do this, this is wrong.
BOTOX BABE	Don't tell me what I'm feeling is wrong.
BRANDON	Erin, don't.
BOTOX BABE	Look at me and tell me you don't feel it too.
BRANDON	(HE LOOKS DIRECTLY AT HER AGAIN AND FALTERS) It's probably me, but is ... is this working? It ... is anybody worried?
BOTOX BABE	I'm not worried.
BRANDON	Is anybody worried?

VOICES OFF	No ... no ...
DIRECTOR	(OUT OF VIEW) Well let's go for the kiss, and ...

BRANDON LEANS TOWARDS THE ACTRESS, LOOKING CONFUSED AND DISGUSTED. HE CLOSES HIS EYES AND MOVES IN FOR THE KISS.

OLD WOMAN HOME HELP

THE OLD WOMAN'S GRANDSON ARRIVES AND LOOKS INTO THE EMPTY LIVING ROOM.

GRANDSON	Hello, Nan.

THE OLD WOMAN EMERGES FROM THE KITCHEN.

OLD WOMAN	There he is.
GRANDSON	You all right?
OLD WOMAN	Come up and see me?
GRANDSON	Yeah.
OLD WOMAN	Come up and see me, ain't ya?
GRANDSON	Yeah.
OLD WOMAN	Yeah, I noticed that. 'Ere, is it cold outside?
GRANDSON	Er, not very.
OLD WOMAN	I can tell it's cold outside 'cos it's cold in here, see. It's gotta be cold outside if it's cold in 'ere, innit? I mean, it stands to reason, don't it? If it's cold in here it's gotta be cold outside, and it is cold in here, it must be cold outside. Put a couple of bars on that fire if you like, darling.
GRANDSON	No, I'm all right actually, Nan.
OLD WOMAN	I don't mind, go on. Put a couple of bars on that fire, warm yourself up. (HER GRANDSON TURNS ON THE FIRE.) Huh! That's it. Hah!

SHE SITS DOWN, PANTING.

Ain't it hot?

Cor, I'm roasting! ... Oh I can't breathe in here, it's so warm ... Oh I'll have to take a pair of these tights off ...

HER GRANDSON GETS UP TO TURN THE FIRE OFF.

That's it. 'Ere, 'ere, she was up 'ere today, weren't she?

GRANDSON	Who's that?
OLD WOMAN	Home help.
GRANDSON	Oh good.
OLD WOMAN	Yeah, Latka something, innit?
GRANDSON	Elena.
OLD WOMAN	Who is it?
GRANDSON	Her name's Elena.
OLD WOMAN	Yeah, yeah, she's from, er ... she's from somewhere, ain't she?
GRANDSON	Is she?
OLD WOMAN	Yeah. Oh yeah, definitely, yeah. What is it? Czechoslovakia innit, or something ... Bulgaria ... ahhh, it's one of them oddmark countries anyway.
GRANDSON	Poland.
OLD WOMAN	Who is it?
GRANDSON	She's from Poland.
OLD WOMAN	Yeah, well I don't like her and that's it.
GRANDSON	Oh God.
OLD WOMAN	I said to her, 'look, darling, I'm not being funny, I don't mean nothing by it, but I don't want you coming up here no more if you don't mind.'
GRANDSON	Oh Nan, you didn't.
OLD WOMAN	She said to me, 'Mrs Taylor, you mustn't be so proud.' I said, 'what you talking about?' She said, 'd'you not want me coming up here no more because you feel your independence slipping away?' I said, 'no, I don't want you coming up here no more because you're a fucking thief!'
GRANDSON	Nan, she's not stealing from you.
OLD WOMAN	What you talking about? Of course she is. I watch her when she thinks I ain't looking. 'Andfuls of gear she takes.
GRANDSON	No she doesn't.
OLD WOMAN	'I'm just going to do some ironing for ya.' 'Oh all right, love,' I say. She was stuffing 'em in her bag. It's a wonder I've got a stitch of clothing to call me own.
GRANDSON	She's not taking your clothes.
OLD WOMAN	She's nicking me food an' all, ain't she?

GRANDSON	I doubt it.
OLD WOMAN	She's nicking me food. I mean, I wouldn't mind, I don't begrudge 'em having something to eat ... Nah. I always say to her, 'would you like a nice corned beef sandwich now you're here, love?' 'Oh, no thank ya,' she says. Then when me back's turned she's fucking shovelling it down her.
GRANDSON	She's from Social Services.
OLD WOMAN	Cunning little bastard!
GRANDSON	She'll probably make a complaint about you now.
OLD WOMAN	Good. Let her. Dirty low life! (CACKLES)
GRANDSON	It's not funny, Nan.
OLD WOMAN	Oh shut up, you. You give me earache you do.
GRANDSON	Nan, seriously, you can't go around making complaints about people when they've done nothing wrong.
OLD WOMAN	Ah-ah-ah-ah, it's me programme. Oh it's on now. Oh I love this, I do. Oh, you seen this? That fat girl off *Emmerdale*, huge big frame.
GRANDSON	*You've Been Framed*?
OLD WOMAN	Yeah.
	You seen it? Oh, she goes round with a cine camera and she takes pictures and then she shows it to you on the telly. Oh it's comical, it is. Mind you, she don't half know some fucking stupid people.
	Have a look. (CACKLES)

AGA SAGA WOMAN EGG

THOMAS AND CHLOE ARE IN THE KITCHEN, EATING BOILED EGGS.
MUMMY WALKS IN.

THOMAS	Mummy, I've just dropped the egg cleaver on the floor.
MUMMY	Thomas, you really are a silly sausage. Pop it on the side and Alice can put it in the dishwasher when she gets home from walking Maximus.
THOMAS	But Mummy, you don't understand, Chloe hasn't topped her egg yet.
	DOOM MUSIC.
MUMMY	Oh, crisis. Well pass me the phone, Thomas, maybe we can catch her. Well come on, quick sticks. Well that silly girl never has her mobile phone

	turned on ... Oh, Alice, what luck we've caught you. Look, we're having a bit of a situation right here.
CHLOE	Mummy, my egg can't breathe, I think it's going to discolour.
	DOOM MUSIC.
MUMMY	Look, darling, I know, just calm down. Mummy's taking care of it ... Alice, what is the shortest cycle on the dishwasher? ... Six minutes. Oh salvation. And how soon can you get here?
THOMAS	Tell her to take public transport.
MUMMY	Oh that's good thinking, Thomas. Alice, take a taxi and get here as soon as you can.
CHLOE	Mummy, my egg.
MUMMY	And call the school and tell them Thomas and Chloe won't be in today. Now calm down, we're going to be okay here.
CHLOE	Mummy, will Alice be okay?
THOMAS	She's bound to worry about us, she's only human. But there's nothing we can do about that right now.
CHLOE	No. Do you think we're cursed?
MUMMY	Oh my God, we're all going to die!
THOMAS	Now I don't want you girls to panic. We're just going to have to be brave and sit this one out.
	DOOM MUSIC

NEW PARENTS CAR PARTY / 1

A CAR PULLS UP IN FRONT OF A HOUSE. TWO PEOPLE ARE WAVING FROM THE FRONT DOOR.

KAREN	(FROM BACK SEAT) Oh look, they're at the door.
	A BABY CRIES. SHE IS IN HER CAR SEAT IN THE FRONT PASSENGER SEAT OF THE CAR.
KAREN	Turn the engine back on.
BEN	What?
KAREN	Turn it on.

THE BABY STOPS CRYING. KAREN WINDS DOWN HER WINDOW.

NICK	Happy birthday! Food's nearly ready. How about a drink?
BEN	That'd be great.
LIZ	(LAUGHS) Do ... d'you want us to bring it out?
KAREN	Um, yeah.
BEN	It's just she's only just this minute gone off. We don't want to risk it.
LIZ	Well, why don't we just bring her inside. You can put her in our room.
KAREN	Are you mad? She's asleep, we can't move her, that's insane.
LIZ	Well, don't worry, it'll be another few minutes. I've done us a trout dauphinoise.
NICK	Yeah, thank God for Jamie Oliver, eh. Changed our lives.

NICK AND LIZ DISAPPEAR INSIDE.

BEN	I think I'll just pop in and use their loo. Shall I see you in there?
KAREN	No, because, um, d'you remember that baby I had six months ago? Well, for the first time in thirty-six hours she appears to be asleep, and if I move her she'll probably wake up, and when she wakes up I'm likely to kill you and then kill myself. So no, I don't think I will see you inside.

HOW MANY HOW MUCH WEIGHT

KATE AND ELLEN ARE WORKING AT THEIR DESKS. ELLEN IS EATING A SLICE OF CAKE.

KATE	Is that cake?
ELLEN	Yeah, it's Sarah's birthday cake.
KATE	Oh, I thought that was cake.
ELLEN	It's lovely.
KATE	Is everyone having cake? What is it, chocolate and buttercream?
ELLEN	Chocolate fudge.
KATE	Chocolate fudge cake. I used to love that.
ELLEN	Hmm?
KATE	I said I used to love that.
ELLEN	Sorry, do you mind if I just finish this email?

KATE	I'm not having any cake ... I'm cutting down.
ELLEN	Sorry, do you want me to move it. I didn't mean to tempt you.
KATE	No, no, no, no, it's fine, it's fine, because I'm in the zone. And when I'm in the zone I'm in the zone.
ELLEN	God you're lucky. I haven't got any willpower.
KATE	I've been really strict with myself since last Monday.
ELLEN	Well done.
KATE	It's just dropping off.
ELLEN	Good for you.
KATE	Guess how much weight I've lost?
ELLEN	Oh!
KATE	How much weight have I lost since last Monday?
ELLEN	I've no idea.
KATE	Okay, have a guess.
ELLEN	I don't know.
KATE	Come on, look at me, have a guess.
ELLEN	Well, I didn't think you needed to lose any weight.
KATE	Boring, whatever. How much, just guess.
ELLEN	It's difficult to say.
KATE	Don't be annoying, just guess how much weight I've lost.
ELLEN	I wouldn't like to.
KATE	Just guess.
ELLEN	A stone and a half?
KATE	A stone and a half! A stone and a half in a week!
ELLEN	Oh yeah. Of course. Ten pounds?
KATE	Ten pounds! I haven't got dysentery.
	Come on!
ELLEN	Five pounds.
KATE	Right, forget it.
ELLEN	Three? Three pounds ... You've lost three pounds.
KATE	I've lost two pounds.

ELLEN	That's a good start.
KATE	Yes. It is.
ELLEN	Keep up the good work.

KATE GRABS THE CAKE AND SHOVES IT INTO HER MOUTH.

KATE	Happy now?

FRIGHTENED WOMAN MOBILE

MARGARET IS IN THE BEDROOM.

MARGARET	Michael?

MICHAEL ENTERS.

MICHAEL	Yes? You all right?
MARGARET	I can't find my mobile.
MICHAEL	Oh.
MARGARET	I had it just a second ago. It's like Beirut in here. Can you call it from yours?
MICHAEL	Er, yes. I don't know, what are we gonna do with you, eh?
MARGARET	Ssssh! Just let me listen.

PHONE RINGS.

MARGARET	(SCREAMS) Gosh, it made me jump.

NEW PARENTS CAR PARTY / 2

BEN AND KAREN ARE EATING THEIR SOUP IN THE CAR.

KAREN	Stop slurping. God! Soup's so bloody noisy. They wouldn't make soup if they had a baby of their own.
BEN	It's Jamie Oliver.
KAREN	Well it's too bloody noisy. And it could do with some pepper.

NICK AND LIZ KNOCK ON THE CAR WINDOW. BEN'S SOUP SPILLS INTO HIS LAP AND HE SCREAMS SILENTLY. KAREN WINDS DOWN THE WINDOW.

BEN	That was lovely.
LIZ	We brought you a present.
KAREN	Oh, thank you. Daddy, could you just take that?

SHE PASSES IT TO BEN.

LIZ	Will you be joining us for the main course?
NICK	Of your birthday lunch?
BEN	Er ...
KAREN	Um, well, it depends. Is it going to be noisy?
LIZ	Sorry?
KAREN	Well, the main course, is it very loud?
LIZ	Well it's trout, but it's dead.

KAREN PASSES HER SOUP BOWL THROUGH THE WINDOW.

KAREN	Thank you.

HOW MANY HOW MUCH EXTRAS

KATE AND ELLEN ARE WORKING AT THEIR DESKS.

KATE	I love Easter, don't you? Hot cross buns, Easter eggs.
ELLEN	I always eat too many.
KATE	Those big old biblical epics on the telly.
ELLEN	They're a bit long for me.
KATE	No, no, that's the best bit. Takes up the whole afternoon. *Ben Hur* – I'll never get enough of that. Charlton Heston, all those extras. I watched a documentary about the making of it.
ELLEN	Did you?
KATE	Hmm. Guess how many extras were in that film?
ELLEN	Oh ...
KATE	How many extras do you reckon are in *Ben Hur*?
ELLEN	I've never seen it all the way through.
KATE	You wouldn't have to, just guess.
ELLEN	I have no idea.

KATE	You'll never guess.
ELLEN	Exactly.
KATE	But try.
ELLEN	Jesus Christ!
KATE	He was a speaking part. How many extras?
ELLEN	I don't have a clue.
KATE	Come on, how many bloody extras?
ELLEN	I don't know.
KATE	It doesn't matter, just have a guess.
ELLEN	I can't think.
KATE	It's just a bit of fun. Guess.
ELLEN	A quarter of a million.
KATE	A quarter of a million, in one film! Half a million sandals!
ELLEN	A thousand?
KATE	I don't think so.
ELLEN	Four thousand.
KATE	Right, it broke the world record for most extras in a film. How many?
ELLEN	Thirty thousand?
KATE	Not that many.
ELLEN	Ten thousand?
KATE	Eight. Eight thousand.
ELLEN	Eight thousand. Gosh, that's loads.
KATE	Yes it is.
ELLEN	How many do you think there were in *Gladiator*?
KATE	Oh, get a life!

PAUL & SAM SPANIEL

PAUL AND SAM ARE IN BED, READING.

SAM	Did you speak to Lisa today?
PAUL	Nah.
SAM	You didn't speak to Lisa at work?
PAUL	Nah, I ain't see her.
SAM	No?
PAUL	Not Lisa, no.
SAM	Oh ... Not Lisa ... oh yeah, Lisa.
PAUL	Lisa who?
SAM	Dunno. I never knew her surname ... What is Lisa's surname?
PAUL	Lisa who?
SAM	I dunno.
PAUL	Give her a ring.
SAM	Who? Lisa?
PAUL	Yeah.
SAM	No, no, I don't like to. I mean, she might not even be called Lisa.

THEY GO BACK TO THEIR READING.

SAM	I might get us a dog.
PAUL	What, now?
SAM	No! Weekend.
PAUL	What do we want to get a dog for?
SAM	Well they're good company, ain't they?
PAUL	Yeah, that's true.
	What sort of dog we gonna get?
SAM	I thought one of them ones with the ears.
PAUL	They've all got ears, babe.
SAM	No, no, the ones with the big floppy ears. Prince Charles spaniel.
PAUL	Oh yeah, oh they're sweet, ain't they?
SAM	Yeah ... 'Ere, I just thought.

PAUL	What?
SAM	That's a bit much, innit?
PAUL	What?
SAM	Calling a spaniel Prince Charles just 'cos it's got big ears.
PAUL	He's probably used to it by now.
SAM	Yeah.
PAUL	No! I'll tell you what, it's not Prince Charles, it's King Charles.
SAM	No, no, he's still definitely only a prince.
PAUL	No, the dog with the big ears is called a King Charles spaniel, not a Prince Charles spaniel ...

THEY LAUGH SILENTLY.

PAUL	What are you like?
SAM	Don't, I'm gonna pass out!
PAUL	What am I gonna do with you?
SAM	Oh my God. Why does it always happen to me?
PAUL	You are a one off.
SAM	That was classic me.

THEY LAUGH SILENTLY.

SAM	Pass me that phone before I die.
PAUL	Who you ringing? ... You are mental.
SAM	Shelley?
PAUL	Ohhh! 'Ere we go.
SAM	(ON PHONE) Shelley, you are not gonna believe this ...

NEW PARENTS CAR PARTY / 3

BEN AND KAREN ARE EATING THEIR MAIN COURSE IN THE CAR.

BEN	You'd better open the present.
KAREN	Don't you dare, don't you dare. Just open the card.
BEN	It's rude.
KAREN	Just open the card.

BEN OPENS THE CARD. 'CONGRATULATIONS' BY CLIFF RICHARD BLARES OUT AS A BIRTHDAY GREETING. HE SHUTS THE CARD IN A PANIC. NICK AND LIZ CLIMB INTO THE BACK SEAT.

LIZ	We thought it would be probably best if we joined you.
KAREN	Oh, this is lovely.
LIZ	Well it's surprisingly easy to ...
KAREN	Sssh, could you just keep it down a bit because we've only just got her off.
NICK	Oh, don't mind us.

BEN UNCORKS A BOTTLE OF WINE.

KAREN	Are you doing this on purpose?
BEN	Karen, it's a bottle of wine, what am I supposed to do?
KAREN	Well maybe you could slap her in the face and wake her up properly.
NICK	Oh, did you like the card?

HE OPENS THE CARD AND THE SONG BLARES OUT. KAREN GRABS THE CARD AND RIPS IT UP.

LIZ	Well, thanks for a lovely evening.
NICK	Yes, thanks so much. Next time you should come over to our car.

NICK AND LIZ LEAVE THE CAR. THE DOOR SLAMS, RE-ACTIVATING THE CARD. THE BABY WAKES UP SCREAMING.

FRIGHTENED WOMAN TOAST

MARGARET IS IN THE KITCHEN, POURING HERSELF A GLASS OF ORANGE JUICE. THE TOAST POPS UP.

MARGARET	(SCREAMS)

SHE DROPS HER GLASS, THEN CALMLY BUTTERS THE PIECE OF TOAST.

ENIGMATIC COP SCRAPYARD / 1

TWO PLAIN CLOTHES POLICE OFFICERS ARE IN A SCRAPYARD, STANDING NEXT TO A BODY.

AMANDA	They say death has many faces, Whittaker.
WHITTAKER	Do they, Ma'am?
AMANDA	Oh yeah. Facially, you know ... it's a thing ... What's the name of this joker?
WHITTAKER	Barry Wheatley, Ma'am. Used to work for the Anderson Brothers.
AMANDA	How do you know he still doesn't?
WHITTAKER	Because he's dead, Ma'am.
AMANDA	Is he?
WHITTAKER	Yes, Ma'am.
AMANDA	Yeah, but is he?
WHITTAKER	Yes, Ma'am.
AMANDA	Yeah, but is he really?
WHITTAKER	Yes, Ma'am, he's definitely dead.
AMANDA	Let's look at this from a different angle.
WHITTAKER	I don't quite know what you mean, Ma'am.
AMANDA	Suppose for one moment, Whittaker, suppose none of this exists. You, me, we could all be figments of someone's imagination.
WHITTAKER	Whose imagination, Ma'am?
AMANDA	Could be yours, Whittaker, could be mine. Could be old Mrs Dawkins who runs a pie and mash shop down the Old Kent Road.
WHITTAKER	But I'm not exactly sure where you're going with this, Ma'am?
AMANDA	It took Adam and Eve one minute to fall from grace in the Garden of Eden, and yet growing out a layered bob can take forever.
	You haven't got a clue where I'm going with this, have you, Whittaker?
WHITTAKER	Well ...
AMANDA	(SINGING) 'I'm gonna use my arms, I'm gonna use my legs, gonna use my style, gonna use my senses, gonna use my fingers, gonna use my, my imagination, whooo, 'cos I'm gonna make you see, there's nobody else here, no one like me, I'm special ...' Whittaker?

WHITTAKER	(JOINING IN RELUCTANTLY) 'Special.'
AMANDA	'So special.'
WHITTAKER	'Special.'
AMANDA	'I'm gonna have some of your attention, give it to me.'
WHITTAKER	'Ooooh,
	Why do you look so sad?'
AMANDA	Whittaker!

HOW MANY HOW MUCH HOUSE

KATE AND ELLEN ARE WORKING AT THEIR DESKS.

KATE	Oh my God, they just accepted our offer.
ELLEN	What offer?
KATE	On the flat we want.
ELLEN	Oh well done.
KATE	They were asking 165,000 for it. Guess how much we got it for?
ELLEN	I don't know.
KATE	Just guess.
ELLEN	Er, one six three five hundred?
KATE	Yeah.

ENIGMATIC COP SCRAPYARD / 2

AMANDA AND WHITTAKER ARE SITTING IN THE CAR, NOISILY EATING CHOCOLATE BISCUITS. AMANDA OCCASIONALLY GLANCES DISPARAGINGLY AT A SHEEPISH WHITTAKER.

END CREDITS

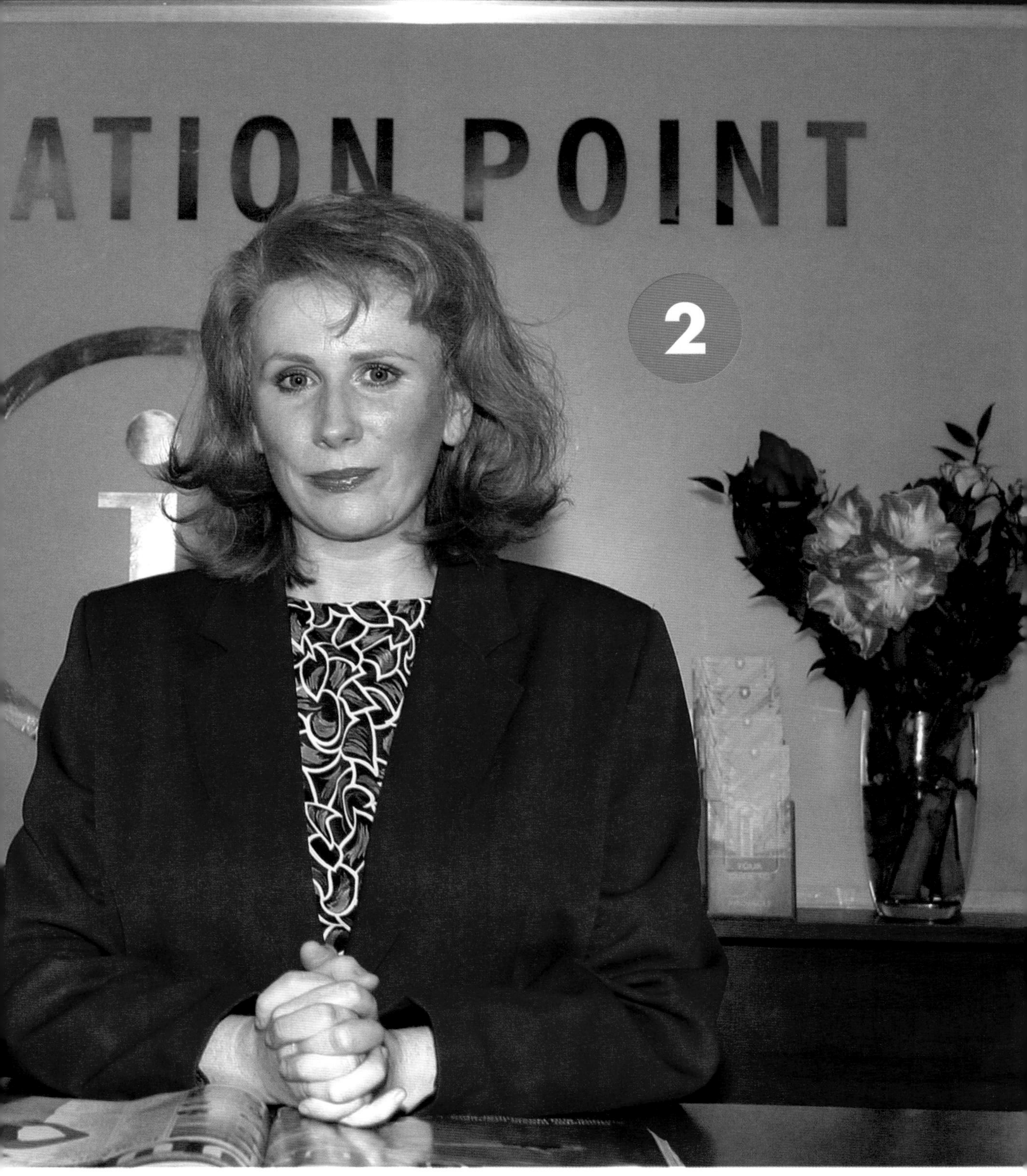
ATION POINT
2

SERIES 1   EPISODE 2

OPENING TITLES / THEME MUSIC

FRIGHTENED WOMAN   BIRTHDAY

MARGARET AND MICHAEL ARE IN THE LIVING ROOM. MARGARET OPENS A BIRTHDAY CARD.

MARGARET   It's from Martin and Vicky.

SHE OPENS ANOTHER CARD. SHE LAUGHS AND SHOWS IT TO MICHAEL.

MARGARET   Typical, Paula.

SHE OPENS A THIRD CARD. AN IMAGE POPS OUT OF THE CENTRE.

MARGARET   (SCREAMS) Oh, it's from your mum.

INFO WOMAN   LOST MOTHER

STELLA IS BEHIND THE INFORMATION COUNTER OF A LARGE SHOPPING CENTRE, READING A MAGAZINE. A WORRIED-LOOKING SHOPPER APPROACHES HER.

JUDY   Excuse me, I've lost my mum.

STELLA   Oh I'm really sorry to hear that. It just creeps up at you at the most peculiar times, doesn't it? Did she have a good innings?

JUDY   She's not dead, I just can't find her.

STELLA   Oh my God! (LAUGHS) Oh I'm sorry, I thought you meant ...

JUDY   It's okay, we ... we just got split up somewhere along the way.

STELLA   Oh I see.

GOES BACK TO READING MAGAZINE

JUDY   Sorry, is it possible to make an announcement?

STELLA   I don't see why not. What would you like to say about it?

JUDY   No, I mean, do you have a speaker system or something?

STELLA   A speaker system?

JUDY   Yes, to make an announcement about my mother.

STELLA   A speaker system to make an announcement about your mother. They'd

	probably think that was a bit of a waste of money, unless she gets lost here on a regular basis.
JUDY	Well, okay, do you have a meeting point?
STELLA	Well I know some people meet out the front near the bus stops but … they're mainly kids.
JUDY	No, I mean, do you have a meeting point for lost people?
STELLA	Well if they're lost they probably won't find it.
JUDY	She'll be eighty-three at the weekend, I … I don't know what to do.
STELLA	I wouldn't have a surprise party … She doesn't want any sudden shocks at that age, does she?
	Does she like muffins?
JUDY	What?
STELLA	You know those shops that sell muffins and cookies?
JUDY	I don't know, is there one of those shops on this floor?
STELLA	Oh, I'm not sure.
	SHE SNIFFS THE AIR.
	You can usually smell them, can't you?
JUDY	What, the muffins?
STELLA	No, old people.
TANNOY	Will customer Judy Wallis please make your way to the third floor café where your mother is waiting for you.
STELLA	Somebody must be lost.

BERNIE PHOTOCOPIER

BERNIE ENTERS SISTER'S OFFICE, CARRYING TWO MUGS.

BERNIE	You wanted to see me, Sister?
SISTER	Yes, come in, Bernie, sit down.
BERNIE	I've bought you a toffee-flavoured Choc-o-Lite, Sister, on the off chance.
SISTER	Not for me, thank you, Bernie.
BERNIE	Right, should I ask Mark if he wants one, only I'm not sure I could manage two. Unless this is gonna be a long meeting, in which case I might just get a Snickers from the machine as well.

SISTER	No, Bernie, just put the drinks on the desk and sit down.
BERNIE	Right. One of these has got three sugars in it ...

SHE PUTS MUGS ON DESK.

SISTER	Bernie, do you know why I've asked to see you today?
BERNIE	Would it be about last night?
SISTER	Yes, I'm afraid it is about last night ... It would seem your birthday stunt may have gone unnoticed had the Xerox machine not jammed. You can imagine Doctor Barker's ... shall we say, surprise ... when trying to photocopy his memos this morning he was presented with forty black and white A3 enlargements of your bottom.
BERNIE	Well, I can explain that, Sister, actually, you know, how that came about.
SISTER	Not only that, it now seems the copier has gone into shock and can print nothing but A3 enlargements of your bottom. Sister O'Brien is having to copy out the rotas by hand as we speak.
BERNIE	Right, I mean, I can explain that, Sister, no problem, you know, how that came about, like.
SISTER	Please, be my guest.
BERNIE	Right.

SHE SAYS NOTHING.

Oh, what now? Well, I mean, there was no harm done. You know what us girls are like when we get together. I bet you're a bit of a dark horse yourself when you get going, you know what I mean?

I didn't mean to upset anyone.

SISTER	Look at it from my position, Bernie. What am I supposed to tell Doctor Barker when he asks why there are several dozen copies of your backside circulating on various male wards?
BERNIE	It was just for the craic, Sister.
SISTER	Is that supposed to be funny, Bernie?
BERNIE	No, Sister.

SHE SUDDENLY GETS THE JOKE.

Oh my God – the crack!

SHE TAKES A SIP OF HER DRINK AND SNORTS WITH LAUGHTER.

Oh no, that's still too hot.

SISTER	We've also had a Mister Blackwood who's complained about you.
BERNIE	He's complained about me?
SISTER	Something you said while giving him a blanket bath ... something about a boat.
BERNIE	'Sweet mother of Jesus it's like trying to raise the Titanic.' (LAUGHS) I'm sorry, Sister.
SISTER	I really feel you've let us all down this time, Bernie, not just yourself. I'm afraid I've no choice but to give you a written warning.
BERNIE	(SINGING) 'Raindrops and roses and whiskers on kittens, Bright copper kettles and warm woollen mittens, Brown paper packages tied up with string, These are a few of my favourite things.'
SISTER	Bernie!
BERNIE	'When the dog bites, When the bee stings ...'
SISTER	Bernie, Bernie, what are you doing?
BERNIE	I'm just trying to lighten the situation.
SISTER	Take these, make sure you read them, sign them both, keep one and hand the other in at the main office. Now if you'd like to get back to your work.

BERNIE GOES TO LEAVE, THEN SNEAKS BACK FOR HER DRINK. SHE TAKES A SIP.

BERNIE	Oh God, this one's yours.
SISTER	Get out!

BERNIE RUNS FOR THE DOOR.

FRIGHTENED WOMAN
POST-IT NOTE

MARGARET WALKS INTO HER OFFICE AND SITS DOWN AT HER DESK. A POST-IT NOTE FROM JULIE IS STUCK TO HER COMPUTER SCREEN.

MARGARET	(SCREAMS)

SHE PICKS UP HER PHONE AND DIALS.

Julie, it's Margaret. Did you want me?

OLD WOMAN CHARLES MANSON

THE OLD WOMAN EMERGES FROM THE KITCHEN AS HER GRANDSON ARRIVES.

OLD WOMAN	Is that you, darling?
GRANDSON	Hello, Nan.
OLD WOMAN	'Ere he is.
GRANDSON	You all right?
OLD WOMAN	Yeah, lovely. You come up and see me?
GRANDSON	Yeah.
OLD WOMAN	Come up and see me, ain't ya?
GRANDSON	Yeah.
OLD WOMAN	I noticed that. Oh you are a good boy. You are a darling child.
GRANDSON	'Ere, Nan?
OLD WOMAN	Yeah?
GRANDSON	You seen Jean lately?
OLD WOMAN	Who?
GRANDSON	Jean.
OLD WOMAN	Jean?
GRANDSON	Yeah, have you seen her?
OLD WOMAN	Jean who?
GRANDSON	Jean. Jean.
OLD WOMAN	Who's Jean?
GRANDSON	Well how many Jeans do you know?
OLD WOMAN	I don't know no Jeans.
GRANDSON	What d'you mean you don't know any Jeans. Jean from over the road. Jean Baker, you went to school with her mother.
OLD WOMAN	Oh yes. Is she called Jean?
GRANDSON	You know she is.
OLD WOMAN	What about her?
GRANDSON	Have you seen her?
OLD WOMAN	No. What's happened to her?

GRANDSON	Nothing's happened to her, I'm asking you if you've seen her lately.
OLD WOMAN	I ain't seen her.
GRANDSON	You've not seen Jean?
OLD WOMAN	No.
GRANDSON	You've not seen Jean from over the road?
OLD WOMAN	No.
GRANDSON	Are you sure?
OLD WOMAN	Course I'm sure, what's the matter with ya? I ain't seen no one, have I? I ain't seen a living soul, I ain't been outside me door.
GRANDSON	So you've definitely not seen Jean?
OLD WOMAN	Oh what are you, a fucking dunce or something?
	I haven't seen no fucking Jean, may God forgive me for swearing. Now you made me do that.
GRANDSON	All right.
OLD WOMAN	Well you're obsessed with the woman, ain't ya?
GRANDSON	Well, no, it's just that I saw her on my way over here and usually she's very friendly, but today she just ignored me. Are you sure you haven't seen her?
OLD WOMAN	Who?
GRANDSON	Jean.
OLD WOMAN	Oh yes, I seen her.
GRANDSON	I knew you had. What did you say to her?
OLD WOMAN	Ain't she got fat?
GRANDSON	Nan!
OLD WOMAN	Oh, ain't she fat, that woman. Ooh, you seen her lately? Oh she is a size. Great big walloping article. Oh, you seen it? She looks like an elephant walking along the street. Great big fat arse hanging off her. What a liberty. I shouldn't have to look at that. She's got a fat back an' all, ain't she? She's got a fat back, the woman. Great big fat dirty hairy sweating back. Oh no, terrible, innit? Oh that is very unfeminine on a woman. Ah, ah, ah, ah. Don't you say things like that about people. Oh, no. Not up my house, dear, no, no. She has got an eating disorder.
GRANDSON	Has she?

OLD WOMAN	Course she has, she can't fucking stop. (CACKLES)
GRANDSON	Nan, what did you say to her?
OLD WOMAN	What? I never said nothing to her.
GRANDSON	You didn't say anything?
OLD WOMAN	No.
GRANDSON	Nothing you might have forgotten?
OLD WOMAN	No, not me, dear.
GRANDSON	Nothing to upset her?
OLD WOMAN	No, no.
GRANDSON	Are you sure?
OLD WOMAN	Oh it's like a mental illness with you, innit? How many more times? On my first Holy Communion, by all the saints in Heaven, as God is my judge I never said nothing to her ... Except what you said.
GRANDSON	What?
OLD WOMAN	Well I just told her what you said, that's all.
GRANDSON	What d'you mean what I said, what you talking about?
OLD WOMAN	You know, what you said about her husband, that's all I said.
GRANDSON	I didn't say anything about her husband.
OLD WOMAN	Yes you did. You said her husband looks like a murderer. That's all I said.
GRANDSON	What? No I didn't.
OLD WOMAN	Now don't you lie to me, son. May I never move, you sat there and you said her husband looks like Charles Manson.
GRANDSON	I said her husband looks like Charles Bronson.
OLD WOMAN	Ohhh! I thought you said Manson. Only I see a programme about him. That's what made me think of it, see. You've seen what he's done, ain't ya? Oh, terrible, that is. That is dreadful.
GRANDSON	Oh my God.
OLD WOMAN	Well that's what I'm trying to tell ya! Stop talking about people. Mind your own business. Keep that out of it (POINTS TO NOSE) and keep that shut (POINTS TO MOUTH). I mean, the poor man, he can't help what he looks like, can he? I mean, all right, he's got a moustache, don't mean he's gonna fucking kill no one.

GRANDSON	I don't believe you, Nan.
OLD WOMAN	Oh, she was terribly upset when I told her that, the woman. Well it's not a nice thing to hear, is it, you know, and it was unexpected an' all, you see, that's what shocked her. And to top it all, I don't think she sees the resemblance herself. (CACKLES)

INFO WOMAN JUMPER

STELLA IS BEHIND THE INFORMATION COUNTER OF A LARGE SHOPPING CENTRE, READING A MAGAZINE. A SHOPPER APPROACHES HER.

SHOPPER	I've brought this top back, but the shop I bought it from has closed down.
STELLA	Oh, bad luck.
SHOPPER	What?
STELLA	I hate that, it's exactly the sort of thing that happens to me.
SHOPPER	Well, what am I supposed to do with it? It's the wrong size.
STELLA	You could try wearing it over your shoulders with the sleeves knotted.
SHOPPER	No, you don't understand, it's no good to me, I don't want it.
STELLA	Oh that's very kind ... Um, oh, I don't ... don't really think that would suit me.
SHOPPER	No, I want to take it back to the shop. Do you know where they've gone?
STELLA	Who's that?
SHOPPER	The people that run the shop.
STELLA	Well if the shop's closed down, they've probably just gone home.

THE WOMAN WALKS OFF.

PAUL & SAM CATALOGUE

PAUL AND SAM ARE IN THE BEDROOM, GETTING READY TO GO OUT.

SAM	You won't believe what's happened to me today.
PAUL	What?
SAM	Well, when I tell you this, that's it, you'll leave me.
PAUL	I'll pack my bags, shall I?
SAM	Yeah, you'd be right to.

PAUL	Come on, let's hear it.
SAM	This is a classic.
PAUL	What you gonna say?
SAM	When you left this morning, you said to me, didn't you, you said, 'what you got on for today?'
PAUL	That's right, yeah.
SAM	And I said, 'well I think I'll go out early, avoid the crowds,' because I wanted to take your Bermudas back to Marks's.
PAUL	Well what's happened?
SAM	I come back about twenty-five to twelve, and as I put the key in the door I've noticed something on the floor.
PAUL	What, on our floor?
SAM	Yeah, like a note or something.
PAUL	Well it couldn't have been the post.
SAM	No, course not.
PAUL	That came before I left.
SAM	Came before you left, didn't it? No, it was like a letter thing.
PAUL	Oh, not a love letter, was it?
SAM	Shut up, love letter!
PAUL	Oh I don't like the sound of this. Who was it? That George Clooney, I suppose?
SAM	Yeah, yeah, he was begging me to run away with him again.
PAUL	What d'you mean again? What, you run away with him before, did ya?
SAM	What?
PAUL	Eh?
SAM	Shut up, have I.
PAUL	Your face.
SAM	I bet I've gone all red now, ain't I?
PAUL	Oh look at you, you look like a beetroot, you do.
SAM	He won't want me now, will he?
PAUL	Not looking like that.
SAM	He'll say, not today, thanks, and send me home.

PAUL	Yeah, back to muggins here.
SAM	Oh you poor sod. It weren't really him. It was from the Post Office.
PAUL	What they want?
SAM	Well it was one of them 'we called today' things but you weren't here.
PAUL	No!
SAM	Yes! That's what I thought ... I thought we weren't expecting nothing, were we?
PAUL	I don't think so.
SAM	Yeah we were.
PAUL	Were we?
SAM	Have a think.
PAUL	I dunno.
SAM	You'll die when I tell ya.
PAUL	I can't think.
SAM	What have I been waiting for? What's the one thing I've been waiting to be delivered?
PAUL	Not your catalogue?
SAM	Me catalogue!
	THEY LAUGH SILENTLY.
PAUL	You ain't gone out the day they've delivered your catalogue?
SAM	Went out early, didn't I?
PAUL	Oh you make me die!
SAM	I should be locked up, shouldn't I?
PAUL	So what d'you do?
SAM	Well I've had to ring 'em up, ain't I?
PAUL	Oh what must they think?
SAM	They must think I'm a lunatic.
PAUL	What d'you say?
SAM	I said, oh I was so embarrassed. I said, 'look, I'm sorry but I weren't home when you came round my house this morning to deliver me catalogue.' I said, 'I've been waiting for it for ages, I can't believe I forgot. Only I went out early to run a few errands and it completely slipped me mind.' I said, 'you must think I'm mental.'

PAUL	What they say?
SAM	Well it was only one of them recorded voices, weren't it, and I didn't know.
PAUL	It weren't?
SAM	Yeah. I'm chatting away, ain't I, and then it said 'press two to speak to an operator.'
PAUL	What you talking to recorded voices for, babe?
SAM	I dunno.
	When I've realised I've gone off, ain't I? I couldn't stop, I was laughing so much.
PAUL	Oh I wish I'd been there.
SAM	Oh my God. When I finally got through to someone I said to the woman, 'don't laugh but I've been talking to that recorded voice thinking it was someone at the other end, only you came round to me house to deliver something and I'd gone out early not thinking.' She said, 'that's all right, we can come back tomorrow.' I've got off the phone, I've had to sit down I was so worn out.
PAUL	How are you not famous?
SAM	I genuinely do not know.

DRUNK ESTATE AGENT

A COUPLE ARE BEING SHOWN ROUND A PROPERTY BY THE SELLER AND THE ESTATE AGENT.

MALE BUYER	Oh this is lovely.
FEMALE BUYER	It's nice. It's very nice.
SELLER	Thank you. We think it's nice.
AGENT	Nice. It's certainly nice. It's very, very nice. I've just been out in the garden and I tell you something, they've made it very nice.
SELLER	Thank you. Well it was overgrown when we bought it, but Terry's very good with plants.
AGENT	Terry your husband? Aaahhhh!
AGENT	Right, fancy making an offer?
MALE BUYER	Huh, well, we haven't …

AGENT	It's on for ... what's it on for?
SELLER	Two hundred and fifty thousand.
AGENT	Two ... Is it really?
SELLER	Yes. You valued it for us.
AGENT	Did I really?
SELLER	Yes. It's very competitively priced for the market.
AGENT	Thank you.
SELLER	You're welcome.
AGENT	She'll take two forty for it because, let's face it, you're gonna have to spend a couple of thousand pounds on it just to get rid of the smell of (SNIFFS) sex.
MALE BUYER	Could we, er, have a look round?
AGENT	Oh it's pretty standard. Three bedrooms ... well, two and one cupboard you could stick a kid in. Have you got any children?
FEMALE BUYER	No.
AGENT	Oh really? I'm sorry, me and my big mouth.
MALE BUYER	Oh no, no, it's ... it's all right, we ... we can have children, it's just we decided against it.
AGENT	Right.
SELLER	Why don't I show you the kitchen.
MALE BUYER	Yeah, okay, thank you.
	THEY MOVE INTO THE KITCHEN.
FEMALE BUYER	Oh I love those units.
MALE BUYER	Chrome works so well in here. Oh I love it.
SELLER	Thank you.
AGENT	Jesus Christ! What the hell have you done in here?
SELLER	Terry put them in.
AGENT	Terry your husband?
SELLER	Before he left.
AGENT	Ahhh!
	THE AGENT PULLS OUT A SLIDING CUPBOARD WITH SHELVES.
	Silent Witness ...

49

SHE PUSHES IT IN AND SLIDES IT OUT AGAIN, LAUGHING SILENTLY.

MALE BUYER	I think they're great though. I love the chrome in the kitchen.
AGENT	Well that would explain the no-children policy then.
FEMALE BUYER	I'm sorry?
AGENT	Well you know what they say about a man who likes a bit of chrome in his kitchen ...
MALE BUYER	No, what do they say?
AGENT	Likes a bit of cock up his arse.
MALE BUYER	You have a bad attitude and a filthy mind.
AGENT	I thank you.
	D'you dream about it? Do you dream about it?
MALE BUYER	Now look ...
AGENT	No kids, drives a big black Chereokee jeep, likes chrome, not to mention the cheap aftershave and the cropped hair. You big old bender!
MALE BUYER	You are a disgrace to your profession.
AGENT	Don't be ridiculous, I'm an estate agent.

SHE SLUMPS AGAINST THE COUNTER.

LAUREN PARTY

LAUREN IS SITTING ON A BENCH IN A SHOPPING CENTRE. LIESE WALKS UP TO HER.

LAUREN	All right? What you doing all dressed up for?
LIESE	Going to that party, ain't I?
LAUREN	You ain't got no business wearing that. What party?
LIESE	Darren's party, innit? It's gonna be a mash up.
LAUREN	I don't know nothing about no party.
LIESE	You do. You thick or something? He told us about it last week, didn't he? Party's tonight. Saturday, innit?
RYAN	Alright?
LAUREN/LIESE	Alright.
RYAN	You ready, Liese?

LIESE	Er, yeah, listen, right. She didn't know there was a party at all.
RYAN	I know.
LIESE	What d'you mean, you know?
RYAN	She ain't invited.
LIESE	What?
LAUREN	Am I bovvered?
LIESE	Oh, don't worry about it.
	You know, just come along, they won't mind.
RYAN	No, he will mind, he don't like you, you're not invited, mate.
LAUREN	Am I bovvered though?
LIESE	But what you gonna do?
LAUREN	Nothing, 'cos I ain't bovvered.
LIESE	Well yeah, but you could just ...
LAUREN	Do I look like I'm bovvered?
LIESE	No I know, but why don't you ...?
LAUREN	Do I look like I'm bovvered though?
LIESE	All right, but I don't think he ...
LAUREN	No, but does my face look bovvered?
LIESE	Why don't ...
LAUREN	Is this face bovvered?
LIESE	Well yeah, but why ...
LAUREN	Is this face bovvered?
LIESE	Why don't you just ...
LAUREN	'Cos I ain't even bovvered.
LIESE	D'you want me to ring?
LAUREN	No, because I'm not even bovvered.
LIESE	But ...
LAUREN	Ask me if I'm bovvered.
LIESE	Well ...
LAUREN	Ask me if I'm bovvered.
LIESE	Are ...
LAUREN	Ask me if I'm bovvered.

ARE YOU CALLING ME A PIKEY?

LIESE	Why?
LAUREN	Ask me if I'm bovvered.
LIESE	That's ...
LAUREN	Ask me if I'm bovvered.
LIESE	Are you bovvered?
LAUREN	No, who told you I was bovvered?
RYAN	She don't care, just leave it.
LIESE	Yeah she does though.
RYAN	She don't give, mate.
LIESE	Yeah, but she is bovvered.
RYAN	Look, we got to chip, mate.
LIESE	Yeah, but I want her to come though.
RYAN	She can't pitch up looking like that anyways, innit?
LAUREN	Are you calling me a pikey?
	Are you calling me a pikey though?
RYAN	No, I'm just saying ...
LAUREN	Are you disrespecting me?
RYAN	No, I'm just saying ...
LAUREN	Are you disrespecting my family?
RYAN	Look, I just ...
LAUREN	Are you calling my mum poor?
RYAN	Oh listen ...
LAUREN	Are you calling my dad a wino?
RYAN	Look, just calm down, right.
LAUREN	No, because my dad's not even a wino.
RYAN	It's cool, right.
LAUREN	But he ain't even a wino though.
LIESE	That was well out of order, I ain't going now.
RYAN	What?
LIESE	You're disrespecting people, I don't need it.
LAUREN	Innit though?
RYAN	But I didn't ...

LIESE	I don't need it, mate.
RYAN	But I didn't mean nothing by it.
LAUREN	She don't need it.
RYAN	Look, I just like ...
LAUREN	She don't need it, mate.
RYAN	Now wait a minute.
LAUREN	She ain't going though.
RYAN	But the thing is ...
LAUREN	You're on your jack though.
RYAN	Look, can ...
LAUREN	You're on your jack, mate.
RYAN	Right, I'll go without you then, I'm busting it.
LAUREN	Yeah, well, she ain't bovvered.

HE POINTS TOWARDS A DRUNK SEARCHING THROUGH A BIN.

RYAN	I think your dad's come to pick you up, innit?

ELAINE FIGGIS, WOMAN OF COURAGE DEATH ROW WIFE / 1

ELAINE IS PICTURED HARD AT WORK IN THE BAKERY.

VOICE OVER	Elaine Figgis is thirty-four and lives in York. She works part-time in a local bakery. Over the past few years she has been corresponding via the internet with people from all over the world. She refers to them as her global family. Her latest pen pal, however, has proved to be something special. Although they have never met, Elaine is about to travel alone to America where they intend to marry.

ELAINE IS AT HOME, PACKING HER SUITCASE.

INTERVIEWER	(OUT OF VIEW) How long will you be away?
ELAINE	Well, all in all, just over a week, but even that's caused a few disruptions. I've asked my friend Jackie to cover my line dancing classes. She's not actually qualified to teach, but, um, she and her husband Rex were regional champions 98/99, plus she's got those little boots with the lights in the heel, which I think will give her some status within the group.

SHE PICKS UP A FRAMED PHOTOGRAPH.

Jeremiah Wainwright the third, that's his full title.

INTERVIEWER (OUT OF VIEW) But his other title, the title the media have given him, is ...?

ELAINE The Cleaver. That's right, yes. Unfortunately a few very small-minded people have called him that.

INTERVIEWER (OUT OF VIEW) Jeremiah can't come to England, can he? He'll never be able to visit you in your bakery because he's in Texas on Death Row, isn't he?

ELAINE If you want to call it Death Row.

INTERVIEWER (OUT OF VIEW) What would you call it?

ELAINE No, yes, it's Death Row.

INTERVIEWER (OUT OF VIEW) So tell me about Jeremiah?

ELAINE What can I say? He is a beautiful, beautiful person.

INTERVIEWER (OUT OF VIEW) Most people would call him a cold-blooded serial killer.

ELAINE I know, Tanya, and believe me, there is hope for those people.

INTERVIEWER (OUT OF VIEW) You say you've fallen in love with this man, that's one thing, but how do you condone mass murder?

ELAINE Life is a journey, Tanya, and sometimes we make a wrong turning, I know I have in the past. Does that make me a bad person?

INTERVIEWER (OUT OF VIEW) He abducted, tortured and murdered eight people.

ELAINE You don't know him like I know him. Nobody does.

INTERVIEWER (OUT OF VIEW) He also ate two of them.

ELAINE Have you never done anything you regret?

INTERVIEWER (OUT OF VIEW) I've never eaten anyone.

ELAINE So far.

Look, I do realise this isn't the typical way that two people meet and fall in love, but, you know, sometimes things happen in life that nobody can explain. I mean, some people really can't believe it's not butter.

INTERVIEWER (OUT OF VIEW) Elaine, let's be honest. The man's a criminal. He's more than that, he's a cannibal, he's a dangerous lunatic. A serial killer who's been put on trial, found guilty and is now incarcerated in a dirty, lonely prison cell, waiting to be put to death.

ELAINE You're making it all sound a bit negative, Tanya.

There's always too many ready to judge. When people hear about Jerry's chosen path they can't wait to jump on the bandwagon. 'Ooh you're marrying a cannibal, oh, he ate two people.' No he didn't. He ate a bit of one of them, when he was a student, which is the time when most of us are experimenting with something new. I know for a fact my cousin once tried hashish.

INTERVIEWER	(OUT OF VIEW) And you honestly think a man like this is capable of love?
ELAINE	Not before. That's because up until he had met me, nobody had ever shown him love. I taught Jerry how to love himself. As Danny Kaye once said, 'you can't love the world until you've settled for yourself', or as my dad used to say, 'the man who can give himself a hug every day truly has the arms of a gibbon.'
	But, er, yeah, today I am Elaine Figgis. Tomorrow I shall be Mrs Jeremiah Wainwright the third. It's been a long wait. Hasn't always been easy, but it's definitely been worth it. True love will conquer all.
INTERVIEWER	(OUT OF VIEW) Now I'm only asking because it's what people will be thinking. Will you have any conjugal rights during your visit?
ELAINE	No. Penitentiary regulations don't allow for that sort of thing, but in a way it doesn't really matter. Obviously our relationship's never been based on anything physical, and I suppose you could say it's been a meeting of minds more than anything else. Plus for twenty-four hours a day he has to wear a muzzle, so ... no.

INFO WOMAN GLAZIER

STELLA IS BEHIND THE INFORMATION COUNTER OF A LARGE SHOPPING CENTRE. A SHOPPER APPROACHES HER.

MAN	Hello, I'm looking for a broken window service, someone reliable.
STELLA	Wouldn't have thought you'd found anybody too reliable that goes around breaking windows.
MAN	No, no, I need someone to replace a couple of windows.
STELLA	Oh, I don't know of anyone. I've got a cousin who once got rid of an old sofa for me, but he lives in Leeds, I'm afraid.
MAN	No, no, I need a professional.
STELLA	Like a hit man?

MAN	No, no, a professional window replacement service.
STELLA	Oh! (SHE LAUGHS) I am sorry. You mean like a glazier?
MAN	Yeah, yeah, exactly.
STELLA	Well there's a very good company that does same-day commercial and domestic installations and repairs and they're called Heart of Glass.
MAN	Oh right, excellent. And they're in this shopping centre?
STELLA	They're in this shopping centre, are they?
MAN	Sorry, I thought you just said they were.
STELLA	Oh no, I don't think so. They're based near my cousin in Leeds. Oh no, I don't know of a glass company in the shopping centre, I'm afraid. Is there anything else I could help you with?
MAN	Yes, er, I also need a blind specialist.
STELLA	Somebody who fits and supplies blinds?
MAN	Yes.
STELLA	No, we don't have one of those either ...

THE MAN LEAVES.

OLD WOMAN PICCALILLI

THE OLD WOMAN AND HER GRANDSON ARE IN THE LIVING ROOM.

OLD WOMAN	D'you get my piccalilli? No, you didn't bother, did ya? No. I asked you to get me a little jar of piccalilli, a little bit, that's all I wanted. I don't want a bucket load of it, do I? Just a little bit to have with me boiled bacon. Oh, 'cos it goes on lovely ... it's tangy, but ... nah, you didn't bother, did ya? Nah, it's too much trouble I suppose, was it? I didn't think it was too much to ask, but no, it's too much trouble, innit, eh?
	Too much trouble for you, innit, eh? Too much trouble for you?
GRANDSON	I'll get it now.
OLD WOMAN	What! I don't want it now! Don't you bring it up here now, don't you bring it in this house. You do, I'll tip it in the fucking bin. I'd choke on it, you bring ... No, no, it's too late now. No, too fucking last minute dot com now. No, no. Go on, piss off out of it, you. What's the matter with ya, keep hanging round me for?

59

GRANDSON	All right, I'll be off then.
OLD WOMAN	You going then, darling?
	Oh that's it, I'll see you tomorrow though? Yeah.
GRANDSON	Ta-ta.
OLD WOMAN	Ta-ta, sweetheart. See you tomorrow. Yeah.

HER GRANDSON LEAVES.

That's it, leave me on me own!

FRIGHTENED WOMAN
MICROWAVE

MARGARET IS IN THE KITCHEN WATCHING THE MICROWAVE TIMER COUNT DOWN TO NOUGHT. THE MICROWAVE BEEPS.

MARGARET   (SCREAMS)

ELAINE FIGGIS, WOMAN OF COURAGE DEATH ROW WIFE / 2

ELAINE LEAVES HER HOUSE, CARRYING HER SUITCASE. SHE WAITS FOR A BUS.

END CREDITS

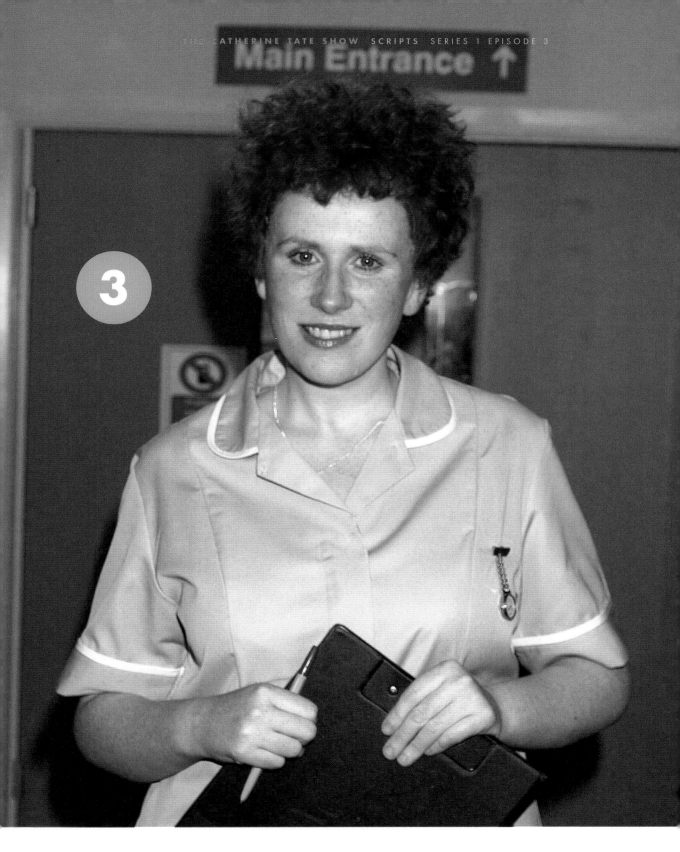

SERIES 1   EPISODE 3

OPENING TITLES / THEME MUSIC

LAUREN CONDUCTOR

LAUREN IS ON A TRAIN.

CONDUCTOR	All change, please. Train's terminating soon … All change.
LAUREN	Are you talking to me?
CONDUCTOR	Yes, it's the last stop.
LAUREN	Am I bovvered?
CONDUCTOR	Pardon?
LAUREN	Am I bovvered though?
CONDUCTOR	This is the last stop.
LAUREN	But am I bovvered?
CONDUCTOR	D'you hear what I said?
LAUREN	D'you hear what I said?
CONDUCTOR	I said you have to get off.
LAUREN	D'you hear what I said though?
CONDUCTOR	Look, love, I'm not gonna argue with you …
LAUREN	What did you call me?
CONDUCTOR	I didn't call you anything.
LAUREN	Did you call me 'love' though?
CONDUCTOR	I just asked you to get off the train …
LAUREN	I ain't your love though.
CONDUCTOR	You have to get off.
LAUREN	Are you disrespecting me?
CONDUCTOR	This is the last stop.
LAUREN	Are you disrespecting me though?
CONDUCTOR	D'you understand what I said?
LAUREN	D'you understand what I said though?
CONDUCTOR	If you don't get off the train I'll call the police.

LAUREN	Am I bovvered?
CONDUCTOR	I'm warning you.
LAUREN	Do I look bovvered?
CONDUCTOR	It's up to you.
LAUREN	Look at my face, is it bovvered?
CONDUCTOR	Look, I'm not arguing.
LAUREN	Look at my face. Is it bovvered though?
CONDUCTOR	This train's not going anywhere.
LAUREN	Yeah, but is my face bovvered?
CONDUCTOR	This is the last stop and you have to get off.
LAUREN	I ain't bovvered.

THE CONDUCTOR GIVES UP AND WALKS AWAY. LAUREN WAITS FOR A MINUTE THEN GATHERS UP HER BAG AND RUNS OFF.

AGA SAGA WOMAN OLIVE OIL

THOMAS AND CHLOE ARE PLAYING CHESS IN THE LIVING ROOM. MUMMY ENTERS AND SITS DOWN.

THOMAS	Oh Mummy, how did it go last night?
MUMMY	Oh darling, aren't you sweet to ask me that.
CHLOE	Was it a triumph? Was it stellar?
MUMMY	Well, you know Mummy will always tell you the truth, don't you?
CHLOE	Of course we do, we have no secrets.
MUMMY	And it's because I want you to grow up to be brave little soldiers that ... I'm going to be honest with you and tell you that ... that last night Mummy almost ran out of extra virgin olive oil.
	DOOM MUSIC.
THOMAS	Darling, tell all.
MUMMY	It was horrific. I was stranded in the kitchen and we were having guests for supper. I opened the cupboard and I was down to the last four bottles.
CHLOE	Mummy, you're shaking.
MUMMY	I just could not cope. You know, the reality is so different to anything you

63

	can imagine and I was blindsided by it. It just completely floored me.
THOMAS	We had no idea.
CHLOE	Are you okay talking about this?
MUMMY	Oh yes, I'm fine, darling, you know really I'm fine. It ... it happened and I got through it, I had to get through it. I had bruschetta in the Aga, I had olives marinating in the larder, I had sea bass on the griddle ... I was going to need at least another litre for drizzling alone.
THOMAS	What did you do?
MUMMY	I knew I had to do something, I knew I had to get help, and somewhere in the chaos and the despair I suddenly ... I suddenly felt this surge of strength, a calm rise within me.
CHLOE	How amazing.
MUMMY	It was actually ... I had the presence of mind to phone Daddy, and thank God I did, because he was fantastic. He said to me, don't worry, because I can buy some from the shop on my way home. And he did.
CHLOE	Did he really?
MUMMY	He did, yup, he absolutely did, just like that. He came in like a knight in shining armour and saved my life.
THOMAS	Cometh the hour, cometh the man.
MUMMY	He was fantastic. I shudder to think what would've happened if I hadn't been able to reach him.
THOMAS	What if he'd been driving through a tunnel and lost his signal? You'd have had to get in the car and drive to the shops yourself.
MUMMY	Sssssh! Don't let's go upsetting ourselves.
THOMAS	Gosh, it really does put everything into perspective, doesn't it?

FRIGHTENED WOMAN SNEEZE

MARGARET AND MICHAEL ARE IN THE LIVING ROOM, READING. MICHAEL
SLURPS HIS DRINK.

MARGARET	(SCREAMS)
	SHE COMPOSES HERSELF. MICHAEL CLEARS HIS THROAT.
MARGARET	(SCREAMS) For goodness sake!

SHE COMPOSES HERSELF AGAIN. MICHAEL SNEEZES.

MARGARET   (SCREAMS) Michael, honestly! I thought we moved to the country for a bit of peace and quiet.

ENIGMATIC COP WAREHOUSE

TWO PLAIN CLOTHES POLICE OFFICERS ARE IN A WAREHOUSE, STANDING NEXT TO A BODY.

WHITTAKER   What're you thinking, Ma'am?

AMANDA   I'm thinking, how about this ... Suppose, just for the sake of argument, that the bullet didn't enter the body.

WHITTAKER   But it did, Ma'am. He's dead and it's because of the bullet going straight through his heart.

AMANDA   Yes I know that, Whittaker, but for the sake of argument let's say the bullet did not enter the body.

WHITTAKER   Well that would mean that Stevens would still be alive.

AMANDA   Exactly. If there was no bullet Stevens would still be very much alive.

WHITTAKER   But he's not, Ma'am, he's dead.

AMANDA   I know that, Whittaker, but just suppose there was no bullet, what would that mean?

WHITTAKER   Well, it would mean that Stevens would still be alive and we wouldn't be here investigating his murder.

AMANDA   Exactly.

WHITTAKER   I'm not exactly sure where you're going with this, Ma'am.

AMANDA   I want you to shoot me with the murder weapon, Whittaker.

WHITTAKER   What?

AMANDA   Take this and shoot me in the heart.

SHE PASSES HIM A GUN.

WHITTAKER   Ummm ...

AMANDA   Just do it, it'll be perfectly okay. I just need to be certain that a bullet in the heart is enough to kill someone.

WHITTAKER   I think ... no, I'm sure it will kill you, Ma'am.

AMANDA	Just squeeze the trigger.
WHITTAKER	I really don't want to kill you, Ma'am.
AMANDA	How do you know you'll kill me?
WHITTAKER	Because this is a forty-four Magnum and I'm standing a foot away from you.
AMANDA	Ohhh, Whittaker, Whittaker. Just when I thought you were making progress.

PAUL & SAM NOT TURNED UP

PAUL AND SAM ARE IN BED, READING.

PAUL	D'you go to the café at lunchtime?
SAM	Yeah.
PAUL	D'you see Donna?
SAM	I've not told you about Donna, have I?
PAUL	What?
SAM	I didn't see her today.
PAUL	You didn't see Donna?
SAM	I didn't see her.
PAUL	Well why didn't you see her?
SAM	She didn't turn up.
PAUL	She didn't turn up?
SAM	No.
PAUL	What d'you mean, no?
SAM	She weren't there.
PAUL	Where was she?
SAM	I dunno.
PAUL	So what d'you do?
SAM	Well I've waited, ain't I?
PAUL	Well yeah, you'd have to wait, wouldn't ya?
SAM	I'm sitting there waiting for her.
PAUL	And did she turn up?

SAM	She's not turned up.
PAUL	And you're waiting for her?
SAM	I'm waiting for her. I'm sitting there.
PAUL	On your own?
SAM	I'm on me own, ain't I?
PAUL	No!
SAM	Yeah, that's what I'm telling ya.
PAUL	Stop it.
SAM	I'm telling you, I'm sitting there on me own waiting for her.
PAUL	And she's still not turned up?
SAM	She's still not turned up. And I'm sitting there waiting for her on me own like a nutter.
	THEY LAUGH SILENTLY.
PAUL	Oh don't make me laugh.
SAM	I can't believe it.
PAUL	Was Vicky working?
SAM	Well she'd seen me walk in, ain't she?
PAUL	So she's been watching ya?
SAM	Yeah, she's been clocking me the whole time.
PAUL	Oh how funny.
SAM	She's seen me come in and look round for Donna.
PAUL	She knows Donna's not there ...
SAM	Oh yeah, she knows Donna's not there.
PAUL	But she's let you carry on looking round.
SAM	She has let me carry on.
PAUL	I bet she was laughing, weren't she?
SAM	She was in fits.
PAUL	Oh what must you have looked like?
SAM	I dunno.
	THEY LAUGH SILENTLY.
PAUL	So what's happened?

SAM	Well I've ordered me lunch, ain't I?
PAUL	Well you'd have to, wouldn't ya?
SAM	I've ordered me tuna mayo baguette and a cappuccino, and I thought shall I have a Rocky Road Crunch for afters, and I thought no I'd better not because I had a bag of Snack-a-Jacks on the way to work this morning. I thought, don't take liberties, Sam.
PAUL	Oh here we go.
SAM	I know. But that ain't it. I've looked down, what they given me?
PAUL	What?
SAM	You won't believe this. What am I looking at?
PAUL	What have they done?
SAM	They have presented me with a cheese and sun-dried tomato panini and a frapaccino. I'm sitting there, me sandwich is hot, me coffee's cold, she still ain't turned up. What is my life like?
	THEY LAUGH SILENTLY.
PAUL	Who served you?
SAM	Gino, he's out of control.
PAUL	Oh I'd've loved to have seen that.
SAM	I said to Vicky, 'wait till I tell my Paul, he'll love this.'
PAUL	It's like a film sometimes, your life, innit?
SAM	D'you know, that is exactly right.

BUNTY TROPHY

BUNTY IS SITTING IN A PUB. GEOFF WALKS UP AND PUTS TWO PINTS ON THE TABLE.

GEOFF	Right, Stella ...
BUNTY	That'll be yours.
GEOFF	And a pint of Armstrong.
BUNTY	Oh! Perfection.
GEOFF	Hmm.
BUNTY	Ohhh! D'you know, there's only one thing better than a pint of real ale.

GEOFF	Two pints.
BUNTY	Oral sex.
	I was only joking.
GEOFF	Right, Bunty, love, we'd, er ... we've got your award here, but, er, before we send it to the engravers, we just need you to, er, approve the inscription, eh?

HE HANDS THE AWARD TO HER.

BUNTY	'Presented to commemorate twenty-five years of unfailing service to the Doncaster Spinners. Bunty Carmichael, a major Majorette.' Oh Geoff, it's beautiful. It's more than beautiful. It's lovely.
GEOFF	Well, you've had a long run with the Spinners and it's, er, only fair you bow out in style.
BUNTY	Bow out? What d'you mean, bow out?
GEOFF	Bunty, look, don't start, you know we've spoken about this before.
BUNTY	No, we've spoken about whether I want to go into the individuals, and I've told you time after time, I don't. I'm a team player, Geoff, you know that.
GEOFF	Yeah, I know, and we all admire your enthusiasm.
BUNTY	Enthusiasm? Oh, oh, is that what I've got, enthusiasm?

SHE HOLDS UP A SASH OF MEDALS.

You don't get those for enthusiasm, Geoff.

Sheffield 1992, best original twirl. Eastbourne 1981, best overall presentation. Halifax 2001, best combination twirl. Hull 1989, endurance champion.

That's not a sash with medals on it, Geoff. Blood, sweat and tears, that's what that is. Blood, sweat and tears.

GEOFF	Look, nobody's questioning your ability, you're the best we've got. It's just that without you the average age of the team is twelve.
	You know yourself you'd be better suited with a display team that've got members nearer your own age. I mean, what about drum corps?
BUNTY	Drum corps? Are you serious?
GEOFF	They're doing very well in the regionals, and I just bumped into Douggie Hicks last night. He's in dire need of twirlers.
BUNTY	Yes, exactly, regionals. They're doing very well in the regionals. I'm national, Geoff, you know I am. I'm on the brink of European.

GEOFF	Look, it's not just your age we've got to consider, Bunty, there are other things as well.
BUNTY	Such as?
GEOFF	Well, I mean, safety.
BUNTY	Meaning?
GEOFF	Your new display twirl.
BUNTY	The big dipper. What about it?
GEOFF	The big dipper. I mean, your baton's going up twenty-five foot in the air.
BUNTY	Geoff, you know when I catch that throw it brings the house down.
GEOFF	Yes, I know it does, but when you don't catch it you're bringing children down.
	You're lucky we've not been sued.
BUNTY	Twenty-five years! I don't know what to say.
GEOFF	All right, er, look, look, what about teaching?
BUNTY	Geoff, what I do you can't teach. Bury St Edmunds 1989, when I broke the four hundred twirls per minute barrier, there was an official enquiry to see if my baton had been electronically enhanced. After the all clear MC Alan Amos christened me the twirlminator.
	How am I gonna teach that?
GEOFF	I don't know.
BUNTY	And it's not just about ability. What about dedication? D'you remember Bradford '94, when I broke both wrists going for the speed record? Doctor told me I wouldn't twirl for six months. Next Saturday, where was I? I was there on the front row with both hands in plaster, blowing a whistle and doing high kicks.
	But if that's not good enough for you, Geoff, well that's fine by me.
GEOFF	Bunty, love ...
BUNTY	No, Geoff, don't ... You've said enough ... Cheers.
	SHE WALKS OUT. ON HER WAY TO THE DOOR SHE PUTS 'TUBTHUMPING' BY CHUMBAWUMBA ON THE JUKEBOX.

VALLEY GIRL / 1

VALLEY GIRL	So I'm like 'euw' and he's like 'wow' and I'm like 'dude' and he's like 'cool' and I'm like 'so' and he's like 'well' and I'm like 'fine' and he's like 'great' and I'm like 'dah' and he's like 'what?' and I'm like 'no' and he's like 'yes' and I'm like 'bye' and he's like 'oh?'

BERNIE NEW NURSE

BERNIE ENTERS THE WARD AND SPOTS THE NEW NURSE, CAROLE.

BERNIE	You must be Carole. How's it going?
CAROLE	Oh hello.
BERNIE	I'm Bernie.
CAROLE	Hi, Bernie.
BERNIE	Oh, you just moved from St Anne's, haven't you?
CAROLE	Yeah, that's right.
BERNIE	Oh, how you doing? Settling in all right?
CAROLE	Yeah, great, thanks.
BERNIE	You all right? Not having any bother with any of the porters?
CAROLE	No, everyone's made me feel really welcome.
BERNIE	Oh grand. Because you know one or two of them can be a little bit frisky, if you know what I mean ... 'specially Malcolm in A&E. I mean, you have to give him the old green light, but after that he won't take no for an answer. He's got big hands, you know what I'm saying?
CAROLE	I hear you've got the busiest A&E department in the region. I wouldn't mind a bit of experience there.
BERNIE	Oh, you'll get experience there, all right, you know what I mean? (LAUGHS) There's a lovely black guy, Colin, security, works nights. My God, he's one big lump of a man.
CAROLE	Right, when I said experience, I was referring to nursing.
BERNIE	Oh God, will you listen to me? (SNORTS) You must think I'm a right whore. No, I just mean, you know, they're a decent bunch of lads, you know, for the craic, you know.
CAROLE	Right, well, I think that's my lunch so I'd better get on.

BERNIE	Oh right, yeah yeah, you going to the canteen? Oh, here, I'll walk down with you. 'Cos you know, I was just saying to big Karen on the desk, we need a bit of new blood in here, you know what I mean, something young with a bit of life. I tell you, it's nigh on impossible to get anyone to go on the pull with these days. What d'you say, Carole, me and you, few Bacardi Breezers, couple of big navvies down the Archway Tavern, you know what I mean?
CAROLE	Er, I've got a partner, so probably not.
BERNIE	Yeah yeah, oh yeah, I mean, haven't we all though, you know what I mean, but you know, just 'cos you're on a diet it doesn't mean you can't dribble over the menu, does it? (LAUGHS)
	Ac ... actually, Carole, I should probably warn you, um, there's been a few problems on Queen Elizabeth Ward.
CAROLE	Really?
BERNIE	Yeah, yeah. Old fella in for a brain scan keeps exposing himself to the female staff.
CAROLE	Oh my God.
BERNIE	Yeah, I know, yeah ... Actually, when I say old, he's not really old, he's probably about late fifties, you know, obviously taken quite good care of himself.
CAROLE	Bernie, this is very serious.
BERNIE	I know.
CAROLE	Who else knows about this?
BERNIE	Oh he doesn't do it all the time. Um, Thursday nights are usually the best. I think there's some sort of sexy programme on Channel Four he likes, certainly puts the lead in his pencil, you know what I mean? (LAUGHS)
CAROLE	Bernie, I don't think you realise how serious this matter is. And to be honest, it sounds as though you're encouraging him.
BERNIE	Oh no, believe me, Carole, he doesn't need any encouragement ... He's like a puppy in a sausage factory. I mean, fair play to him, it's not the biggest one I've ever seen on the ward, but you know what they say – if it's more than a mouthful, it's a waste. (LAUGHS)
CAROLE	Bernie, since I started here on Monday I have tried not to listen to the rumours about you, but it seems everything they say is true.
BERNIE	Oh thanks, Carole, that's really sweet.

CAROLE	That wasn't a compliment. I've had to go round the ward and redo all the beds you made this morning. Half of them hadn't even had their sheets changed.
BERNIE	Oh no, no, Carole, no. Between you and me, what I tend to do is, I give 'em a good sniff and if they're not too whiffy I just leave 'em on for another couple of days.
CAROLE	I didn't hear that, Bernie.
BERNIE	(LOUDER) Right, what I tend to do is …
CAROLE	Bernie! … I'm gonna go and get my lunch now. And after that I'm gonna request a meeting with Sister Hughes.
BERNIE	Yeah, Christ, Carole, no worries, yeah, go and get your lunch, yeah. I'm cutting down meself. Got a right slut of a dress for the summer, I'm going to get into it if it kills me.

AN OLD MAN WALKING PAST LOOKS AT HER. SHE LOOKS BACK IN HORROR.

Yeah, you wish!

VALLEY GIRL / 2

VALLEY GIRL	So I'm like so bored and he's like 'hey there' and I'm like 'hey you' and he's like 'wanna hang?' and I'm like 'okay' and he's like 'oh really?' and I'm like 'whatever' and he's like 'supremo' and I'm like 'uh-oh' and he's like 'baby' and I'm like 'excuse me?' and he's like 'you want me' and I'm like 'seriously' and he's like 'totally' and I'm like 'na-ahhh' and he's like 'yuh-aah' and I'm like 'no way' and he's like 'you bet' and I'm like 'I don't think so' and he's like 'yeah right' and I'm like 'loser' and he's like 'slut'.

OLD WOMAN WINDOW CLEANER

THE WOMAN'S GRANDSON ARRIVES AND WALKS INTO THE LIVING ROOM.

GRANDSON Hello, Nan.

OLD WOMAN Here he is. (LAUGHS) You come up and see me?

GRANDSON Yeah.

OLD WOMAN You come up and see me, ain't ya?

GRANDSON Yeah. Bought your Guinness.

OLD WOMAN Oh, you are a good boy.

GRANDSON You all right?

OLD WOMAN No I'm not, I'm fucking raving.

GRANDSON What's the matter now?

OLD WOMAN They still ain't been to do me windows, 'ave they? I waited in all day. They said they'd be here by twelve o'clock but there's no sign of 'em. I sat here on me own like a poor unfortunate.

GRANDSON Well you know what the council are like.

OLD WOMAN I'm frightened out of me life people are gonna think I'm lousy. They'll take one look at them windows and think this is a doss house. I wouldn't mind, if I could get up there I'd do 'em meself, but I can't climb, see.

GRANDSON Well I'll do it for you.

OLD WOMAN No you won't. Not having you breaking your neck, no, no, you can let that lot do it. No-good layabouts. Three times I've rang her, that Roberts woman.

GRANDSON Who's she?

OLD WOMAN District 'Ousing Officer or something, innit? Aah, great big office she's got and she's getting paid for sitting there and scratching herself.

Oh it makes me wild. And I wouldn't mind but you can bet your life they're gonna send round some poor silly cods who don't know shit from clay. Last one they sent, he didn't bring his stepladder, so he couldn't reach the tops of me windows. They don't want the work, see.

GRANDSON Oh come on, Nan, why don't I just do it, I'll just get on the chair.

OLD WOMAN Don't you dare. Don't you dare! I'm not having you risking your life. No, no. Oh no, wouldn't they like that? Oh yes, yes, that would suit them, wouldn't it, eh? Everyone doing their own windows, people climbing up and falling out and killing themselves.

GRANDSON	It won't take two minutes.
OLD WOMAN	Don't you get on that chair. If you get on that chair I won't let you through that door any more. On me first Holy Communion I won't let you up here.
GRANDSON	All right, all right, sorry, I'm sorry.
OLD WOMAN	That's it. See what they do to me? Fucking lowlifes!
	THE DOORBELL RINGS.
OLD WOMAN	Here, I bet that's them now. What's the time? Look at the time, half past four. Twelve o'clock they said they'd be here. Oh they make you sick!
GRANDSON	I'll go, Nan, stay here, please.
	HE ANSWERS THE DOOR AND RETURNS WITH THE WINDOW CLEANER.
	It's these in here, I think.
CLEANER	Oh I'm sorry to be so late, Mrs Taylor.
OLD WOMAN	Oh, what's that? That someone at the door?
GRANDSON	Nan, it's the window cleaner from the council.
OLD WOMAN	Who is it?
CLEANER	I know you've been waiting, I do apologise.
OLD WOMAN	Oh, was that today? Oh I didn't realise that was today.
CLEANER	Yeah, yeah, Wednesday, you know I'm sorry, I'm two men down this week, I've had to do the whole of the nursing home on me own.
OLD WOMAN	Oh don't worry about me, darling, I don't take no notice. I mean, it don't matter to me if it ain't done today.
CLEANER	Oh no, it's no trouble at all.
OLD WOMAN	Oh. Here, don't worry about filling up your bucket with water, son, no, just wipe 'em over, that's all they need. Would you like a cup of tea? Get the fella a cup of tea, he's gasping.
CLEANER	I'm fine actually, the ladies at the nursing home kept me well supplied.
OLD WOMAN	Did they? (CACKLES) Poor dears. Have a sandwich then.
CLEANER	That's very kind but I won't, thanks.
OLD WOMAN	I've got a lovely bit of boiled bacon in there.
CLEANER	No, really, I'll just nip to the van, get me stepladder and I'll, er, get up the top of the windows.
OLD WOMAN	Oh don't worry about that, darling, you can't see up there, no one's gonna be looking at my windows anyway.

CLEANER	Sure? It's no problem.
OLD WOMAN	No, no, that's lovely what you done there, that's all I want. Oh I'm very much obliged to you, sweetheart. Truly I am.
CLEANER	All right, well that didn't take long. I'll be off then.
OLD WOMAN	Ahhh, all right, sweetheart. Take care. Thank you very much. Much obliged to you, I really am, I mean that.

SHE SHOWS THE WINDOW CLEANER OUT THEN COMES BACK INTO THE LIVING ROOM.

What a fucking liberty!

Look at the state of them windows. He ain't touched 'em. He ain't touched 'em! Ooh I shall be on the phone tomorrow morning a bit lively. He had to go and do the nursing home! What do they care? All that silly old lot. Half of 'em are sitting in their own piss. The rest of 'em are smearing the walls with shit! What do they care if their windows are clean or not?

GRANDSON	Why didn't you just let him ...
OLD WOMAN	Get up there and do them windows, you. I'll have people talking about me now.
GRANDSON	I thought you said ...
OLD WOMAN	Get on that chair at once you no-good noncepot!
GRANDSON	I thought you said it was too dangerous?
OLD WOMAN	Don't be such a fucking old Mary-Ann.

FRIGHTENED WOMAN HICCUPS

MARGARET AND MICHAEL ARE IN THE LIVING ROOM. MARGARET IS PAINTING HER NAILS. SHE HICCUPS.

MARGARET	(SCREAMS)

SHE COMPOSES HERSELF, THEN HICCUPS AGAIN.

MARGARET	(SCREAMS)

SHE HOLDS HER BREATH TO GET RID OF THE HICCUPS, THEN GOES BACK TO PAINTING HER NAILS. SHE HICCUPS.

MARGARET	(SCREAMS)

ELAINE FIGGIS, WOMAN OF COURAGE DEATH ROW WIFE / 3

ELAINE LEAVES HER HOUSE, CARRYING HER SUITCASE. SHE WAITS FOR A BUS.

VOICE OVER	Elaine Figgis is thirty-four and lives in York. She's travelled over four thousand miles to Dallas, Texas, to marry a man she's never met. Jeremiah Wainwright the third is a convicted murderer and notorious cannibal. He is currently on Death Row awaiting execution.
	ELAINE IS ALONE IN A PRISON WAITING ROOM. SHE IS WEARING HER WEDDING DRESS.
ELAINE	It's strange how fate can bring two people together. I was surfing on the internet, that just means looking, and I typed in midsummer murders and up came midsummer murderer and I thought, oh what's that, and then I read his little ad and I dropped him a line, and here we are. I'd no idea that in less than two years we'd go from simple pen pals to husband and wife. It's funny, isn't it? I was only after a signed picture of John Nettles.
INTERVIEWER	(OUT OF VIEW) How was the journey?
ELAINE	Well, the taxi driver turned up but wouldn't let me in his cab. He'd seen an article about me in the local paper. I mean, everyone's entitled to their own opinion, but it's not very nice being pushed out of someone's car and being called a nutter on the happiest day of your life, is it?
	I missed the direct flight, so it was nineteen hours by Greyhound bus from Atlanta to Georgia, but I did sit next to a very nice man from Louisiana called Buck. He gave me his number ... I shan't be ringing him, of course.
INTERVIEWER	(OUT OF VIEW) How did you feel when you finally arrived in Texas?
ELAINE	It was very emotional actually. I mean, I felt as if I'd come home, which is odd because I was actually born in Twickenham. Mind you, Texas, Twickenham, it's the same initial − T. I hadn't thought that before.
	I suppose it was the realisation that I was walking on the same ground as my beloved. I mean, not literally, obviously, he's strapped to a board most of the day.
	But, you know, breathing in the same air, it's a once in a lifetime feeling.
	THE INTERVIEWER INDICATES A PLASTIC BAG BY ELAINE'S SIDE.
INTERVIEWER	(OUT OF VIEW) Is that a wedding present?

ELAINE	Yeah. Just a little love token. Last minute whiz round Duty Free, if truth be told ... I thought ... I thought this might be fun.
	SHE BRINGS OUT AN ORNAMENTAL BEAR DRESSED AS A POLICEMAN.
	And then I thought no, get him something he really likes ... so I bought him that (HOLDS UP A PACKET OF SHORTBREAD) – he's a slave to shortbread.
INTERVIEWER	(OUT OF VIEW) What do your friends think of this?
ELAINE	Oh, you can imagine what they say, can't you? 'You're doing the wrong thing', 'it'll never work', 'it's a ridiculous idea', 'you're mad'. But to be honest, I think that's always going to be the case when a woman marries someone considerably younger.
INTERVIEWER	(OUT OF VIEW) You think that's their concern?
ELAINE	Oh they're not concerned, they're not concerned at all. To be honest, it's just jealousy, that's all it is.
INTERVIEWER	(OUT OF VIEW) Could it be ...
ELAINE	(SINGING) 'I'm falling in love with you baby.' Sorry, me and my friend Jenny used to do that all the time. Go on.
	A BUZZER SOUNDS.
ELAINE	Oh, all right, that'll be me then.
INTERVIEWER	(OUT OF VIEW) Good luck.
ELAINE	I've had more than my fair share of luck. It's down to me now.
	SHE DISAPPEARS THROUGH A DOOR. A SHORT TIME LATER THE BUZZER SOUNDS AGAIN AND SHE IS BACK. SHE HOLDS UP HER FINGER TO DISPLAY THE WEDDING RING.
INTERVIEWER	(OUT OF VIEW) Was everything all right?
ELAINE	Yeah, yeah. All done and dusted.
INTERVIEWER	(OUT OF VIEW) Is that it?
ELAINE	Well yeah, yeah. I mean, I knew it was going to be a short service because, um ... well, he's a big lad and it's difficult to gauge the amount of sedative to give him. I mean, they ... they don't want to kill him, but on the other hand they don't want him lashing out with all the excitement. So it was a quick I do and, um, well, and that was it really. Um, I can't stand it when weddings drag on though, can you?
INTERVIEWER	(OUT OF VIEW) Will you be seeing Jerry later today?

ELAINE   No, um, no, he hasn't got another visiting order now for about four weeks. So it's back to good old Blighty. I might ask the pilot if he could tie some tin cans round the back of the plane.

No, actually that would be dangerous.

I just ... I think we should go. Shall we? We could ... no, I think we should just go.

VALLEY GIRL / 3

VALLEY GIRL   So I'm in this bar and he comes over it and I'm thinking oh my God and he's like 'hi' and I'm like 'hi' and he's like 'are you on your own?' and I'm like 'yes' and he's like 'no way' and I'm like 'it's true' and he's like 'I don't believe you' and I'm like 'come on' and he's like 'I'm serious' and I'm like 'cut it out' and he's like 'am I embarrassing you?' and I'm like 'can we stop?' and he's like 'I saw you come in' and I'm like 'okay' and he's like 'can I get you a drink?' and I'm like 'that'd be great' and he's like 'what do you want?' and I'm like 'a soda' and he's like 'is that all?' and I'm like 'what do you mean?' and he's like 'on its own' and I'm like 'yes' and he's like 'don't you drink?' and I'm like 'no' and he's like 'why not?' and I'm like 'it's none of your business' and he's like 'I'm only asking' and I'm like 'well you started it' and he's like 'calm down' and I'm like 'I'm sorry' and he's like 'don't be' and I'm like 'why should I?' and he's like 'back off' and I'm like 'fuck you!'

FRIGHTENED WOMAN CRISPS

MARGARET IS IN THE LIVING ROOM. MICHAEL ENTERS AND GIVES HER A BAG OF CRISPS. SHE OPENS IT.

MARGARET   (SCREAMS. TAKES OUT A TOKEN) Oh, I've won another bag.

END CREDITS

4

SERIES 1 EPISODE 4

OPENING TITLES / THEME MUSIC

PAUL & SAM ZIMBABWE

PAUL AND SAM ARE IN THE BEDROOM.

SAM	I see Jackie today.
PAUL	Did ya?
SAM	Yeah.
PAUL	Has she seen Shelley?
SAM	No.
PAUL	She ain't seen Shelley?
SAM	She ain't seen her.
PAUL	Well how d'you know?
SAM	She told me.
PAUL	Well what's she say?
SAM	She said 'I ain't seen her.'
PAUL	What … she told you she ain't seen her?
SAM	Well I asked her, I said, 'you seen Shelley?' She said 'no.'
PAUL	She said no?
SAM	She said 'no, she's gone on holiday.'
PAUL	She's gone on holiday?
SAM	She's gone on holiday.
PAUL	What's she gone on holiday for?
SAM	I dunno.
PAUL	Where's she gone, Ibiza?
SAM	I said, 'where's she gone, Ibiza?' She said 'no, she's gone Zimbabwe.'
PAUL	She's gone Zimbabwe?
SAM	She's gone Zimbabwe.
PAUL	What's she gone Zimbabwe for?
SAM	I dunno.

PAUL	I thought she was going Ibiza.
SAM	I said, 'I thought she was going Ibiza.' She said 'no, she's gone Zimbabwe.' I said, 'what's she go Zimbabwe for?' She said, 'I dunno.'
PAUL	It's funny, innit?
SAM	I couldn't believe it.
PAUL	Where is Zimbabwe?
SAM	I dunno.

BACKHANDER WOMAN
WINDSCREEN

CAROLE IS IN THE BACK OF A MINICAB.

CAROLE	Just on the high street's fine. How much will that be?
DRIVER	Er, about twelve quid.
CAROLE	Oh great.
	A WINDSCREEN WASHER APPROACHES AS THEY PULL UP AT SOME LIGHTS. HE STARTS TO PUT SOAP ON THE SCREEN.
DRIVER	No, no, it ... it's washed. I've just ...
WASHER	Just a quick wash.
DRIVER	No, it's ... it's clean. Please?
	THE WINDSCREEN WASHER WALKS OFF, LEAVING SOAP ALL OVER THE WINDSCREEN.
CAROLE	Oh they don't take no for an answer, do they?
DRIVER	No. It's ... it's unbelievable. Every day they do that, every day I have to say no.
CAROLE	You know what you could do ...
DRIVER	What's that?
CAROLE	Well you could just get out of your car and say 'no, no, no, no! I said no!' And then just get his pail of water and sling it right over his greasy, flea-ridden head. And he'll be like 'ow that's hot, ow, ow that's hot, ow that's hot.' And then just give him one backhander, one swift backhander right across his steamy red face.

DRIVER	Well ...
CAROLE	Hitler-worshipping pikey scum.
	Actually, just round the corner's fine. Was it twelve pounds?
DRIVER	Er, no, no, just, er, call it ten.

BUNTY FLASHDANCE

BUNTY IS SITTING ALONE IN THE PUB, WEARING HER MAJORETTE'S HAT.
GEOFF ARRIVES.

GEOFF	Am I late?
BUNTY	No, bang on time as usual, Geoff.
GEOFF	Oh, er, have we got company?
BUNTY	No, it's two for one on Theakston's tonight.
GEOFF	Oh, well then, er, shall I have that one and, er, get the next round in?
BUNTY	Er ... well I've nearly finished this one, so ...
GEOFF	Right, I'll ju... um, actually, no, I won't bother, I can't stop for long. Now, we ... Bunty, look, d'you want to take your hat off?
BUNTY	Well, thing is, Geoff, it's a new one and I'm trying to break it in before the Leeds Nationals.
GEOFF	May ... maybe just for this meeting, huh?
BUNTY	You're the boss.

SHE TAKES OFF THE HAT.

GEOFF	Now, as you know we've got your big presentation to organise at some point. I just wanted to go through a few last minute details.
BUNTY	I've told you, Geoff, I don't want anyone making a fuss.
GEOFF	Come on now, how many people do you know that have been a majorette for twenty-five years? Most kids have had enough by the time they're fifteen.
BUNTY	What can I say, Geoff? I love spinning a baton. It's me life.
GEOFF	Aye ... I think we should let you know the line-up for Leeds.
BUNTY	Fire away.
GEOFF	Okay, front row I've got Lauren, Ashleigh, Danielle and little Gemma Graham.

BUNTY	Right, can I stop you there, Geoff. Gemma Graham on the front row? Shouldn't she be in tiny tots?
GEOFF	She was in tiny tots last year, and there are no awards in tiny tots.
BUNTY	I'm sorry, Geoff, but Gemma should be in tiny tots. This could be the tip of the ice cube. I mean, if you put her in the main team this year who knows what her demands will be next year.
GEOFF	Bunty, she won't have any demands, she's six. I'm putting her in the main team and that's that.
BUNTY	But come on, Geoff, on the front row, Gemma Graham! Isn't she going to look a little bit foolish with one year's twirling experience standing next to me on the front row?
GEOFF	You're not on the front row this year.
BUNTY	Right ... Well, well I suppose second row is better than nothing.
GEOFF	You're not on the second row either.
BUNTY	Oh, I see ... Well, is there anything else I should know?
GEOFF	I'm sorry, love, I didn't mean to tell you like that. It's just that you're thirty-one. Every year we think you're going to, you know, call it a day with the Spinners, but every year you just keep coming back. I'm sorry, love, but we all feel the time is right now for you to leave the Spinners ... Bunty, love, are you all right?
BUNTY	Oh, Geoff, you really don't understand, do you? It's not about medals or trophies, it's not about getting me picture in the local paper. Yes, I may be a legend in some people's eyes, but I have to step into me catsuit one leg at a time just like everyone else. It's about marching shoulder to shoulder with your fellow majorettes.
	It's about watching each other's back when a high throw goes up. It's about having that sixth sense that tells you that even though you can't hear the music properly, you know you're more or less in step with everybody else.
	It's a feeling there are no words to describe. When twenty-five individual majorettes become one living breathing animal with the instinct of a fox and the grace of a soaring kestrel ... I'm a Doncaster Spinner, and you'll never know how proud I am to say that. And if the Spinners ask me to leave, well, I'd go.
	And of course I'd carry on living, but, believe me, Geoff, my heart would die.

GEOFF	I'm sorry, love, it's over.

BUNTY PUTS ON HER HAT AND WALKS OUT. ON HER WAY TO THE DOOR SHE PUTS 'ALL BY MYSELF' BY HARRY NILSSON ON THE JUKEBOX.

PAUL & SAM CAFETIÈRE

SAM IS IN THE BATHROOM, TALKING TO PAUL IN THE BEDROOM.

SAM	Oh, you don't know what's happened to me today.
PAUL	What?
SAM	I've not told you, have I?
PAUL	No.
SAM	Oh it was so funny, you won't believe what I've done.
PAUL	What happened?
SAM	You won't believe what I've done, it was so funny.
PAUL	What have you done?
SAM	I can't believe it.
PAUL	Come on, what have you done this time?
SAM	I can't tell you.
PAUL	What d'you mean, you can't tell me?
SAM	You'll die. When you know what I've done you will die.
PAUL	You've got to tell me.
SAM	I nearly died, it was so funny.
PAUL	What have you done?
SAM	I've not told you, have I?
PAUL	You ain't said a word.
	SAM RUNS INTO THE BEDROOM.
SAM	Eight o'clock this morning I've gone into work. I've put the kettle on, to make a cup of tea.
PAUL	Yeah?
SAM	Well I've gone back to me desk and I'm sorting through some stuff, and all of a sudden I can hear something behind me.

PAUL	What's behind ya?
SAM	Well I thought, what's behind me? And I've turned around, ain't I, like that, have a look, and it's only Shona, innit?
PAUL	What's she doing there?
SAM	She's standing by the kettle and she's laughing.
PAUL	Well what's she laughing for?
SAM	I said to her, 'what you laughing for?' She said to me, 'I thought you were gonna make a cup of tea.' I said 'I am, I just put the kettle on.' She said, 'no you ain't.' I said, 'what you talking about, you just seen me do it.' She said, 'it ain't plugged in.' I said, 'what d'you mean it ain't plugged in?' She said, 'you've plugged in the cafetière instead.'
	THEY LAUGH SILENTLY.
PAUL	You didn't plug the kettle in?
SAM	I ain't plugged it in. I've gone to make the tea, I've put the water in the kettle, I've put the tea in the pot, I've put the pot on the side and I have plugged in the cafetière instead.
PAUL	Why didn't you plug the kettle in, babe?
SAM	I dunno. Well we have fell about. She said to me, 'I don't believe you, you're going mad, ain't you?' I said, 'I think I am, ain't I?'
PAUL	You're going mad.
SAM	I am going mad. But then it's dawned on me what must have happened.
PAUL	What?
SAM	You know what I've done, don't ya?
PAUL	No.
SAM	I've suddenly realised ... I've got the leads mixed up.
PAUL	Is that what's happened?
SAM	Well it must be, mustn't it. I mean, it makes sense, don't it?
PAUL	Well I suppose it would.
SAM	I've told Shona and she's looked at me like that (FACE) ... She said, 'I don't believe you, what are you like,' it was so funny. She told the other girls in the office and they have collapsed. They have absolutely collapsed. Mary, who works by the fax, she's wet herself she's laughing so much. Pauline from Personnel, she can't breathe she thinks it's so funny.

And by this time poor Shona's nearly choking. It was absolute bedlam. She said to me, 'you are a liability, what are you like?' I said, 'well, you know what I'm like.' She said, 'I know what you're like.' She knows what I'm like.

THEY LAUGH SILENTLY.

PAUL   What's a cafetière?

SAM   I dunno.

BACKHANDER WOMAN
WHOLEFOOD SHOP

CAROLE HAS JUST BOUGHT LUNCH IN A WHOLEFOOD SHOP.

CAROLE   Um, d'you mind if I sit here?

WOMAN   Oh no, not at all.

CAROLE   Gosh it's busy in here today, isn't it?

WOMAN   Yeah. Is it always like this?

CAROLE   Yeah, it's very popular.

A MAN EMERGES FROM THE KITCHEN AND ADDRESSES THE DINERS.

MAN   Okay, er, anyone who's already paid for vegetarian lasagne, I'm sorry, guys, it's all gone, er, but you can have aubergine bake or butternut squash risotto for the same price.

WOMAN   Oh no, I don't believe it.

CAROLE   Oh, was that you? Oh, how annoying.

WOMAN   Oh well, never mind.

CAROLE   You know what you could do ...

WOMAN   What?

CAROLE   Well you could just go up there, grab the dirty little soap dodger by the scruff of his hemp shirt and say, 'listen Moon Unit, why don't you pay as much attention to how many veggie lasagnes you've got left as you do to trying to save the whale or whatever it is you do when you're not rolling around in shit. You stinking, unicycle-riding, tofu-eating hippy.'

              And then get a big bloody steak and he'll be 'no, no, I don't eat meat,'

and then poke it right down his throat so he can't breathe, and then just give him a backhander, just one swift backhander right across his scabby vegetarian face.

WOMAN	I think I might just get something else.
CAROLE	The aubergine bake is lovely.

NEW PARENTS DRIVING

KAREN AND BEN ARE DRIVING IN THE CAR. THEIR BABY IS ASLEEP.

BEN	In future, why don't you just admit you can't read maps and save us the trouble of getting lost?
KAREN	In future, why don't you make it clear that the little squiggly blue lines are different to the little squiggly green ones.
BEN	I'm sorry, I forgot that you have to have every painfully obvious little thing explained to you.
KAREN	No I don't.
BEN	Things that everybody else would take for granted ...
KAREN	No they wouldn't.
BEN	Just in case you balls it up.
KAREN	All right, I won't interfere next time.
BEN	Can I have that in writing?
KAREN	You can do it all yourself.
BEN	Good.
KAREN	See how you like it then. See how you get on.
BEN	Well we'd get to places a lot sooner, I know that much.
KAREN	Shut up.

THE BABY CRIES.

BEN/KAREN	(SINGING) 'No one else can make me feel,
	The colours that you bring,
	Stay with me while we grow old,
	And we will live each day in springtime.'

THE BABY QUIETENS DOWN.

BEN	I mean, why can't you just admit defeat and say I don't know what I'm doing, I think we may be lost.
KAREN	Oh shut up, Ben, you're like an old woman.
BEN	Instead of pretending for two hours ... Two hours! Jesus Christ!
KAREN	All right, all right, you've made your point. Little man.
BEN	What?
KAREN	Little man syndrome, that's what you've got.
BEN	Don't be stupid.
KAREN	I'm a short, short little man, I get all angry about things when actually I just want to be a bit taller.
BEN	You're pathetic.
KAREN	Maybe I am, but at least I can see above the dashboard.
BEN	Good for you. Shame you can't fit in the back seat though.
KAREN	What d'you mean by that?
BEN	Ooh nothing.
	THE BABY CRIES.
BEN/KAREN	(SINGING) ''Cos loving you, Has made my life so beautiful, And every day of my life, Is filled with loving you.'
	THE BABY QUIETENS DOWN.
KAREN	Are you saying I'm fat?
BEN	I didn't say that.
KAREN	Are you saying I'm fat?
BEN	All I'm saying is that maybe you're a little bit sensitive about still having a jelly belly.
KAREN	Excuse me?
BEN	Well, you know, it's been six months, you probably thought you'd be back in those jeans by now.
KAREN	What has that got to do with anything?
BEN	Instead of pouring yourself into those maternity slacks every morning.
KAREN	Concentrate on the road, you evil little dwarf.

THE BABY CRIES.

BEN/KAREN	'La la la la lah ...'
BEN	Calm down, we'll soon be at Dunkin' Donuts.
KAREN	Midget!
BEN/KAREN	'Doo doo be doo ahhhhh.'

PAUL & SAM HUMAN RESOURCES

PAUL AND SAM ARE IN THE BEDROOM.

SAM   It's been such an absolutely mental day today, you wouldn't believe it. Lunchtime, right, Hayley says to me, 'what d'you fancy?' And I said, 'well I was thinking about a jacket potato,' and she said, 'I'm in half a mind to go Pret a Manger,' and I said, 'well why don't I walk down with you 'cos it's on the same way?' In the end we've ended up sharing jacket potato, cottage cheese and a salad nicoise, so it's all worked out quite well. We've gone back to work, we've got in the lift. Next thing I know, the lift's stopped, the doors have opened, she's walked out, I've followed her out, I've taken one look around me ... I'm only on the fifth floor, ain't I? I'm only on the fifth floor in Human Resources.

PAUL   You don't work in Human Resources, babe.

SAM   I know.

        I'm on the fifth floor in Human Resources, I'm supposed to be down on the third in Personnel. Well, we have gone off into uncontrollable hysterics. She said to me, 'what you doing up here, you don't work up here?' I said, 'you know what I've done, don't you? I've only followed you out, ain't I.' She said to me, 'you're a lunatic. What you gonna do now?' I said, 'I think I'll just walk back down.'

        THEY LAUGH SILENTLY.

PAUL   What's Human Resources?

SAM   I dunno.

        THE PHONE RINGS. SAM ANSWERS.

SAM   Hello? ... *Allo ... Oui, je sais ... c'est moi ... il est né le divine enfant* (SAM BREAKS INTO FLUENT FRENCH.) ... *Je t'embrasse ... Je t'embrasse. A*

	tout à l'heure ... Oui, c'est ça ... Oui, je sais ... Salut.
PAUL	Who was that?
SAM	I dunno.

HOW MANY HOW MUCH KIDS

KATE AND ELLEN ARE WORKING AT THEIR DESKS.

KATE	You want kids, don't you?
ELLEN	Yeah, one day. We have spoken about it. It would be nice.
KATE	Jenny Topley's just had another one.
ELLEN	Has she?
KATE	Yeah, I'm surprised she's got time for anything else.
ELLEN	It's not her first then?
KATE	Jenny Topley? Her first? You know Jenny Topley.
ELLEN	Do I?
KATE	Jenny Topley from the canteen, you've heard me speak about her loads of times.
ELLEN	Oh yeah.
KATE	Guess how many kids she's got now?
ELLEN	Oh.
KATE	How many kids has she got now?
ELLEN	I wouldn't have a clue.
KATE	Well then have a guess. You've heard me talk about her, she's always pregnant.
ELLEN	I really have no idea.
KATE	Yes you do. Come on. Jenny 'kids R us' Topley. How many? Just guess.
ELLEN	I don't know.
KATE	Come on, how many kids has she got now?
ELLEN	I have no idea.
KATE	Just have a guess.
ELLEN	Twelve?
KATE	Twelve! Who has twelve kids? She's a woman, not a cat.

ELLEN	All right, three?
KATE	Jenny Topley, three! She's been pregnant all her adult life.
ELLEN	Five.
KATE	Five. Am I speaking another language? No, she hasn't got five.
ELLEN	All right, eight.
KATE	Seven. She's got seven kids.
ELLEN	Seven, wow, that's a lot of kids.
KATE	Yes it is ... Seven more than you'll ever have, you barren old crow.

BACKHANDER WOMAN MIME

CAROLE IS IN THE PARK, WATCHING A MIME ARTIST.

WOMAN	I just don't see the point of it myself.
CAROLE	Well there's a long history of street theatre in this area.
WOMAN	Yeah, I've seen them here before. Not this one though. Just can't see what he's supposed to be doing.
CAROLE	Actually, it does get on your nerves a bit, doesn't it? Makes you want to walk up to him, get him in a headlock and say, 'what in the name of Christ are you doing with your life? Mincing around like a big old Mary-Ann, dressed like some sort of deviant. You're nearly fifty, for God's sake, what do your children say? "Oh, my daddy hangs around public places wearing make-up and scaring people."' Someone should just give him a backhander. One swift backhander right across his saggy-jowled, painted old face. That'd bring him to his senses, wouldn't it?
WOMAN	I quite like the man that does the juggling here though.
CAROLE	Yes, he is wonderful.

LAUREN NOTE

LAUREN WANDERS INTO A CLASSROOM AND APPROACHES A TEACHER
SITTING AT A DESK.

TUTOR Hello, Lauren, how can I help you?

LAUREN Yeah, I got, like, this to give you, innit.

TUTOR Thank you ... Er, one second, Lauren ... This is a note requesting you to be excused from games.

LAUREN Yeah, that's why I'm giving it to you, is it.

TUTOR But why are you giving this to me? You should give this to Miss Harris.

LAUREN No, because, like, I tried to find her, yeah, but she weren't there or nothing.

TUTOR Lauren, you have to find Miss Harris and give this to her, okay? As your form tutor I can't excuse you from a subject that I don't teach.

LAUREN Am I bovvered?

TUTOR I'm sorry?

LAUREN Am I bovvered though?

TUTOR Look, I can't help you.

LAUREN I'm not bovvered though.

TUTOR This has nothing to do with me.

LAUREN Not bovvered though.

TUTOR Lauren, you're not even listening to me.

LAUREN Yeah, but am I bovvered?

TUTOR I don't know where you get this attitude.

LAUREN Are you talking about my family?

TUTOR I beg your pardon?

LAUREN Are you disrespecting my family?

TUTOR All I'm saying is ...

LAUREN Are you disrespecting my family though?

TUTOR I never mentioned your family.

LAUREN Are you ignoring my family?

TUTOR Lauren ...

LAUREN Are you ignoring my family though?

TUTOR	Lauren, you're a bright girl.
LAUREN	But do I care?
TUTOR	You could do well.
LAUREN	Do I care though?
TUTOR	If you just applied yourself.
LAUREN	But I don't care, mate.
TUTOR	You're just wasting my time. Now, look, go and find Miss Harris or you're gonna be marked absent.
LAUREN	But do I look bovvered?
TUTOR	No, Lauren, you don't look bovvered, and I'm sure you'll agree, neither do I.
LAUREN	But am I bovvered?

SHE KNOCKS OVER A POT PLANT AND LEAVES.

HOW MANY HOW MUCH HOLIDAY

KATE AND ELLEN ARE WORKING AT THEIR DESKS.

KATE	Have you had your holiday yet?
ELLEN	Yeah, we went to Cornwall.
KATE	Nice. I booked my holiday this morning.
ELLEN	Good for you, you deserve a break.
KATE	Two weeks.
ELLEN	Brilliant. Listen, do you mind if I just get on with this, sorry.
KATE	Egypt, Cairo, land of the Pharaohs. The pyramids.
ELLEN	Wow, sounds amazing.
KATE	Yeah, we get there by boat all the way down the Nile, boiling hot apparently.
ELLEN	Lovely.
KATE	Tutankhamun.
ELLEN	Do you mind if I just finish this?
KATE	Four stars. Bang in the middle of Cairo.
ELLEN	Brilliant.

KATE   En-suite bathroom, camel rides, waiters in local costumes.

ELLEN   Sounds like you've done really well.

KATE   Packed lunches on the excursions.

ELLEN   Wow.

KATE   Guess how much I paid for all that?

ELLEN   Oh.

KATE   How much did I pay for all that?

ELLEN   I've no idea.

KATE   Just have a guess.

ELLEN   I really don't have a clue.

KATE   Doesn't matter. Just have a guess. En-suite bathroom.

ELLEN   I really don't know.

KATE   Take a wild guess. Camel rides.

ELLEN   I really wouldn't like to.

KATE   Have a guess, have a guess.

ELLEN   I don't know.

KATE   Doesn't matter, it won't kill you, have a guess.

ELLEN   I can't think.

KATE   Say a number.

ELLEN   Eighty pounds.

KATE   Eighty pounds! Eighty pounds! I'm going to Egypt, not phoning it.

ELLEN   Sorry, I've never been to ...

KATE   You couldn't go to Croydon for that.

ELLEN   Two hundred pounds.

KATE   Have you been listening? It's the holiday of a lifetime.

ELLEN   Five hundred.

KATE   Right, have you ever been on a camel?

ELLEN   Six fifty.

KATE   Seven hundred.

ELLEN   Seven hundred!

KATE   And eleven pounds.

ELLEN	Actually, did you say packed lunches on the excursions? That's really reasonable.
KATE	Yes, it is.
ELLEN	I'm sure you'll have a lovely time.
KATE	Shove it up your arse.

OLD WOMAN MEALS ON WHEELS

THE OLD WOMAN'S GRANDSON ARRIVES.

GRANDSON	Hello, Nan.
OLD WOMAN	Oh, here he is. You come up and see me?
GRANDSON	Yeah.
OLD WOMAN	You come up and see me, ain't ya?
GRANDSON	Yeah.
OLD WOMAN	Oh you are a good boy. You want something to eat?
GRANDSON	No, I'm all right thanks, Nan.
OLD WOMAN	What d'you want, a sandwich?
GRANDSON	No, I've just eaten.
OLD WOMAN	We'll have a quick sandwich then, eh?
GRANDSON	No, I don't want anything.
OLD WOMAN	Well you've got to have something, ain't you, eh? Cup of tea at least.
GRANDSON	All right, I'll have a coffee.
OLD WOMAN	What?
GRANDSON	I'll have a coffee.
OLD WOMAN	Oh I ain't got time for coffees. Now come on, clear all that lot up, I'm expecting company.
GRANDSON	Who you expecting?
OLD WOMAN	It's Thursday, innit? Meals on wheels.
GRANDSON	Well it's only Brenda, it's hardly royalty.
OLD WOMAN	Ah-ha, well that's where you're wrong, see. Because I've got meself a new chap, ain't I? (CACKLES). Got meself a new chap bringing up me dinners.

WHAT A FUCKING LIBERTY!

GRANDSON	Nan, what you talking about? What's happened to Brenda?
OLD WOMAN	Don't talk to me about that dirty thieving bastard.
GRANDSON	What have you done now?
OLD WOMAN	I've got rid of her. Oh I got meself a new chap. Oh you wanna see him. Lovely head of hair he's got. He's called Gavin and he's better than that thieving shithouse that was robbing me blind.

THE FRONT DOOR BANGS SHUT.

GRANDSON	Oh, who's that?
OLD WOMAN	Here, yeah, that'll be him now.
GRANDSON	You've not given him a key to the flat, have you?
OLD WOMAN	Course I've given him a key to me flat, who do you think he is, Harry fucking Houdini!

GAVIN ENTERS AND STARTS A FULL SONG AND DANCE ROUTINE. HE PASSES THE MEAL TO JAMIE.

GAVIN	(SINGING) 'I won't dance, don't ask me,
	I won't dance, don't ask me,
	I won't dance madam with you,
	My heart won't let my feet do things they should do.'
OLD WOMAN	(CACKLES)
GAVIN	(SINGING) 'So if you hold me in your arms,
	I won't dance.'

HE FINISHES AND SITS NEXT TO JAMIE ON THE SOFA.

OLD WOMAN	Ahhhh! What did I tell you, eh? Have a look.
GAVIN	Oh, how are you keeping?
OLD WOMAN	Yeah, lovely.
GAVIN	Now, I've got you something special this week.
OLD WOMAN	Yes.
GAVIN	There was only one left and I saved you it.
OLD WOMAN	Oh you are a good boy, coming up all this way.
GRANDSON	I'm Jamie, Mrs Taylor's grandson.
GAVIN	Yes. Yes, I can see you are. You're obviously a whole family of lookers, aren't you?

OLD WOMAN	Yeah, he's very short.
GAVIN	I bet you've broken a few hearts with those eyes. I say, princess, I bet he's broken a few hearts with those eyes.
OLD WOMAN	Er, yeah, he's got glasses but he won't wear 'em. He'll be blind by the time he's thirty.
GAVIN	Now while I remember, here's your tights.
OLD WOMAN	Ohhh.
GAVIN	And your change.
OLD WOMAN	Oh you are a good boy, ain't ya, eh. Now listen, I've got a nice bit of salmon in that fridge, you take that, have it for your dinner.
GAVIN	Oooh.
GRANDSON	Nan, that salmon's for you, you asked for it.
OLD WOMAN	Mind your own business, you. He gets on my nerves, he does, keep coming up here. I can't make him out. I mean, you'd think a boy of his age'd be interested in girls, but no.
GAVIN	I wouldn't worry about it, I was the same at his age.
GRANDSON	I am interested in girls.
OLD WOMAN	(CACKLES)
GRANDSON	Nan, when Gavin's gone I'd like a word with you, please.
OLD WOMAN	Make us a cup of tea, we're gasping.
GAVIN	I can't stay anyway.
OLD WOMAN	No?
GAVIN	Got a rehearsal tonight.
OLD WOMAN	Oh.
GAVIN	So got to get over to Dulwich after I've finished feeding my girls.
OLD WOMAN	Oh you are a good boy, ain't ya, running about after people. Oh what a darling.
GAVIN	So ...
OLD WOMAN	Yeah?
GAVIN	I'll see you next week.
OLD WOMAN	Not if I see you first. (CACKLES) Oh ta-ta sweetheart, ta-ta.
	GAVIN LEAVES.

OLD WOMAN	Oh, what did I tell ya? Oh what a smashing feller. Oh we do have a laugh. Look at that, and he's brought me tights up an' all. What a darling, eh, I don't know what I'd do without him. Huh!

SHE EXAMINES THE PACKET OF TIGHTS.

	American tan? American fucking tan? Who does he think I am, Carmen Miranda?
GRANDSON	Oh, I thought he was your new chap.
OLD WOMAN	Can't even get me a simple pair of tights, the lazy, fat, bug-eyed fairy.
	And what's this eh? What's he brought me up here? Not lamb. Not fucking lamb, is it? Oh that's all I need, innit. Oh don't turn me stomach. And look at it, not even a drop of gravy on it either.
GRANDSON	Nan, you like lamb.
OLD WOMAN	Listen, this would never have happened with Brenda.
	That's you, that is, making me get rid of her. You got shot of me lovely Brenda, didn't ya? Just so's you could sit there making eyes at that bow-legged, humpty-backed freak show.
	Coming up here, worrying the fucking life out of me with song and dance routines. Oh they want shooting, they really do.
GRANDSON	Nan, you like lamb, you know you do.
OLD WOMAN	(MIMICKING) 'Nan, you like lamb, you know you do' ... Shut up, go in there and get me some mint sauce, you, you useless poof.
	Come on, it's getting cold.

HOW MANY HOW MUCH SANDWICH

KATE AND ELLEN ARE WORKING AT THEIR DESKS.

KATE	I got my lunch from that new sandwich shop. Avocado, tomato on wholemeal, soya mayonnaise.
ELLEN	Three pound twenty.
KATE	Lesbian.

NEW PARENTS

BEN AND KAREN ARE STOOD BY THE SIDE OF THEIR BABY'S COT, SINGING AND DANCING FOR ALL THEY'RE WORTH. THE BABY IS STARING BACK AT THEM.

END CREDITS

5

SERIES 1 EPISODE 5

OPENING TITLES / THEME MUSIC

LAST HIT WOMAN BOARDROOM

A GROUP OF MEN AND WOMEN ARE SAT AROUND A BOARDROOM TABLE.

GALLAGHER	So I think that just about brings us up to date with the Woods and Payne contract. Sandra, do you have anything to add?
SANDRA	Not really, Roy, I've got a meeting with Alistair Payne now, so I'll pass on any further information I get. Er, besides that, I think it's worth mentioning again that without your initial lead we wouldn't be dealing with Woods and Payne in the first place.
GALLAGHER	Well, now that we've got them, let's make sure we keep them.
SANDRA	Absolutely. Last hit.

SANDRA SIDLES UP TO GALLAGHER, HITS HIM, THEN RUNS OFF.

AGA SAGA WOMAN BRIE

THOMAS AND CHLOE ARE BAKING IN THE KITCHEN. MUMMY IS STANDING BY THE FRIDGE DOOR.

MUMMY	Thomas, did you want a Coca-Cola? Do you want a Coca-Cola? If you want a Coca-Cola let me know now before I close the cooler door.
THOMAS	Um ...
MUMMY	Well look, I've closed the cooler door now so it's too late. If you want a Coca-Cola you'll have to get it on your own. Chloe, do you want a Coca-Cola?
CHLOE	No thanks.
MUMMY	Right. Darling, darling, what did Mummy tell you, not with a metal spoon, you'll bruise the dough.

SHE HANDS HIM A WOODEN SPOON.

THOMAS	But it's only panini, Mummy.

MUMMY	Now come on, let's do it properly. Now, are you putting olives in yours?
THOMAS	Yes.
MUMMY	Right, well, that's fine, but you'll have to wait because there's only one olive fork because Chloe's using it right now, aren't you, Chloe?
CHLOE	Well actually no, I'm still waiting for my olives to temper.

THE PHONE RINGS. MUMMY ANSWERS IT.

MUMMY	Hello? Hello, Jacques ... We're fine, how are you? Yah ... Yah ... No I don't want to sit down, just tell me what's happened ... Right ... Right ... Um, listen, Jacques, I'm gonna have to call you back. Yes, they're here with me now.
	No, they're fine, they'll be fine. Yes, thank you, I'm fine. I'll get back to you this afternoon. And Jacques, thank you, I know this wasn't an easy call to make ...

SHE HANGS UP.

Thomas, Chloe, I've got something to tell you ... You know Daddy left for Paris this morning on business? That was Jacques, Daddy's European PA. I've got some bad news. Daddy hasn't been able to find any good Brie this trip.

DOOM MUSIC.

THOMAS	But Mummy, it's the school picnic tomorrow.
MUMMY	I know, Thomas. Thomas, I know.
CHLOE	Has he tried Le Bon Marché?
MUMMY	Yes of course, Chloe, he'll have tried Le Bon Marché first.
THOMAS	I think we have some Wensleydale left over from Ginny's christening.
MUMMY	Oh Thomas, don't be silly, it's a Parisian picnic, do you want all the other children to laugh at you?
THOMAS	No.
MUMMY	No of course you don't. Now come on children, think.
CHLOE	What about Roquefort? That eats well with some good bread.
MUMMY	Good, Chloe, that's it. Now pass Mummy the phone book. Come on, quick sticks. And Thomas, get me two Nurofen and a glass of Pellegrino. I'm getting one of my heads.

LAST HIT WOMAN LIFT / 1

SANDRA AND PAYNE ARE WALKING DOWN AN OFFICE CORRIDOR.

SANDRA	Well we certainly have enough to be getting on with here.
PAYNE	I need the results of that data by Friday afternoon. I trust you can meet that deadline?

THEY STOP BY A LIFT.

SANDRA	I tell you what, Mr Payne, why don't we say ten o'clock Friday morning, proofed and on your desk. No point in waiting till Saturday to start the weekend.

THE LIFT DOORS OPEN. PAYNE STEPS IN.

PAYNE	Friday morning it is. You have my numbers if you need me.

SANDRA LUNGES THROUGH THE DOORS JUST AS THEY ARE SHUTTING AND HITS PAYNE.

SANDRA	Last hit!

LADY CLOWN ORIGINAL

THREE CLOWNS IN FULL COSTUME ARE ATTENDING A CLOWN WORKSHOP LED BY MATTHEW.

MATTHEW	What we'll do now is have a short informal test, as per clown key stage two. I'll be working with you one on one starting with, er, Jill. Thanks. Okay, Jill, let's begin with a little test of the basics from the first term.
JILL	It's just such a relief to feel normal again.
MATTHEW	Okay, so, er, let's push on and look at some of the skills you've learnt so far. D'you remember the walk, Jill, the clown's walk?
JILL	Yes I do.
MATTHEW	Okay, so let's try that ...

THEY PERFORM THE WALK SIDE BY SIDE.

Good ... And into the trip.

THEY PRETEND TO TRIP UP.

JILL	Oooh!

MATTHEW	Ohhh, excellent Jill.

JILL IS LOOKING DAZED.

JILL	This is how they found me, you know. Slouched over the steering wheel like this.
MATTHEW	Okay, Jill ... So, er, what do we do when we've done a trick? How do we present ourselves?

THEY STAND TOGETHER, ARMS IN THE AIR.

JILL	Yes, that's right.
MATTHEW	Yeah? Good. Give us some jazz hands, Jill.
JILL	Oh yes ... Oh God.
MATTHEW	What's the matter?
JILL	It's the whiplash.
MATTHEW	Okay, don't worry, Jill, just, er, try and keep your mind on the task in hand, yes. D'you remember the trick where you surprise yourself by accidentally squeezing the horn?
JILL	Yeah, I do, I love this trick.
MATTHEW	Let's see that then.

JILL HONKS THE HORN.

MATTHEW	Ohh ... (LAUGHS)
JILL	If he had had one of these, I might have heard him.
MATTHEW	Right, er, how about your uniform, let's start at the top. How's your wig?
JILL	It's great.
MATTHEW	Yeah?
JILL	It's big, it's curly, it's very bright. If he'd have been wearing one of these, I might have seen him.
MATTHEW	What about your squirty flower, let's have a go at that. Okay.
JILL	I've been practising this.

JILL SQUIRTS WATER INTO MATTHEW'S FACE.

MATTHEW	On me. Ooh gosh.
JILL	They're still there, you know. Bit withered, but ...
MATTHEW	What are?

JILL	The flowers tied to a tree.
MATTHEW	Okay, one last thing. D'you remember the bucket trick?
JILL	Yes, that's my favourite.
MATTHEW	Let's see that … Good … Good … Ohhh, excellent Jill. Very funny.
	JILL THROWS A BUCKET FULL OF PIECES OF SILVER PAPER.
JILL	Oh God.
MATTHEW	What now?
JILL	It looks like shattered windscreen.

LAST HIT WOMAN LIFT / 2

SANDRA	Sorry, Anthony. Um, I was just wondering, have you seen that at all …
	SHE HITS ANTHONY AND RUNS INTO THE LADIES' TOILET.
	Last hit!

BERNIE MR WILLIS

BERNIE SPOTS A MAN IN THE HOSPITAL CORRIDOR.

BERNIE	Are you still hanging around here?
WILLIS	Er, yeah.
BERNIE	You're never out of this hospital, are you?
WILLIS	Not at the moment, no.
BERNIE	You was here all last week as well, weren't you?
WILLIS	Yeah, well my mum's very ill so I'm here quite a lot at the moment.
BERNIE	Oh it's a worry, isn't it?
WILLIS	Yeah.
BERNIE	I just had a few days off myself. And by Christ I needed it. It's a bit difficult trying to fill your time when you're used to being rushed off your feet though. I watched *Ready Steady Cook* for a few tips, and I got one – don't watch it, it's shite.
	Mind you, in saying that there was this great hunk of a lad doing the

111

cooking, James something or other I think his name was. Cockney lad, I think, and I thought to meself, by Christ I'd like to baste his turkey for him, you know what I mean? You know what I mean though? He reminded me of Gerald, my Gerald. He could cook. My God he could cook – pies, cakes, pastries, anything, he'd just whip it up, you know, and he just, he just ... whip it right up, you know what I mean? I shouldn't have let him get away. It's a bit tricky when they leave you for a man though.

Do you go out much yourself?

WILLIS   Er, not recently, no.

BERNIE   I went out last night. I went out last night with the girls, karaoke, great craic. They're all saying to me, 'go on, Bernie, give us a song.' So I did me Bonnie Tyler, 'cos I'm holding out for a hero as well, you know what I mean? God, I was ripe for it last night, you could've taken me really. Had all me Pamela Anderson gear on. Getting loads of male attention, as usual. And in the end the girls, they all say to me, 'God almighty, Bernie, cover yourself up. You're fat, you're obnoxious and you're making us all feel sick.' Yeah, sick with envy more like, you know what I mean. (SNORTS)

You should come out with us tonight. I get off at half past seven, you could meet me outside Casualty. You can show me a good time. Have you any plans at all?

WILLIS   No, I'm ...

BERNIE   Oh well then, that's set. Half ... half past seven outside Casualty. You can just come along for the ride – you know, the ride.

WILLIS   Er, no, I'm ... I'm waiting for my mother to come out of the operating theatre, so I'm ...

BERNIE   Oh Jesus, I've a head like a sieve today. Um, it's bad news, I'm afraid. Your mother passed away ten minutes ago. I'm very, very sorry, Mr Wallace. I'll send a nurse through and she'll ... she'll send you ... she'll send you in.

WILLIS   Well, er, sorry, Wallace, my name's Willis.

BERNIE   What? Your name's Willis?

WILLIS   Willis.

BERNIE   Not Wallace?

WILLIS   Not Wallace, no.

BERNIE   Oh my God, are you sure?

WILLIS	Yes.
BERNIE	Willis, Willis, Willis, let's have a look – of course it'd kill 'em to put these in alphabetical order, wouldn't it? Oh, wait a minute now ... oh, here you are, no yours is alive.
	There you go now, oh, close shave there, wasn't it, eh? Right, right, oh no, hang on, hang on a minute. Willis, you say, is that with the I.S.?
WILLIS	Yes.
BERNIE	Oh God, no, she's dead too. I think. Is that on the same line as that? I dunno. Oh this is useless, isn't it? Oh God, look, we'll get your number, we'll just ring you this afternoon, is that all right?
	Don't ... don't forget what I said though. Half past seven in Casualty.

LAST HIT WOMAN CAR ACCIDENT

ANTHONY IS WAITING FOR THE LIFT. THE DOORS OPEN AND SANDRA GETS OUT.

ANTHONY	Oh hello.
SANDRA	Hello.
	ANTHONY HITS SANDRA THEN DASHES INTO THE WAITING LIFT.
ANTHONY	Last hit!
	SANDRA SCREAMS AND DASHES DOWN THE STAIRS TO CATCH HIM. SHE SPOTS HIM AND CHASES HIM THROUGH THE FOYER. HE RUNS INTO THE ROAD AND IS HIT BY A CAR.
MAN	Yeah, ambulance please.
	SANDRA REACHES ANTHONY AND KNEELS DOWN NEXT TO HIM.
MAN	Don't touch him till the ambulance arrives.
	SHE QUICKLY TAPS HIM.
SANDRA	(WHISPERING) Last hit.

BUNTY STALKER

BUNTY IS SITTING ALONE IN THE PUB. GEOFF ARRIVES.

GEOFF	Oh, you're here already. I thought I was early. Can I get you a drink?
BUNTY	No, I'm fine.
GEOFF	Pint of Armstrongs?
BUNTY	I don't think I could keep it down, Geoff.
GEOFF	Best not then ... So, how have you been?
BUNTY	How do you think I've been?
GEOFF	Well I won't keep you long. As I said on the phone, I've got a photocall with the *Echo* at six.
BUNTY	Oh yes, I've heard all about your new majorette. Melanie whatshername.
GEOFF	Melanie Watkins.
BUNTY	Yeah. And I hear you've made her captain already. So I get chucked out of the Doncaster Spinners on a Monday and Melanie Watkins gets my majorette captain title by the Friday. My God I bet she looks like the cat that got the cream.
GEOFF	Bunty, she's nine.
BUNTY	Oh yeah, and does she realise she'll be on the majorette scrapheap by the time she's thirty?
GEOFF	We'll probably bring it up nearer the time.
BUNTY	So, you asked me to come here and here I am. As usual someone shouted shit and I've jumped on the shovel.
GEOFF	I do appreciate you coming.
BUNTY	Well let me tell you now, Geoff, if you've brought me here to try and talk me into teaching, you're wasting your time.
GEOFF	The reason I've asked you here has nothing to do with you teaching.
BUNTY	Good, because to be honest, Geoff, I haven't got the time these days. Since the Spinners dumped me, I've not stopped. I'm busy most nights of the week now, and even busier Saturday mornings.
GEOFF	Yes, Bunty. We know you are.
BUNTY	What's that supposed to mean?
GEOFF	You've been seen.

BUNTY	I don't know what you're talking about.
GEOFF	Right, Saturday morning marching practice, you were seen watching us from your car wearing dark glasses with a blanket on your head. The NMA awards in Manchester, you were seen on the front row wearing a false nose and a moustache.
	Sunday morning, we were playing as a curtain raiser for the rugby and somehow you were a touch judge. Bunty, come on, it's not fair what you're doing, you're frightening the kids, they're having nightmares.
BUNTY	I tried. I tried to stay away, Geoff. But I'm a majorette. It's in me blood.
GEOFF	I know you are, and you're a bloody good one, but it's just that we can't have you marching with a team of ten year olds. It looks like we've had you on hormones.
BUNTY	I'm a Doncaster Spinner. D'you know what it's like knowing you're never gonna march ten abreast spinning a baton to the 'Eye of the Tiger' ever again?
GEOFF	Come on, Bunty, there's a big wide world out there. I mean, you're thirty-one years old. I mean, d'you not want a family?
BUNTY	I had a family, Geoff. I had a family. And look what they did to me. Well, I'll just get on with me life as if the last twenty-five years just never happened. It can't be that difficult. You're obviously doing it.
	BUNTY WALKS OUT. ON HER WAY TO THE DOOR SHE PUTS 'EYE OF THE TIGER' ON THE JUKEBOX.

LADY CLOWN FACE PAINTING

THE CLOWNS ARE PAINTING FACES ON THREE CHILDREN.

MATTHEW	Okay, you should be just about finishing up now, so paints down, please. Honker, let's have a look at your little man.
	HONKER TURNS HIS LITTLE BOY ROUND TO SHOW A TIGER FACE.
HONKER	Meeee meee.
MATTHEW	Oh fantastic, Honker, well done.
HONKER	Meeee meee.
MATTHEW	Cheer up, Boo, it's your turn ...

BOO TURNS HIS LITTLE GIRL ROUND TO SHOW A FLOWER FACE.

Oh, Boo, well done. Okay, Jill, let's see what you've got for us.

JILL TURNS HER LITTLE GIRL ROUND TO SHOW A FACE COVERED IN SCARS AND BLOOD.

JILL   You should've been there.

LAST HIT WOMAN AMBULANCE

ANTHONY IS WHEELED INTO THE BACK OF AN AMBULANCE. SANDRA IS WALKING ALONGSIDE HIM.

WOMAN   He's in very good hands, you don't have to worry.

JUST AS HE IS PUSHED INTO THE AMBULANCE, HE TAPS SANDRA.

ANTHONY   (FAINTLY) Last hit.

PARAMEDIC   Excuse me, love.

SANDRA   Oh no! No, no, no, no.

WOMAN   Calm down ...

SANDRA   No, no, no ...

WOMAN   Look, it'll be all right.

SANDRA   Please, please let me in the ambulance, please.

WOMAN   Look, keep quiet.

SANDRA   Look, please, you don't understand, he's getting away, he's getting away ... Please move, move, move!

No! Stop that ambulance!

SHE CHASES THE AMBULANCE DOWN THE STREET.

MARTIN WEBB TRAIN

MARTIN IS ON A BUSY TRAIN, MAKING A CALL FROM HIS MOBILE PHONE.

MARTIN   Hi Jane, it's Martin Webb, can you put me through to Mark Warriner please? Thank you ... Marky, you bastard! Martin Webb, how goes it? ... Oh, good night, yeah, real good night. Got hammered, completely hammered, yeah. Only had four hours' sleep. Yeah. I'm on the train now, yeah, I'm just gonna get me head down, I think, you know, catch a few zeds before you bastards get your hands on me.

Yeah ... Oh I thought you'd never ask. We, er ... we won Best Regional. Yeah, yeah, result, yeah. Well I ... yeah, yeah, of course, I think I've still got a bit of blood running through me alcohol vessels. Yeah, yeah.

Well, free beer, weren't it? Yeah, yeah, absolutely twatted, yeah.

Marky, Marky, are you on your own? Here, listen. I copped off as well ... Hey, shut it, gobshite! That's for me to know and you to find out. Yeah, yeah, mental. Er, look ... Oh no, no, no, no, you go, yeah, yeah, no I'm on the ... yeah, I'm trying to get me head down. All right, mate, I ... I'll speak to you later. All right. And Marky we ... Oh!

HE RE-DIALS.

Hi Jane, it's Martin Webb, can you put me through to Richard Bolton please? Thank you, my darling, you are a gentleman and a scholar. Don't mean anything, I ... it just means thank you.

(TO THE OTHER PASSENGERS) Phew! I tell you, it's women like that that get you ...

Dicky! How goes it? You bastard. Martin Webb, yeah, oh storm, absolute storm. Yeah, we won, er, two awards, yeah, Best Regional and, er, some other blo... yeah, probably a load of old shit, but hey, I'll take the glory, no probs. Yeah, yeah, hey, well I think the, er, company card's gone into meltdown. Yeah, well we were on the old champagne from seven, weren't we? Yeah, yeah, mental, yeah. Listen, I ... Oh no, you're all right, no, no, I've got to go as well, yeah.

No, er, no, I'm trying to get me head down, yeah, for a bit. All right, mate, I'll speak to you later, yeah. Hey, I'll tell you what, I'll give you a ring if I've still got a bit of blood running through me alco ... Hello?

(TO THE OTHER PASSENGERS) Signal! ... Re-ee-dial. When the crowd said Bo Selecta.

Hello Jane, it's Martin Webb, er, can you put me through to, er, Rob Mullett please? Er, Chas Smith then? Kev Marv? Well I ... sorry, who hasn't gone to lunch yet? Richard who? Oh no, no, yeah, no, I know who you mean. Yeah, yeah, put ... yeah, he'll do, yeah. Thank you ...

Ricardo, you fat bastard! Martin Webb, how goes it? We ... Martin Webb

... Second floor. Look, d'you know Barry Cheeseman? Yeah, exactly, I'm a big pal of his, yeah. Look, can you get a ... can you get a message to Perry Blenkinsop for me please, right? Can you tell him, right, that we just ... we won everything, right. Just tell him that, and if you ask him not to ring me because, like, I'm coming back from London, I'm on the train, I'm trying to get me head down for a ... well, you can ask ... you can give him the mess...

Whoa whoa whoa, pal, hey hang on, d'you know who you're talking to? Well I'll tell you, you're talking to a man, right, that spent yesterday afternoon playing golf with Ralph Harvin, yeah, right, spent two hundred quid on a new suit from Oxford Street, right, that's in London, yeah. Well, slept with a prostitute ...

Yes, well I didn't know she was a prostitute, you know, but I'd probably have spent that amount of money on her anyway, so ... technicalities. Well, not exa ... yeah, have you got to go? Yeah, well I've got to go first, bye! Yes!

HE RE-DIALS.

Hiya, you all right? What ... yeah, what you doing? Right, d'you want anything from the ... the thingy, a sandwich or owt? All right. List ... listen, I might ... I might come and sit in smoking with you. It's a bit dead in here. Yeah. All right. I ... all right, no, I've got me inhaler, I'll be all right. All right. All right, Mam, I'll see you in a minute.

Hey hey, Mam, this will kill you ... no, you're all right, I've got to go as well, yeah, all right.

HE PULLS A FACE AT THE WOMAN SITTING NEXT TO HIM.

LADY CLOWN BALLOONS

THE CLOWNS ARE PRACTISING THEIR BALLOON TWISTING SKILLS.

MATTHEW   Okay, three, two, one, stop twisting. Okay, Honker?

HONKER HAS MADE A RABBIT.

HONKER   Meeee meee.

MATTHEW   Hey! Okay, Boo ...

IT TOOK ADAM AND EVE ONE MINUTE TO
FALL FROM GRACE IN THE GARDEN OF EDEN
AND YET GROWING OUT A LAYERED BOB
CAN TAKE FOREVER.

BOO HAS MADE A DOG.

Well done, very good. Hey, it's long, isn't it? Wipe your face ... Jill, let's see what you've got for us.

JILL HAS MADE A NOOSE.

ENIGMATIC COP RIVERSIDE

TWO PLAIN CLOTHES POLICE OFFICERS ARE BY THE SIDE OF A RIVER, STANDING NEXT TO A BODY.

WHITTAKER   That's the fifth headless body we've pulled out of the river this month. No fingerprints, it's been in the drink too long. There's obviously some psycho out there.

AMANDA   Not necessarily, Whittaker. The lady who did this may be every bit as sane as you or I.

WHITTAKER   Why do you think it's a lady, Ma'am?

AMANDA   Because statistically there are more ladies than chaps in London. Now I can't be certain, but logically the perpetrator of these crimes is more likely to be a lady than a chap.

WHITTAKER   It's going to be a nightmare to identify the bodies. No heads, no fingerprints.

AMANDA   I would've thought that would've made it easier.

WHITTAKER   How's that, Ma'am?

AMANDA   Think about it, Whittaker. How many people in London do you know without heads or fingerprints?

Anyone like that would stick out a mile.

WHITTAKER   Well, er, when they were alive they would've had heads and fingerprints, Ma'am.

AMANDA   The cause of death in these cases may not necessarily be decapitation.

WHITTAKER   So you mean they were killed before they were decapitated?

AMANDA   You know, technically it is possible to live without a head. You know the phrase about headless chickens running around.

WHITTAKER   They don't live for very long, Ma'am. They fall over after a few seconds. You couldn't live a normal life as a chicken without a head.

AMANDA	I couldn't live a normal life as a chicken without a head! Don't be too sure.
WHITTAKER	Look, no, not you, Ma'am, a chicken.
AMANDA	Well then, are you saying that a chicken's life is a normal life? What's normal about having feathers and eating grain?
WHITTAKER	I'm not exactly sure where you're going with this, Ma'am?
AMANDA	You're still learning, aren't you, Whittaker?
WHITTAKER	I like to think I do a good professional job.
AMANDA	I used to go to embroidery classes when I was a child. And I learnt more about being a detective from those embroidery classes than I ever did at ... that place where I learned to be a detective.
WHITTAKER	I don't understand, Ma'am.
AMANDA	One day you will, Whittaker. One day you will.

LAST HIT WOMAN HOSPITAL

SANDRA ENTERS ANTHONY'S HOSPITAL ROOM.

NURSE	I'm sorry you've been waiting so long. It really should only be family but we're having problems contacting them.
SANDRA	Oh that's okay, I just want a minute.
NURSE	Well I'll be back in a second, then I'm afraid you'll have to leave.
SANDRA	Yes of course.
	SHE SITS BY THE BED.
	Anthony, it's Sandra Graham from Fullston's. I don't know if you can hear me but I just want to say I'm so sorry. I know this is all my fault. If you can hear me, please give me a sign, just to let me know you're all ...
ANTHONY	(COUGHS)
SANDRA	Oh you're all right, you're all right ...
	Last hit.
	SHE HITS HIM ON THE HEAD AND RUNS FROM THE ROOM.

OLD WOMAN POUND SHOP

THE OLD WOMAN AND HER GRANDSON ARE SHOPPING.

OLD WOMAN	It's a lot of rubbish, innit?
GRANDSON	It's a pound shop, Nan.
OLD WOMAN	Oh what a load of old shit.
GRANDSON	Nan!
OLD WOMAN	I wouldn't give you a thank you for any of it.
GRANDSON	Well come on then, let's go.
OLD WOMAN	Hang on, hang on. What's this?
GRANDSON	It's a Bustomatic. Dramatically increases bust size in only five minutes a day.
OLD WOMAN	What a load of old shit. How much is it?
GRANDSON	It's a pound.
	SHE SHOUTS OVER TO THE SHOP ASSISTANT.
OLD WOMAN	How much this, love?
GRANDSON	They're a pound.
OLD WOMAN	Er, I'm talking.
SHOPKEEPER	Everything's a pound.
OLD WOMAN	Everything's a pound? Oh well, that ain't bad, is it? Oh that's very reasonable ... I don't know where I'll put it all but I'll take it off your hands for a pound.
GRANDSON	No, Nan, it's a pound per item.
OLD WOMAN	What, each?
SHOPKEEPER	Every single thing is a pound. It's a pound shop.
OLD WOMAN	What, twenty shillings? Oh that's scandalous money, that is, innit?
	SHE PICKS UP A GARDEN GNOME.
	How much is that?
GRANDSON	It's a pound.
OLD WOMAN	What is it?
GRANDSON	It's a garden gnome.
OLD WOMAN	What's it do?

GRANDSON	Sits in your garden.
OLD WOMAN	Hah, I'll take a couple of them, they don't eat nothing, do they?
GRANDSON	Come on, Nan, we've gotta go.
OLD WOMAN	Hang on, what's this?
GRANDSON	Er, jam jars, come on, you don't want them.
OLD WOMAN	How much are they?
GRANDSON	They're a pound.
OLD WOMAN	What, for all three?
GRANDSON	Yeah, you get three for a pound.
OLD WOMAN	Oh.
GRANDSON	Look, what d'you want them for? Come on, Nan, we've gotta go.
OLD WOMAN	'Ere, 'ere, I ain't told ya. Oh!
GRANDSON	What?
OLD WOMAN	She's dead then.
GRANDSON	Who?
OLD WOMAN	That Jackson woman, flat above me. Dead.
GRANDSON	What?
OLD WOMAN	Yeah, terrible, innit? Oh it frightens the life out of me, it does.
GRANDSON	Hang on a minute, Mrs Jackson's dead?
OLD WOMAN	Yeah.
GRANDSON	Well how did she die?
OLD WOMAN	She had the (MUMBLES), didn't she?
GRANDSON	What you talking about?
OLD WOMAN	She's dead!
GRANDSON	I know.
OLD WOMAN	Well shut up then.
GRANDSON	Oh my God.
OLD WOMAN	I know, that's what I'm trying to tell ya. I don't even like talking about it 'cos it frightens me so much. Oooh, you don't know what to do to be right, do you, those poor children.
GRANDSON	I can't believe it.

OLD WOMAN	Yeah, well, it's true, she's dead.
GRANDSON	I didn't even know she was ill.
OLD WOMAN	Well she ain't no more. That's it, gone, finished, dead, done, dot com, that's your lot. Offski, ta-ta. Hah!
GRANDSON	Who told you she was dead?
OLD WOMAN	What?
GRANDSON	Who told you?
OLD WOMAN	Oh leave off.
GRANDSON	Who told you?
OLD WOMAN	No one, I don't need telling, I know.
GRANDSON	Oh my God.
OLD WOMAN	Now look, the woman's dead so let her rest in peace.

SHE PICKS UP AN ORNAMENT.

	Little dog. (LAUGHS)
GRANDSON	Mrs Jackson's not dead, is she?
OLD WOMAN	I'll have a couple of them, I think.
GRANDSON	Nan?
OLD WOMAN	Jam jars.
GRANDSON	Nan?
OLD WOMAN	Can't have too many, can ya?
GRANDSON	Nan!
OLD WOMAN	What?
GRANDSON	Mrs Jackson's not dead, is she?
OLD WOMAN	Well I ain't seen her for four days.
GRANDSON	For God's sake.

SHE EXAMINES THE JAM JARS.

OLD WOMAN	Now let me see, are they all in threes? All in threes, are they? ... Oh, I could do with four.
GRANDSON	Look, we've ...
OLD WOMAN	These are a pound, love.
SHOPWOMAN	Do you need a bag?

OLD WOMAN	What?
SHOPWOMAN	Do you need a carrier bag?
OLD WOMAN	Course I need a carrier bag. Where d'you think I'm gonna carry 'em, on me 'ead?
SHOPWOMAN	That's a pound and a penny, please.
OLD WOMAN	What?
GRANDSON	Nan, they charge for carriers because everything's only a pound in the first place.
OLD WOMAN	A pound for a carrier!
GRANDSON	No, Nan, the jam jars are a pound but the carriers are a penny.
OLD WOMAN	You got to pay for the carriers?
GRANDSON	Yeah, look, I've got a pound and a penny here.
OLD WOMAN	What? Don't you dare. When have I ever taken money off you, as God is my judge.
SHOPWOMAN	Do you want the carrier or not?
OLD WOMAN	Oh fucking chill out!

SHE EXAMINES THE JARS AGAIN.

Let's have a look at these.

SHOPWOMAN	Look, excuse me, madam, there's a queue. If you want to look at them, can you go and stand over there, please?
OLD WOMAN	I haven't got time to be standing anywhere. I've got an appointment. People have got better things to do than sifting through old tat in here. Come on, you, you're making me late.

SHE THROWS THE JAM JARS ONTO A STAND.

What a load of old shit!

LAST HIT WOMAN CEMETERY

SANDRA IS AT ANTHONY'S FUNERAL.

WIDOW	Thank you so much for coming.
GALLAGHER	Oh not at all. And you know, if there's anything at all the company can do?
WIDOW	Oh thank you, that means so much. I know he was only with you for a year, but Tony always said how much he loved working at Fullston's.
GALLAGHER	He had such a great future with us. Such a tragic loss. This is Sandra Graham by the way, she was Tony's manager.
WIDOW	Oh, you're Sandra Graham. Well he must have meant you.
SANDRA	I'm sorry?
WIDOW	The last night at the hospital Tony managed to say a few words. He said he had a message for you. It didn't make much sense to us but maybe it will mean something to you.
SANDRA	What did he say?
WIDOW	Well he said to do this (TAPS SANDRA'S ARM) and say 'last hit'.

SANDRA LOOKS AS IF SHE MIGHT FAINT AND TAKES DEEP BREATHS.

GALLAGHER	Sandra, are you all right?
SANDRA	Yeah, I was just, um ...

SHE RUNS BACK TOWARDS THE GRAVE, SCREAMING.

Noooooo! Noooooo! Last hit! Last hit! Last hit! Last hit!

BUNTY

BUNTY IS SEEN IN THE MIDST OF A MAJORETTE ROUTINE, SURROUNDED BY YOUNGER MAJORETTES.

END CREDITS

SERIES 1 EPISODE 6

OPENING TITLES / THEME MUSIC

FRIGHTENED WOMAN
RESTAURANT

MARGARET AND MICHAEL ARE IN A RESTAURANT. THE WAITER HANDS THEM A MENU EACH.

MARGARET   Thank you.

MICHAEL   Thank you.

                Ah, goat's cheese for me, no contest.

MARGARET   Oh, you've not even looked at the others. Deep fried prawns with sweet chilli …

THE WINE WAITER APPEARS FROM BEHIND MARGARET'S BACK AND HANDS HER A MENU.

MARGARET   (SCREAMS) Oh, it's the wine list. How about a nice Rioja?

MICHAEL   Ooh yeah.

HOW MANY HOW MUCH
CORNWALL

KATE AND ELLEN ARE WORKING AT THEIR DESKS.

KATE   You've been to Cornwall, haven't you?

ELLEN   Yeah, we went last year. We went to Tintagel Castle, it was lovely.

KATE   We went this weekend. It's a long old drive, Cornwall.

ELLEN   Yeah.

KATE   One hundred and ninety miles.

ELLEN   Is it really?

KATE   Door to door.

ELLEN   Wow.

KATE   AA reckoned it would take me four and a half hours.

ELLEN	Did they?
KATE	Well it's single lane most of the way.
ELLEN	Course, yeah.
KATE	The A39, caravans, Stonehenge rubberneckers. Four and a half hours, that's about right.
ELLEN	I would've thought so.
KATE	Guess how long it took me?
ELLEN	Oh.
KATE	How long did it take me to get to Cornwall?
ELLEN	Um ...
KATE	Four and a half hours, that's the AA talking. How long did it take me?
ELLEN	Look, I'd love to, it's just I really need to get ...
KATE	Just have a guess. One hundred and ninety miles.
ELLEN	Er, well ...
KATE	Come on. The A39, roadworks at Exeter. How long?
ELLEN	Really don't know.
KATE	Come on, how long did it take me? Just have a guess.
ELLEN	I don't even drive.
KATE	Doesn't even matter, just guess.
ELLEN	Two hours?
KATE	Two hours! Two hours ...
ELLEN	Okay, I don't know.
KATE	... to Cornwall?
ELLEN	Two and a half?
KATE	Two and a half hours! I was in a car, not a jet.
ELLEN	Three. Three and a half hours.
KATE	Right, do you know where Cornwall is?
ELLEN	Yeah, it's right at the bottom.
KATE	Yeah. Four hours.
ELLEN	Four hours.
KATE	And ten minutes.
ELLEN	Well that's ... that's less than they said at the AA.

KATE	Yes it is. It's twenty minutes less.
ELLEN	Did you have a nice time?
KATE	No, it was shit.

ELAINE WAINWRIGHT, WOMAN OF COURAGE DEATH ROW WIFE – EXECUTION

ELAINE IS SHOWN AT WORK IN THE BAKERY, DURING THE BUILD-UP TO THE WEDDING, AND IN HER WEDDING DRESS ON HER WEDDING DAY.

VOICE OVER	Elaine Wainwright is thirty-four and lives in York. She recently travelled over four thousand miles to marry a man she'd never met before. Jeremiah Wainwright the third, a convicted murderer and notorious cannibal, is currently on Death Row awaiting execution. Now back in York, Elaine has been adapting to married life.
	However that is all about to change. We've had a phone call from Elaine. She's discovered that after six false alarms, this morning at seven a.m. Jerry is going to be administered under Texan law with the lethal injection that will kill him for the crimes he has committed against society.
	ELAINE IS AT HOME, IN FRONT OF A MAKESHIFT SHRINE TO JERRY.
INTERVIEWER	(OUT OF VIEW) How are you, Elaine?
ELAINE	Well it's all been a bit of a rush, really. I mean, I did have everything planned the first time I was told Jerry was leaving us, but it's been called off so many times since then I don't know whether he's coming or going … literally.
INTERVIEWER	(OUT OF VIEW) But today's the day?
ELAINE	Yes, I checked his website before I went to bed last night, as I always do, and there's been an update. It's definitely happening for seven o'clock this morning.
INTERVIEWER	(OUT OF VIEW) So it's literally moments away.
ELAINE	Yeah, not long now. I've lit a candle representing Jerry's life, and in a couple of minutes I shall put it out, symbolising the shining light that was Jeremiah Wainwright the third being extinguished by a society that chose not to understand him.

INTERVIEWER	(OUT OF VIEW) Not understand why he tortured and killed eight innocent people?
ELAINE	Yes, I've just said that.
INTERVIEWER	(OUT OF VIEW) So you've been a married woman for just five days now, and in a few short minutes you'll be a widow.
ELAINE	Yeah, it's been a funny old week.
	It's true to say being a married woman has changed my life. When I was at school I made a list of the top ten things I want to do before I die. Getting married was at number one. I've come a long way. I've only got Disneyland to go.
INTERVIEWER	(OUT OF VIEW) It must feel strange, especially as you've been here so many times before.
ELAINE	Yeah, we have had a few false starts. And when I found out it was definitely going ahead this morning, I realised I'd run out of candles. I got these from the shop on the corner. It's only a little one, but you'd be hard pushed to find something they didn't sell.
	AN ALARM SOUNDS.
ELAINE	Oh right, that's my one minute warning. I set the timer on the cooker so I wouldn't have to unplug the alarm clock by my bed. Jerry wouldn't want any fuss.
INTERVIEWER	(OUT OF VIEW) Would you like us to stop filming?
ELAINE	No, no, you're all right, it'll only take a minute. I would like a moment of silence before I blow the candle out, if that's okay.
	THE ALARM CONTINUES TO SOUND.
ELAINE	Sorry, it'll go off in a moment.
	THE ALARM CONTINUES.
ELAINE	Right, sorry, could one of you turn that off because that's quite annoying. If you just press the red switch ...
	THE ALARM IS SWITCHED OFF.
	God bless, Jerry, may all those who misunderstood you and never gave you a chance one day somehow see the error of their ways. Goodnight, angel. (BLOWS CANDLE OUT) D'you know, I've lived that moment a thousand times.

THE CANDLE RE-LIGHTS.

Oh my God, you saw me blow that out, that is a sign.

INTERVIEWER   (OUT OF VIEW) But I think it ... it might be ...

ELAINE   Do you think the injection didn't work? I mean, he's a big lad.

INTERVIEWER   (OUT OF VIEW) Elaine, I think it might be one of those magic candles.

ELAINE   Call it what you will, that is a miracle.

INTERVIEWER   (OUT OF VIEW) No, I ... I mean they're ... they're candles you buy as a joke, they ... they don't blow out.

ELAINE BLOWS THE CANDLE OUT AGAIN. IT RE-LIGHTS.

ELAINE   That's just silly, isn't it? I mean, what use is that to anyone? ... Sorry, could you just put that under a tap for me, please?

SHE HANDS THE CANDLE TO SOMEONE.

INTERVIEWER   (OUT OF VIEW) How are you feeling, Elaine?

ELAINE   Not too bad actually. Now it would be wrong to say being a widow suits me, but I do feel very at one with myself. I feel Jerry's at peace. It's funny, because when I was counting down the seconds I could actually feel it here. (SHE PATS HER HEART)

INTERVIEWER   (OUT OF VIEW) It seems unusual to carry out something like this at one o'clock in the morning. Was there a special reason for that?

ELAINE   One o'clock? Sorry, I don't follow?

INTERVIEWER   (OUT OF VIEW) Well it's seven a.m. here, but with the time difference between here and Texas ...

ELAINE   And they're ahead of us.

INTERVIEWER   (OUT OF VIEW) They're six hours behind.

ELAINE   They're behind? Um, right, sorry, you've confused me now. Um, is he dead or alive?

INTERVIEWER   (OUT OF VIEW) Well if it was meant to be seven a.m. their time, he's still alive. And seven a.m. their time will be one p.m. our time today.

ELAINE   One o'clock this afternoon? Oh isn't it silly. I wonder if Jackie will swap her shift with me? I'm sure she will, she's very good like that.

Oh, right. Well I might just snaffle a few more hours' sleep, I've been up since four. Um, are you ... are you still all right for one o'clock?

INTERVIEWER   (OUT OF VIEW) Yes, one o'clock's fine.

ELAINE	All right, well, er, I'll see you then.
	(TO SOMEONE IN THE BACKGROUND) Sorry, have you got those candles because I might just take them back.

HOW MANY HOW MUCH RUN

KATE AND ELLEN ARE WORKING AT THEIR DESKS.

KATE	What did you do last night?
ELLEN	We went bowling. It was a really good laugh actually, have you ever been?
KATE	Didn't you go to the gym?
ELLEN	No.
KATE	Oh!
ELLEN	I don't go to the gym.
KATE	Oh, I thought you did.
ELLEN	No I don't.
KATE	Don't you feel better after a bit of exercise?
ELLEN	Actually, do you mind if I just finish this?
KATE	Bit stiff this morning though. Didn't have time for a good warm down. You know what it's like after a long run.
ELLEN	Yeah, I bet.
KATE	You need a good warm down.
ELLEN	Right.
KATE	It's really important for the muscles.
ELLEN	Is it?
KATE	Yeah, recovery rates. James was saying. You know how pushy personal trainers can be.
ELLEN	You've got a personal trainer?
KATE	Yeah, yeah, he's making all the difference, you know, really spurring me on, all that running.
ELLEN	I bet.
KATE	Guess how far I ran last night? How far did I run last night?

ELLEN	I have no idea, anything's good, isn't it?
KATE	I don't think so. Have a guess.
ELLEN	I really don't know.
KATE	Think like an athlete. Just guess.
ELLEN	I wouldn't have a clue.
KATE	Doesn't even matter, doesn't even matter, just have a guess.
ELLEN	I can't.
KATE	Come on, you'll be amazed. Have a guess.
ELLEN	I'm not good at this.
KATE	Come on, we're just having a laugh. Guess.
ELLEN	Fifty miles.
KATE	Fifty miles! ... Fifty miles! I said run, not drive.
ELLEN	Thirty miles?
KATE	Thirty miles in one go! Do I look Ethiopian?
ELLEN	Five? Five miles.
KATE	Right, have you ever met me?
ELLEN	Two?
KATE	Eight ...
ELLEN	Wow.
KATE	... hundred metres.
ELLEN	Well that's still good.
KATE	Yes it is.
	Further than you'll ever run, you knock-kneed old trollop.

BERNIE ASSESSMENT

THERE IS A KNOCK AT THE DOOR.

SISTER	Come in.
	ANOTHER KNOCK AT THE DOOR.
SISTER	Come in.
	ANOTHER KNOCK AT THE DOOR.

SISTER	Bernie, come in.
	BERNIE PUTS HER HEAD ROUND THE DOOR.
BERNIE	Sorry, did you say come in?
SISTER	Yes, Bernie, come in, sit down.
BERNIE	I'm sorry I'm late, Sister. I know you said nine o'clock, but I went out for a curry with the lads last night and it turned into a bit of a late one, you know what I mean?
SISTER	As you know, Bernie, you've already had two written warnings this month.
BERNIE	Oh, d'you mind if I take me coat off, I'm sweating beef madras in here?
SISTER	Are you eating, Bernie?
BERNIE	Oh I am sorry, Sister, you must think I'm so rude. Would you like a rhubarb and custard?
SISTER	No thank you. And I'd appreciate it if you didn't eat in this office.
	BERNIE PUTS THE SWEET ON THE DESK.
SISTER	So in light of this I think you'd benefit from an unofficial assessment. Just answer the questions as best you can.
BERNIE	Did you have a nice weekend?
SISTER	How often do you change your uniform?
BERNIE	How often do I change my uniform?
SISTER	Yes, Bernie, it's a simple question.
BERNIE	Well, I sometimes put a bit of tinsel in my hat at Christmas. But besides that I don't really think it's up to me, you know what I mean?
SISTER	What is the difference between a rectal reading and an oral reading when using a digital thermometer?
BERNIE	(SIGHS) ... It's, er ... (MEASURES WITH HER HANDS) ... about two feet. And you probably want to give it a wipe with a damp cloth before you do the second one.
SISTER	The answer is one degree.
	On your morning round you found a patient who's died in the night. What's the first thing that you do?
BERNIE	In fairness, Sister, I haven't started my shift yet, so whoever it is I honestly don't think you can blame me.

SISTER	Bernie, the question is hypothetical.
BERNIE	Sister, I do understand what this is all about, and I just want to say, I didn't kill him, I swear to you.
SISTER	Didn't kill who?
BERNIE	Mr Thompson.
SISTER	Bernie, what makes you say that? Mr Thompson died over a week ago.
BERNIE	I know he did, and believe me, Sister, if I thought a night out would've finished him off I never would've taken him.
SISTER	Taken him where?
BERNIE	Well, as you know, Mr Thompson, he was a great one for the craic, and I promised him if he felt up to it I'd take him out for his birthday, you know, my treat.
SISTER	You took an eighty-one-year-old critically ill patient on a night out? A night out where?
BERNIE	(WHISPERS) Chitty Chitty Bang Bang.
SISTER	Where?
BERNIE	Chitty Chitty Bang Bang.
SISTER	Please tell me it's not true?
BERNIE	Well it's about a flying car, so ... I'd say probably not.
SISTER	You do know this treat, as you call it, may well have contributed to the heart attack later that evening that killed Mr Thompson.
BERNIE	Yes.
SISTER	I have absolutely no alternative but to send you home with immediate effect.
BERNIE	Oh that's really sweet of you, Sister, but to be honest, it was over a week ago now, I think I'm over the worst of it.
SISTER	Would you please leave my office.
	BERNIE PUTS HER COAT ON AND PICKS UP HER BAG, WHICH IS IN THE FORM OF A BIG SHAGGY DOG. SISTER LOOKS HORRIFIED.
BERNIE	It was a present.

LAUREN RYAN

LAUREN AND LIESE ARE IN A SHOPPING CENTRE.

LIESE	D'you go out with Ryan last night?
LAUREN	He blew me out. Can you believe that? I was like, 'are you joking me with this?' And he was like, 'don't start giving me grief,' and I goes, 'well you'd better stop vexing me then.'
LIESE	That is so dry. That boy is taking liberties.
LAUREN	You know what I'm saying? He must think I'm like some sort of lackey or something, waiting round for him.
LIESE	He needs to be told, man.
LAUREN	Right, he's coming, just shut up, shut up, shut up.
	RYAN WALKS UP.
RYAN	Alright?
LAUREN/LIESE	Alright.
RYAN	Listen, I was thinking that we shouldn't see each other no more.
LAUREN	Yeah, that's fine, whatever. Did you bring me that CD you was talking about, Liese?
RYAN	I think I should concentrate on my football and stuff.
LAUREN	Am I bovvered?
RYAN	What?
LAUREN	Am I bovvered though?
RYAN	I just don't think that ...
LAUREN	Don't care 'cos I'm not bovvered.
RYAN	I'm just like really busy, yeah?
LAUREN	Yeah, so am I and I ain't bovvered.
RYAN	We could still have a laugh, you know.
LAUREN	No we can't 'cos I ain't bovvered.
RYAN	I just gotta load on, you know.
LAUREN	Does my face look bovvered?
RYAN	Well it's just like, you know ...
LAUREN	Does my face look bovvered though?

RYAN	We can still hang around.
LAUREN	Is my face bovvered?
RYAN	You can still ...
LAUREN	Bovvered?
RYAN	Well ...
LAUREN	Bovvered?
RYAN	Well, when ...
LAUREN	Bovvered?
RYAN	It's like ...
LAUREN	Bovvered?
RYAN	Well I don't think ...
LAUREN	Bovvered, do I look bovvered though?
RYAN	No you don't look bovvered.
LAUREN	Yeah, that's 'cos I'm not.
RYAN	All right, just forget it, right.
LAUREN	Yeah I will, and don't tell me what to do.
	RYAN LEAVES.
LIESE	Are you alright?
LAUREN	Yeah, I'm fine.
LIESE	He is so lame, you know. That was such a rank thing to do.
LAUREN	Right, just shut up, right, you don't even know anything about it.
LIESE	Yeah, but you shouldn't let him talk to you like that.
LAUREN	But you should shut up though.
LIESE	Well why don't you just go and tell him.
LAUREN	Why don't you shut up though?
LIESE	Yeah, but he want ...
LAUREN	I said I want you to shut up.
LIESE	I was only ...
LAUREN	Just shut up though.
LIESE	Because the thing is ...
LAUREN	Why don't you shut up?

LIESE	No.
LAUREN	Look, I asked you to shut up.
LIESE	Yeah, but ...
LAUREN	Did I ask you to shut up?
LIESE	Yeah, but ...
LAUREN	So the thing is you should shut up.
LIESE	Yeah, but ...
LAUREN	Did I ask you to shut up?
LIESE	Yeah, but ...
LAUREN	Did I ask you to shut up?
LIESE	Yeah, but ...
LAUREN	Have you shut up yet?
LIESE	Yeah.

RYAN COMES BACK.

RYAN	I was just thinking, right ...
LAUREN	I ain't bovvered.

FRIGHTENED WOMAN
CALL ME BACK

MARGARET IS IN HER OFFICE, TALKING ON HER MOBILE PHONE.

MARGARET   Michael, can you call me back on the landline, you know I don't like speaking on the mobile ... Yes, I'm at the office. I'm at my desk now ... Right.

SHE PUTS THE PHONE DOWN AND WAITS.

Oh, come on!

THE PHONE RINGS.

MARGARET   (SCREAMS) Hello, Margaret speaking.

BUNTY RESTRAINING ORDER

GEOFF IS SITTING ALONE IN THE PUB. BUNTY ARRIVES.

BUNTY   Hiya, Geoff, sorry I'm late.

GEOFF   It's not a problem, Bunty, take a seat.

BUNTY   Just gonna go and get a pint, won't be a second.

GEOFF   Bunty, it's fine. Just take a seat, this won't take long.

BUNTY   I really would love a pint, Geoff.

GEOFF   Bunty, just let me say what I'm gonna say, then you can have as many pints as you like.

BUNTY   How was your holiday?

GEOFF   My holiday was fine, thank you. Unfortunately it was spoilt when I got back and I'd heard you'd been up to your old tricks again.

BUNTY   Can I have a sip of your pint?

GEOFF   Last time we were here I made it quite clear your time with the Doncaster Spinners was up. Your leaving was well overdue. So then I go on holiday, I think that'll be that. But oh no, when I get back I'm greeted with this.

HE PUTS A NEWSPAPER ON THE TABLE.

BUNTY   What's that?

GEOFF   This is last Thursday's *Echo*. (HE PICKS IT UP AND READS FROM IT) 'There were dramatic scenes yesterday outside Saint Mary's Junior School, the rehearsal venue of majorette display team the Doncaster Spinners, when Bunty Carmichael, thirty-two, of Mercer Road, held a one-woman protest at her expulsion from the group. Bunty, a majorette with the Spinners since she was six, chained herself to the school gates and sang Bon Jovi's "Living on a Prayer" ... repeatedly until she was let into the Wednesday night rehearsal. Group organiser Geoff Bird, currently on holiday in Benidorm, was unavailable for comment.'

BUNTY   Who told them I was thirty-two?

GEOFF   When are you going to get it into your head, Bunty?

BUNTY   I'm thirty-one!

GEOFF   We can't have you marching with a majorette team full of ten year olds. You look ridiculous.

ACCORDING TO THE RULES THE MINIMUM AGE FOR A DONCASTER SPINNER IS
SIX YEARS OLD. YOU TELL ME WHERE IT SAYS THERE'S AN UPPER AGE LIMIT

BUNTY	I look ridiculous! Gemma Graham dropped her baton three times during the *Star Wars* medley on Saturday. Who looked ridiculous then?
GEOFF	A Saturday demonstration you shouldn't have been involved in. But oh no, you wait till I'm abroad and then you worm your way back in.
BUNTY	The Spinners need me, Geoff.
GEOFF	The Spinners need you to leave them alone.
BUNTY	According to the rules the minimum age for a Doncaster Spinner is six years old. You tell me where it says there's an upper age limit.
GEOFF	There isn't one. Up until now we've been relying on self-respect.
BUNTY	Oh I see, so I'm being penalised because I've got the will to survive.
GEOFF	The only thing you've got is the will to be a bloody nuisance.
BUNTY	Eye of the tiger, Geoff. I've got the eye of a tiger.
GEOFF	Have you? Right, well I'm very pleased for you. And as well as the eye of the tiger you've also got that.

HE PUTS AN ENVELOPE ON THE TABLE.

BUNTY	What's that?
GEOFF	A restraining order, preventing you from going anywhere near the Doncaster Spinners, whether it be in rehearsal or performance.
	I'm sorry, Bunty, love, but ... you really left us no option.
BUNTY	I've been with the Doncaster Spinners for twenty-five years. That's nearly a quarter of me life. Don't let it end like this, Geoff. D'you remember when me mam couldn't afford to let me go on that trip to France when I was fourteen? You told me the Spinners had a whip round to pay for me. I know it was you, Geoff. I know it was you who paid for me to go.
GEOFF	Bunty, don't do this.
BUNTY	You believed in me then, why don't you believe in me now?
GEOFF	Bunty, it's not that I don't believe in you, love, it's just that ... it's time to move on.
BUNTY	Just let me come with you to Leeds for the Nationals and then I'll leave, I promise.
GEOFF	I'm sorry, love, I can't.
BUNTY	D'you remember what you used to say to me when I first joined the Spinners, when I used to say to you, Mr Bird, I can't spin me baton and march at the same time? D'you remember what you used to say to me?

GEOFF	There's no such thing as can't.
BUNTY	If you feel you can give me one more chance I'll be waiting at the top of me street for the minibus, nine o'clock on Friday morning. If you've not turned up by quarter past, well, I'll know you can't.

BUNTY WALKS OUT. ON HER WAY TO THE DOOR SHE PUTS 'DO YOU REALLY WANT TO HURT ME?' BY CULTURE CLUB ON THE JUKEBOX.

FRIGHTENED WOMAN
CHAMPAGNE

MARGARET IS IN THE LIVING ROOM. MICHAEL WALKS IN WITH CHAMPAGNE AND A GIFT.

MICHAEL	Happy anniversary, darling.
MARGARET	We said we weren't doing presents! You are naughty.
MICHAEL	Opening the champagne now, darling.
MARGARET	Okay.
MICHAEL	Doing it right now.
MARGARET	Yes, yes, I heard you. That's fine.
MICHAEL	Cork's coming out now.
MARGARET	Michael, honestly!
	CHAMPAGNE CORK POPS.
MARGARET	(SCREAMS)

HOW MANY HOW MUCH
WHAT AM I THINKING?

KATE AND ELLEN ARE WORKING AT THEIR DESKS.

KATE	Guess what I'm thinking.
ELLEN	One thirty.
KATE	Yeah.
	Freak!

OLD WOMAN UGLY BABY

THE OLD WOMAN'S GRANDSON ARRIVES.

OLD WOMAN	Is that you, darling?
GRANDSON	Hello, Nan.
OLD WOMAN	Here he is.
GRANDSON	You all right?
OLD WOMAN	You come up and see me? You come up and see me, ain't ya?
GRANDSON	Yeah.
OLD WOMAN	Yeah, I noticed that. Ahh, d'you get me shoe polish? Couldn't get it, could ya? I knew you wouldn't be able to get it. I said you wouldn't be able to get it. Didn't have it, did they? I knew they wouldn't have it. Couldn't get it, could ya, no?

HE PUTS THE SHOE POLISH ON THE ARM OF THE SOFA.

	Oh, did you get it? Oh, you did get it, did ya? I didn't think you'd be able to get it. I said you wouldn't get it, but you got it, look at that. You got it. They did have it, did they? Ohh, you did get it. Oh you are a good boy.
GRANDSON	I do me best.

SHE LOOKS CLOSELY AT THE SHOE POLISH.

OLD WOMAN	It's the wrong one. I knew you wouldn't get it.
GRANDSON	Nan, that's the one you always have.
OLD WOMAN	Huh! I see your sister today.
GRANDSON	Did ya?
OLD WOMAN	She's had the baby.
GRANDSON	I know.
OLD WOMAN	She's had the baby.
GRANDSON	I know.
OLD WOMAN	Oh, little girl.
GRANDSON	I know.
OLD WOMAN	She come up here and see me.
GRANDSON	Did she?
OLD WOMAN	Oh, you seen it? Oh, she's come up here, it's only a little dinky thing like

148

that. (CACKLES) Only a little tot no bigger than that. And she's let me hold her. (CACKLES) Ahh, you seen it?

GRANDSON	Yeah.
OLD WOMAN	Have you seen it?
GRANDSON	Yeah.
OLD WOMAN	Have you seen it?
GRANDSON	Yeah.
OLD WOMAN	Ain't it ugly?
GRANDSON	Nan!
OLD WOMAN	Oh, come on, I ain't never seen such an ugly child. It's frightened the fucking life out of me. And ain't it hairy? ... Ooh, I ain't never seen a child with so much hair on it. It's like a big hairy elf looking up at you. Oh, I nearly had a bilious attack looking at it. And they're calling it some funny name an' all, ain't they?
GRANDSON	No they're not.
OLD WOMAN	Calling it some funny name.
GRANDSON	Francesca.
OLD WOMAN	They're calling it Tescos.
GRANDSON	They're calling her Francesca.
OLD WOMAN	Calling the poor child Tescos. Oh, I said, don't call it Tescos, darling, whatever you do, it'll have enough fucking problems looking like that. And it's got a funny shaped head an' all, ain't it?
GRANDSON	Oh, Nan, come on, it was a forceps birth, it was very traumatic for them.
OLD WOMAN	I should think it was traumatic when that came out ... Ooh, I'd have run a mile if that'd been mine.

And it's got a wonky eye, innit? ... It's got a wonky eye, the child. Mind you, it gets that from that ugly git of a father.

He's got that, ain't he? One eye looking at you, the other one looking for you.

Nah, oh that's wrong, that is, I mean the pair of them together, they'll look like they came off *Fraggle Rock*.

Don't you say things like that, no, no, no, not up my house, oh no, no, she's a very good girl to me, she is. She looks after me, your sister. I said to her, 'you all right for money, darling, here y'are, take this tenner, go and buy yourself a pair of tights.' She said, 'I'm all right, Nan.' I said, 'take the money.' She said, 'I don't want the money.' I said, 'take the money.' She said, 'I don't want the money'. I said, 'take the money.' She said, 'I don't want the money'. I said, 'take the money, you'd bleed me dry if you could. Now take that ten pound note, buy that child a bonnet and tie it over its fucking face.'

GRANDSON   Nan!

OLD WOMAN   (CACKLES) She said to me, 'you're wicked, you are, you're a nuisance, we're gonna put you in a home.' No you don't. Ooh, wouldn't you like it, eh? Oh, what? Up there with all the old girls playing ping-pong, sing-along-a-Max-Bygraves, sitting in your own shit!

Not me, love, you ain't slinging me up the nut house. I shall have some champagne with me winkles, thank you very much, and I don't like crumble neither, so you can take that away. I don't like it, ain't eating it, no, no! Filth. Take it away. I don't want it and that's it. In fact you can take the crumble, take the old girls, take Max Bygraves, take your sister, take the fella with the wonky eye, take the fucking lot of you and shove 'em up your arse and piss off out of it! (CACKLES)

GRANDSON   Nan, you've got to stop this. You can't keep talking about people like that.

OLD WOMAN   (CACKLES)

GRANDSON   It's not funny.

OLD WOMAN   (MIMICKING) Oh, it's not funny. (CACKLES)

GRANDSON   Nan, seriously, stop it.

OLD WOMAN   Oh, fucking chill out! (CACKLES)

GRANDSON   Nan, why are you like this?

OLD WOMAN   (SINGING) 'I am what I am,
I am my own a-special creation,
I'll come take a look,
Give me the hook or the ovation,
It's my world,
That I want to have a little pride in,
My world,
And it's not a place I have to hide in,

Your life it's not worth a damn,

Till you can say,

I am what I am!'

Here I go (STANDS UP AND STARTS DANCING ROUND THE ROOM),

'I am what I am!

I don't want praise,

I don't want pity,

Here we go,

I bang my own drum

Some think it's noise but

I think it's pretty,

And so what if I love each sparkle and each spangle,

Why not see things from a different angle,

Your life is a sham,

Till you can shout out,

I am what I am!' (CACKLES)

GRANDSON   Nan, sit down.

OLD WOMAN   Fuck off! (CACKLES)

END CREDITS

END OF SERIES 1

THE CATHERINE TATE SHOW SCRIPTS

SERIES 2

SERIES 2 EPISODE 1

OPENING TITLES / THEME MUSIC

LAUREN CHRISTIAN

LAUREN AND HER CLASSMATES ARE WAITING FOR THEIR TEACHER.

LAUREN	What's this thing we're going on again?
LIESE	Theatre trip, innit. It's going to be well good.
LAUREN	No it ain't, it's gonna be boring.
RYAN	I reckon it might be all right, you know.
LAUREN	Yeah, it'll be a laugh, won't it?
LIESE	Are we getting the tube, 'cause I ain't got my pass with me?
LAUREN	No, we're getting a coach innit, how embarrassing is that?
RYAN	No, coach'll be a laugh, man.
LAUREN	Yeah, it'll be all right, won't it?
LIESE	I forgot to tell ya, d'you know who I saw yesterday?
	THE TEACHER ENTERS
LAUREN	Oh my God, what is she wearing?! What is she wearing? I ain't walking down the street with her looking like that.
LIESE	That is well shameful.
TEACHER	How are we all? Looking forward to a slice of culture?
LAUREN	Miss?
TEACHER	We're all in for a treat today.
LAUREN	Miss?
TEACHER	I'm going to give you your tickets now.
LAUREN	Miss?
TEACHER	And I want you to look after them.
LAUREN	Miss?
TEACHER	And don't lose them. Yes, Lauren?
LAUREN	Miss, I'm not being funny or nothing, but have you seen what you've got on?

TEACHER	Are you suggesting I don't know what I'm wearing, Lauren?
LAUREN	I don't know, Miss, I thought maybe someone had thrown it at you or something.
TEACHER	Well I think it's nice to make an effort once in a while.
LAUREN	No, I don't think it is, Miss.
TEACHER	Now the coach is parked by the main gates.
LAUREN	Are you going out on the street like that, Miss?
TEACHER	Gather up all your belongings.
LAUREN	But are you going out on the street looking like that though?
TEACHER	Yes, Lauren.
LAUREN	Oh my God, what have you got on your feet?! I'm too scared to look.
LIESE	Look at 'em though! Jesus Creepers.
RYAN	That is well bad.
TEACHER	I think it's nice to let your feet breathe.
LAUREN	Are you a Christian, Miss?
TEACHER	Lauren, get your things together.
LAUREN	But are you a Christian though?
TEACHER	We don't have time for this.
LAUREN	Right, but are you a Christian?
TEACHER	Lauren!
LAUREN	Is the Lord your shepherd, Miss?
TEACHER	Sorry?
LAUREN	But is he your shepherd though?
TEACHER	I beg your pardon?
LAUREN	Have you got Jesus in your heart, Miss?
TEACHER	What?!
LAUREN	But is he in your heart though?
TEACHER	Lauren!
LAUREN	Why d'you wear clothes like that then?
TEACHER	Lauren!
LAUREN	Do you like Cliff Richard, Miss?

TEACHER	Lauren.
LAUREN	Are you the Vicar of Dibley, Miss?
TEACHER	Lauren!
LAUREN	But are you the Vicar of Dibley though?
TEACHER	No, of course not!
LAUREN	Are we your flock?
TEACHER	What?
LAUREN	Are we your flock though?
TEACHER	No.
LAUREN	Is it that we are your flock?
TEACHER	No, you're not my flock.
LAUREN	Have you got a friend in Jesus, Miss?
TEACHER	Oh for goodness sake!
LAUREN	Does he want you for a sunbeam?
TEACHER	Look ...
LAUREN	Does he want you for a sunbeam though?
TEACHER	Lauren, enough. You're just wasting time now, not to mention being incredibly rude to me. Now get your things together or I shall suspend you from this trip.
LAUREN	Am I bovvered?
TEACHER	Lauren.
LAUREN	Am I bovvered though?
TEACHER	Look, don't make me do this.
LAUREN	I ain't doing nothing, 'cause I ain't bovvered.
TEACHER	You'll regret this.
LAUREN	No I won't 'cause I ain't bovvered.
TEACHER	I mean what I say.
LAUREN	Do I look bovvered?
TEACHER	I don't understand why you do this.
LAUREN	I don't understand why you wear that!
TEACHER	Lauren!

LAUREN	I don't give, Miss.
TEACHER	Come on.
LAUREN	Don't give, mate.
TEACHER	Now come on.
LAUREN	Don't care, mate.
TEACHER	Lauren.
LAUREN	Don't give, mate.
TEACHER	Lauren.
LAUREN	Don't give, mate.
TEACHER	Lauren.
LAUREN	Don't give, mate.
TEACHER	Stop it.
LAUREN	Aks me if I give. Aks me if I give.
TEACHER	Lauren, stop it!
LAUREN	Don't give, mate.
TEACHER	Lauren!
LAUREN	Don't give.
TEACHER	Stop it!
LAUREN	Don't give.
TEACHER	Come on.
LAUREN	Don't give.
TEACHER	Stop it.
LAUREN	I ain't bovvered.
TEACHER	I don't ...
LAUREN	Don't care.
TEACHER	I'm not, I'm not ...
LAUREN	Do I look bovvered?
TEACHER	No ...
LAUREN	Do I look bovvered though?
TEACHER	No.
LAUREN	Is my face bovvered?

TEACHER	No!
LAUREN	Is my face bovvered though?
TEACHER	No.
LAUREN	I ain't bovvered.
TEACHER	Come on.
LAUREN	I ain't bovvered.
TEACHER	Now ...
LAUREN	Face ...
TEACHER	Lauren ...
LAUREN	Look ...
TEACHER	No ...
LAUREN	Bovvered ...
TEACHER	You ...
LAUREN	Face ...
TEACHER	Now ...
LAUREN	Sandals.
TEACHER	Come ...
LAUREN	Look.
TEACHER	You ...
LAUREN	Bovvered.
TEACHER	Look.
LAUREN	Look at my face. Bovvered ...
TEACHER	Don't ...
LAUREN	Miss ...
TEACHER	Look ...
LAUREN	Bovvered ...
TEACHER	Don't make ...
LAUREN	Bovvered ...
TEACHER	Me ...
LAUREN	I ain't bovvered!
TEACHER	Right! Lauren, you are not going on this trip. You can sit there and get

	comfortable, it's going to be a very long afternoon.
LAUREN	Am I bovvered though?
TEACHER	Not another word!

DEREK FAYE DOCTOR

DEREK IS SITTING IN THE DOCTOR'S SURGERY.

DOCTOR	Right, well I don't think that looks too bad. I think a course of antibiotics should clear that up within about a week.
DEREK	Well yes, you see I'm very sensitive, Doctor. I have to be very careful what I put in my mouth.
DOCTOR	Right. How's your mother, Derek? Are you still living at home?
DEREK	She's very well thank you, Doctor, and yes, I'm still there. Couldn't leave her on her own, not at her age, dear.
DOCTOR	Oh, Derek, I've saved you one of these leaflets. The surgery is starting a new gay men's health clinic on the first Monday of every month. I don't know if that's something that would interest you.
DEREK	I beg pardon?
DOCTOR	It's a new health clinic on Mondays.
DEREK	Yes, I heard that bit.
DOCTOR	For gay men.
DEREK	I beg your pardon? How very dare you? I have never been so insulted!
DOCTOR	Derek, everything said here is completely confidential.
DEREK	What on earth are you insinuating?
DOCTOR	I'm sorry, Derek, I didn't mean to speak out of turn, I just always assumed you were gay.
DEREK	Gay, dear? Who, dear? Me, dear? No, dear. Just because I live with my mother and haven't found the right girl yet, you assume I take it up the arris? How very dare you?!
DOCTOR	I apologise unreservedly.
DEREK	Well yes, I think you should. Twenty-five years I've been coming here and then you suddenly come out with this? Well I find you impertinent. 'Gay men's health clinic'? How very dare you!

DEREK STANDS UP TO LEAVE.

DOCTOR Derek, your um ...

DEREK PICKS UP HIS BAG.

DEREK It's a gentleman's sponge bag.

DEREK AND HIS MALE COMPANION, LEONARD MINCING, PREVIOUSLY UNSEEN, GO TO LEAVE.

DEREK Come on, Leonard, we're off.

SANDRA KEMP THE REFUGE / 1

SANDRA AND TWO POLICE OFFICERS ARE IN AN INTERVIEW ROOM.

POLICE OFFICER Cup of tea?

SANDRA Thank you.

POLICE OFFICER Milk and sugar?

WPC HILLMAN Okay, we've taken a full statement, and in the light of the information you've given us, I don't feel it's safe for you to go back home.

I'm recommending we take you to a refuge where there's other people like yourself.

SANDRA Other people like myself? Is that your answer? Put us all in the ghettos, make sure all the freaks are together? It's not fair, I'm the victim here, not the criminal.

WPC HILLMAN I know, Sandra, but we can't protect you from these bigots twenty-four hours a day. That's why we're offering you a place at the refuge.

POLICE OFFICER HANDS SANDRA A CUP OF TEA.

SANDRA Thank you. I'm just sick of the inbreds in this stupid village sniggering at me behind my back. I thought about moving to London, you know, where people are more accepting, but I thought: no, why should I run and hide? I know it's a cliché, but I am what I am.

POLICE OFFICER Come on, Sandra, don't upset yourself.

SANDRA Don't upset myself?! The people in the village spit at me, the children throw dog muck through the letterbox and you're saying don't upset myself. It's just not fair!

WPC HILLMAN I know, Sandra, but at the end of the day there will always be those who just can't bring themselves to accept people who are ...

SANDRA You can say it, you know.

WPC HILLMAN Ginger.

SANDRA So where is this refuge?

POLICE OFFICER It's just outside Long Riston, about twenty miles from here. We can take you there tonight. We have got hair dye if you don't want people seeing you leave.

SANDRA Do you not think I've tried that? I dyed my hair and my eyebrows black when I was fifteen, but at the end of the day, I've still got freckly arms.

POLICE OFFICER So shall we go then?

SANDRA What's it like? Is everybody there ginger?

WPC HILLMAN Oh not all of them, there are a few normal ... non-ginger people who work there as well. But there's nothing to worry about, they've been trained to work with ginger people. And some of them even have ginger relatives themselves.

POLICE OFFICER We're not saying it's right that you should have to go there, but at the moment, what with the current hate campaigns against ging ... (STARTS TO SAY 'GINGERS' RHYMING WITH 'MINGERS') sorry, ginger people, we think it's the safest course of action right now.

SANDRA CRIES.

WPC HILLMAN Oh come on, love. Now come on. Now don't upset yourself. Come on, let's go. Good girl. Come on.

WPC HUGS HER AND WINCES BEHIND SANDRA'S BACK.

Come on now. Come on, it's going to be all right. There you go, come on now.

Now get that chair wiped down, will you, and make sure someone's here to burn my clothes when I get back.

TACTLESS WOMAN FACIAL HAIR

A PARTY IS TAKING PLACE.

LEE	Ally!
ALLY	Hello. Oh my goodness, I've just been in your garden, it's gorgeous.
LEE	Thank you. Look, I don't believe you've met Yvonne?
ALLY	No, hello. I'm Ally.
YVONNE	Hello.
ALLY	Hi. Oh, you've got something on your face there. Just give it a rub off. Yeah.
YVONNE	(RUBS HER CHEEK) Is that all right?
ALLY	No, I think it's a hair or something, hold on. (ALLY TRIES TO PULL THE HAIR FROM YVONNE'S CHEEK) It's attached. Um ... no, I mean you can't see it, I mean I, I mean I, I can see it, but then I know it's there, I mean he didn't see it. He doesn't know it's there. Oh Christ, there's more. Um. Don't pluck them, two will grow in one.
	So ... my nan had a beard.
	Ooh!

ALLY DROPS TO HER KNEES AND CRAWLS AWAY IN EMBARRASSMENT.

JANICE & RAY
SHIITAKE MUSHROOMS

JANICE AND RAY ARE SITTING ON THE SOFA.

RAY	Well, you might think you've heard everything, listen to this.
JANICE	Well I don't know where to start.
RAY	Well where do you start?
JANICE	We was on our way to see our Valder.
RAY	She'd just moved to Beverley.
JANICE	She used to live on Brandsholme.
RAY	Yeah, they don't need to know that.
JANICE	So anyway, we're on our way to see our Valder and we have to keep stopping because Ray hadn't brought his driving glasses.

163

THE DIRT

BASTARDS

RAY	I'm usually all right, but they'd just put in a new ring road, so ...
JANICE	So anyway, we stopped again to ask for directions and we noticed we were opposite a pub.
RAY	Listen to this.
JANICE	So we thought we'd better have something to eat before we get there, because Valder's one of these vegetarians.
RAY	They don't eat meat.
JANICE	So we cross over to this pub – it looked all right from the outside, didn't it?
RAY	Oh, famous last words.
JANICE	So we gets in and there's a sign saying it was, what do they call it?
RAY	A 'gastropub'. Don't ask.
JANICE	So we sits down and we looks at the menu.
RAY	Listen to this.
JANICE	Well, the first thing on the menu was mushroom soup. Well Ray liked the sound of that, didn't you?
RAY	Yeah, not for long.
JANICE	But then he read what were in it.
RAY	Listen to this.
JANICE	When he read what sort of mushrooms they were.
RAY	This is unbelievable.
JANICE	What were they called?
RAY	Dried shit ache mushrooms.
JANICE	You went mad, didn't you?
RAY	Dried shit ache mushrooms.
JANICE	You don't want that in soup, do you?
RAY	Shit ache mushrooms, dried.
JANICE	You don't want it in anything.
RAY	Now I've eaten everything, right, from Whitby crab to gammon with pineapple on it, so I'm not squeamish, but I am not eating anything that has got dried shit in the title. No way.
JANICE	This is in Beverley.
RAY	The dirty bastards!

PAUL & SAM LOTTERY

PAUL AND SAM ARE IN THE BEDROOM.

SAM	I've not told you about today, have I?
PAUL	What's been happening?
SAM	I can't believe I ain't told you.
PAUL	Told me what?
SAM	Have I told you already?
PAUL	Told me what, babe?
SAM	No, I must have told ya.
PAUL	You ain't told me nothing.
SAM	There is absolutely no way I could have got to … twenty past ten without telling you what's happened to me today.
PAUL	What is it?
SAM	You are gonna die.
PAUL	Oh come on.
SAM	I might as well ring the ambulance now because you are gonna die.
PAUL	Come on, you've got to tell me now.
SAM	I ain't told you, have I?
PAUL	You ain't said nothing.
SAM	This is quality.
PAUL	Come on, what you done this time?
SAM	Lunchtime, right, I'm out with Kerry and gay Simon and we're on our way to Gino's. We get there, we're about to go in and Kerry says she don't want nothing to eat 'cause she's doing the Atkins, all she wants is a packet of Extra Strong Mints. So I said, 'well I'm not that fussed about eating either,' 'cause I'd gone mad and had an M&S wheatgerm tricolore for me breakfast. Then gay Simon says in that case he don't want nothing either, 'cause he ain't eating on his own.
PAUL	What, nobody wanted anything to eat?
SAM	Nobody wanted anything to eat and we're stood outside Gino's like a bunch of nutters!
PAUL	No!

SAM	Well, we've looked at each other like that. (MAKES FACE) As usual, Kerry's the first to go, she starts laughing. I said 'I hope you ain't laughing at me, Kerry Baxter.' Baxter ain't her real name, but she don't talk to her dad no more so she thought she might as well change it. Meanwhile, gay Simon is laughing so much he's collapsed.
PAUL	No!
SAM	He has collapsed. It's one o'clock, the three of us are standing outside Gino's, no one's eating and we are racked with agony.
PAUL	What are you lot like when you get together?!
SAM	Oh but that ain't it.
PAUL	That ain't it?
SAM	That, that is your starter for ten.
PAUL	Oh this is unbelievable.
SAM	So, Kerry says she might as well get her mints from the newsagent. I said I'd go with her, and gay Simon said he'd come too as long as he didn't have to eat nothing. So we get there, Kerry buys her mints, gay Simon gets a newspaper and I buy one of them scratch cards.
PAUL	Oh here we go.
SAM	I know!
PAUL	Millionaires now, are we?
SAM	Shut up! Don't spoil it.
PAUL	Shall I book the holiday now?
	THEY LAUGH SILENTLY.
SAM	Stop it, I'm gonna wet meself!
PAUL	What are you like?!
SAM	You know what I'm like!
PAUL	I know what you're like.
SAM	So, we're in the shop, I'm doing me scratch card, gay Simon's looking at his newspaper, and Kerry's asking the man behind the counter if there's any carbohydrate in a strawberry mini-milk. Then, I've looked down at this scratch card, I've only got three pound symbols.
PAUL	No.
SAM	I swear to God.

PAUL	You won?
SAM	Three pound symbols, I've won me money back.
PAUL	Oh my God!
SAM	But that ain't it. I've give the card to the man behind the counter, he's looked at it like that, he said to me, 'you ain't won, 'cause all the symbols have got to be in a straight line.'
PAUL	Were they not in a straight line, babe?
SAM	No. One of 'em's in the corner, the other one's next to it and I can't remember where the other one is.

THEY LAUGH SILENTLY.

SAM	Well, we have gone off. Gay Simon is doubled up, I'm screaming like a witch and Kerry's got strawberry mini-milk coming out of her nose. It was bedlam!
PAUL	Why does it always happen to you?
SAM	I dunno!

SAM'S MOBILE PHONE BEEPS.

SAM	It's a text from Kerry.
PAUL	Oh 'ere we go. What's it say?
SAM	It says, it says: 'when are we gonna spend your winnings?'

THEY DOUBLE UP WITH LAUGHTER.

SANDRA KEMP THE REFUGE / 2

A POLICE CAR, SIREN ON AND LIGHTS FLASHING, PULLS UP OUTSIDE A REFUGE AT NIGHT. SANDRA IS HURRIED INTO THE BUILDING BY WPC HILLMAN. SHE IS HIDDEN UNDER A BLANKET.

RITA	Hello, Sandra, we've been expecting you. Don't worry, you're safe now. (TO WPC): Would you like to bring Sandra through?
WPC HILLMAN	Um, through to the other room?
RITA	Yes.
WPC HILLMAN	Are there more ... people through there?
RITA	Ginger people? Yes there are. This is a ginger refuge.

WPC HILLMAN	I brought Sandra here because we're short-staffed, but I can't … It's not the smell. It's, it's just that I'm not qualified to work with ginger people. I'm sorry. We'll get your stuff sent on to you, eh.
	WPC HILLMAN LEAVES.
RITA	Sandra, the police are some of the most ginger-phobic people in society. But don't worry, as I said, you're safe now. Come through.
	SHE LEADS SANDRA INTO THE REFUGE.
RITA	Welcome to Russet Lodge.
	THERE ARE GINGER PEOPLE EVERYWHERE.
RITA	Can we join you, Helen?
	RITA LEADS SANDRA OVER TO THE SOFA ON WHICH HELEN, A BRUNETTE IS SITTING.
RITA	This is Sandra Kemp, she's just arrived.
HELEN	Hello.
SANDRA	Hi. (LOOKING AT GINGER CHILD) Oh, she's beautiful, does her mum live at the refuge?
HELEN	I'm her mum.
SANDRA	I don't understand, you're not …
RITA	The ginger gene can skip a generation. Helen is what's known as a carrier. Although carriers can blend into society much more easily than gingers, at some point communities find out and people like Helen are driven out of their homes too.
HELEN	So I'm just like you. I may not be ginger here (SHE TAPS HAIR), but I'm ginger here. (SHE TAPS HER HEART.)

TACTLESS WOMAN STUTTER

A PARTY IS TAKING PLACE.

DAN	I'm glad you could come, it's so nice to see you.
SHAUN	Well, to be honest, I wasn't sure whether I was going to m m m make it tonight.
DAN	Ally!

ALLY	Hello. Come on you two, get on the dance floor!
DAN	Have you two met each other?
ALLY	No, hello, I'm Ally.
SHAUN	Hi, I'm sh sh sh ...
ALLY	Chaka Khan, let me rock you, let me rock you, Chaka Khan.
SHAUN	No, I'm sh sh sh ...
ALLY	Chaka Khan, let me rock you, that's all I want to do.
SHAUN	No, I'm sh sh sh sh ...
ALLY	Chaka Khan, let me rock you, let ...
SHAUN	Shaun.

ALLY REALISES SHAUN HAS A STUTTER.

| ALLY | Hmm? God, no, yeah, no, God. No, I mean I know, yeah no, I was just rapping. Yeah. No, 'cause I know you ... You, you, you're, because you're Shaun with the, hmm. (POINTS TO HIS MOUTH.) |
| | You know it goes if you sing. |

SHE PRETENDS DAN HAS GOOSED HER.

| ALLY | Don't do that! |

SHE LEAVES.

SHEILA CARTER FUNERAL

SHEILA AND SOME OTHER MOURNERS GET INTO A CAR AFTER A FUNERAL.

SHEILA	Beautiful service.
OTHERS	Hmm. Yeah. Yes.
PASSENGER 1	Ninety-eight, you've got to admit, the old bugger had a good innings.
OTHERS	(AMUSED) Yeah. That's true.
SHEILA	I'm sorry, I find that language very disrespectful. I think you should modify your tone.

THE ATMOSPHERE HAS TURNED FROSTY AND NO ONE SPEAKS. ONE OF THE PASSENGERS WHISTLES. SHEILA GLARES AT HIM AND HE STOPS. ONE OF THE OTHER PASSENGER'S MOBILE PHONE RINGS.

PASSENGER 2	Sorry, I thought I switched it off.
SHEILA	Unbelievable!

EVERYONE SITS IN SILENCE. SHEILA LETS OUT A LONG FART. THE OTHER
PASSENGERS LOOK AT HER.

SHEILA	I'm sorry, would you mind moving down? It's very cramped in here.

OLD WOMAN TELEVISION

THE OLD WOMAN IS SITTING IN HER LIVING ROOM. HER GRANDSON
RUSHES IN.

OLD WOMAN	Is that you, darling?
GRANDSON	Hiya, Nan.
OLD WOMAN	Oh sweetheart, thank God for that.
GRANDSON	Are you okay? I came as soon as I got your message.
OLD WOMAN	Oh you are a good boy.
GRANDSON	How are you feeling?
OLD WOMAN	I'm all right, love, yeah, I'll be all right. Just a bit of a shock, that's all.
GRANDSON	Yeah. When did it happen?
OLD WOMAN	Just after one o'clock. I've been sat here not knowing what to do since then.
GRANDSON	I got here as soon as I could, Nan.
OLD WOMAN	No, don't worry, darling, you weren't to know something like this was going to happen, how could anybody know? We all take these things for granted and then one day, bang, that's your lot.
GRANDSON	Yeah. Is it just ITV you can't get?
OLD WOMAN	No, love, it's all of 'em. I've been sat here in silence for the last three-and-a-half hours.
GRANDSON	Have you missed many of your programmes?
OLD WOMAN	Oh you know me, love, I don't really take much notice. It's just nice to have on in the background for a bit of company, that's all, you know.
GRANDSON	Yeah.
OLD WOMAN	Although I suppose I'll never know what happened to Tanisha.

GRANDSON	Who's Tanisha?
OLD WOMAN	Girl on that Trisha this morning, did you see it?
GRANDSON	No.
OLD WOMAN	Oh it's unbelievable. She's getting the fat sucked out of her thigh and injected into her backside. Only a young girl she was, I thought they'd got it the wrong way round at first, but no, she wants to have a bigger arse than she's already got. And if you ask me, it was a fair size to start with. You could show fucking cartoons on it!
GRANDSON	I've got someone coming over to have a look at the telly, he should be here soon.
OLD WOMAN	And I've missed me lovely gay boy, who takes you to an auction and sells all your old shit you were going to throw out. Oh he is clever.
GRANDSON	It might just be the fuse.
	THE DOORBELL RINGS.
GRANDSON	Oh that'll be Danny.
OLD WOMAN	Danny who?
GRANDSON	Oh, Nan, don't start, Danny Shaw.
OLD WOMAN	I don't know no one called Shaw.
GRANDSON	You do, you know his mother, Lou Shaw, she's just come out of hospital.
OLD WOMAN	Not Loopy Lou?
GRANDSON	Don't you dare say that while he's here, she's been very ill.
OLD WOMAN	Not Loopy fucking Lou! They've never let her out again, have they?!
	THE DOORBELL RINGS AGAIN.
GRANDSON	Nan, I'm warning you, he's repairing the telly for free, so don't upset him.
OLD WOMAN	For free?! No thank you. I don't want no charity. You can tell him to piss off out of it. I'd rather sit in the dark.
	DANNY WALKS IN, TOOLBOX IN HAND.
DANNY	(BRIGHTLY) Hello, Mrs Taylor, how are you doing?
OLD WOMAN	Hello, sweetheart, how are you?
DANNY	I'm not too bad thanks. Now, let's have a look at this.
OLD WOMAN	Oh you can take it away, darling, I never really look at it.
GRANDSON	I'll put the kettle on.

DANNY	Did Jamie check the fuse?
OLD WOMAN	Oh don't bother asking him nothing, darling, he ain't got a job.
DANNY	Now I'm not going to charge you for the repair, Mrs Taylor, and I don't want any arguing, okay?
OLD WOMAN	Oh you are a good boy. How's your mum, darling? I ain't seen her about for a while?
DANNY	(WARILY) She's okay, thanks.
OLD WOMAN	Oh. She still up the nuthouse?
GRANDSON	Nan ...
DANNY	Mum went into hospital for a rest, but she's much better now, thanks.
OLD WOMAN	Oh I am pleased, darling, 'cause last time I saw your mother she was down on all fours in the dry cleaners barking like a dog.
DANNY	No, I think you must have her confused with somebody else, Mrs Taylor.
OLD WOMAN	No, Loopy Lou! Everyone knows your mother. I remember when she got barred out of Tesco's when they caught her peeing in the deep freeze. Off her fucking nut, she was! Still, I'm very pleased to hear she's feeling better.
DANNY	There you go, Mrs Taylor. It was just the fuse, so I'll be on my way.
OLD WOMAN	No you won't, son, oh no, no, you'll take something for your trouble.
DANNY	Now we've been through this.
OLD WOMAN	Ah ah ah ah ah ...
DANNY	No I won't take your money.
OLD WOMAN	Now be a good boy.
DANNY	It's only a fuse.
OLD WOMAN	That's not the point. There's fifty pound. (SHE GIVES HIM £50.)
DANNY	Look, I can't take it.
OLD WOMAN	Now you take it and go and treat your mother to a nice new hat.
DANNY	Well thank you, Mrs Taylor, you look after yourself.
OLD WOMAN	Aah, thank you, sweetheart. Very obliged to you coming out at such short notice. Truly I am.
	OLD WOMAN FOLLOWS DANNY OUT. THE DOOR SHUTS BEHIND HIM AND THE OLD WOMAN COMES BACK IN.
OLD WOMAN	Huh! What a fucking liberty! Fifty pound?! Fifty pound?! He weren't here five minutes! Greedy little bastard!

176

GRANDSON	Nan, you offered it to him.
OLD WOMAN	He nearly took me fucking hand off!
GRANDSON	But he was going to do it for free.
OLD WOMAN	Mugged in me own front room. Oh, and he was such a lovely little boy an' all. I remember he used to come up here wearing his little cowboy outfit. Should have fucking kept it on.
GRANDSON	Nan!
OLD WOMAN	And a lot of good you were an' all, stood there worrying about what side your hair's parted, while I'm getting turned over by a man whose mother eats her own shit!!

SANDRA KEMP THE REFUGE / 3

SANDRA IS SITTING ON A SOFA IN THE REFUGE, TALKING TO RITA.

SANDRA	Being ginger is who I am. Why should I deny that?
RITA	You shouldn't. And that's why we're here. We have all sorts of gingers here. Gingers in denial, confused gingers, even militant gingers. But they have one thing in common, they don't need to fear the outside world. They're all welcome to stay here in peace and harmony.
	A FIGHT BREAKS ABOUT BETWEEN TWO WOMEN. CHRISSY IS HOLDING A BROKEN BOTTLE.
CHRISSY	I've had enough of this! I've had enough, this is the last time!
RITA	Put the bottle down.
CHRISSY	What's she doing here? She's not even ginger, she's strawberry blonde.
FRANCES	I've as much right to be here as you.
CHRISSY	Look at her face. She's not even pale.
FRANCES	I'm as ginger as you are.
CHRISSY	How come you're the only one who uses the garden when it's sunny? Oh look, she's getting a tan.
RITA	All right everyone, that's enough. Look at us! Look at us. From strawberry blondes to flame-haired beauties, we are all ginger. And if we can't get on with each other in here, what chance do we have in the real world? 'Duracell, ginger nut, carrot-top, copper knob'. We're used to getting that

kind of abuse every day out there. People asking us to move away from areas where food is being prepared. Total strangers assuming we're Scottish! Forever trawling the streets trying to find a hairdresser's that isn't 'fully booked'. Well not in here. This is a safe haven for everyone and everything ginger. Let's keep it that way.

GINGERS GATHER ROUND AND SING TO A GUITAR.

'I'd like to build the world a home
And furnish it with love
Grow apple trees and honey bees
And snow white turtle doves ...
I'd like to teach the world to sing
In perfect harmony.
I'd like to hold it in my arms
And keep it company.'

AN ANTI-GINGER GANG HAS GATHERED OUTSIDE.

CROWD   'Gingers out! Gingers out!'

GINGERS   'I'd like to see the world for once
               All standing hand in hand.'

END CREDITS

SERIES 2   EPISODE 2

OPENING TITLES / THEME MUSIC

AGA SAGA WOMAN   GEORDIE

THOMAS AND CHLOE ARE EATING BREAKFAST.

THOMAS	There you are, Mummy. We were beginning to think you didn't want your brioche.
MUMMY	Thomas, Chloe, Mummy has something to tell you.
THOMAS	What is it, dear heart? Tell all.
MUMMY	Alice can't come to work today, so Mummy's had to arrange ... for an agency nanny to come round.
	DOOM MUSIC.
CHLOE	Mummy, no!
MUMMY	We must all be very brave.
THOMAS	I don't feel very well.
MUMMY	Be strong, my darlings, because there's something else you should know. Something much worse. This ... person ... the agency are sending us, she's from the North.
	DOOM MUSIC.
MUMMY	Newcastle I'm told, but could be as far as Sunderland. I'm sorry.
	THE DOORBELL RINGS. MUMMY OPENS THE FRONT DOOR.
GINA	Hiya, I'm Gina from the agency. Are you Mrs Montgomery?
	MUMMY CAN ONLY SQUEAK BACK AT GINA. GINA GOES INTO THE HOUSE.
GINA	Hey, I tell you what, I thought I was going to be late, the traffic was that bad. Never mind, here I am, on time, so no worries there.
	You've got a lovely place, Mrs M. You don't mind if I call you Mrs M, do you? Only Mrs Montgomery's a bit of a gobful.
	(TO CHILDREN) Hiya. What do you call yous then? I can see I'm gonna have me hands full with you pair of tykes, aren't I?
CHLOE	Mummy, Mummy, what's she saying?

MUMMY	I don't know, Chloe, but she sounds awfully angry, so don't provoke her in any way. Avoid looking her in the eyes.
THOMAS	Is she going to kill us?
MUMMY	Ssh, ssh, Thomas, Mummy won't let anything happen to you.
GINA	Right, I'll start with the breakfast things, but first, why don't I make us all a nice milky brew? And who fancies a couple of biccies as well, eh?
MUMMY	Run for your lives, children, we're all going to die!!

DOOM MUSIC.

THEY FLEE, LEAVING GINA LOOKING AFTER THEM.

SHEILA CARTER TAXI

SHEILA IS IN THE BACK SEAT OF A MINICAB, STUCK IN TRAFFIC.

SHEILA	Is that air freshener I can smell?
DRIVER	Yes, it's supposed to be vanilla.
SHEILA	It's very overpowering.
DRIVER	I can put it in the glove compartment if it's bothering you.
SHEILA	Would you mind?

HE PUTS THE AIR FRESHENER AWAY. THE RADIO IS PLAYING.

SHEILA	Sorry, do you mind if we don't have the radio on?
DRIVER	Sure, no problem.
SHEILA	I've just got a bit of a headache.

A VAN IN FRONT OF THEM HAS A LOT OF SMOKE COMING FROM THE EXHAUST.

SHEILA	Look at that. Do you mind winding up your window?
DRIVER	Yeah, sure.
SHEILA	Disgusting!

SHEILA LETS OUT A LONG FART. THE TAXI DRIVER IS DUMBFOUNDED AND WINDS DOWN HIS WINDOW AGAIN.

| SHEILA | It's very cold in here. Could you put your heating on? |

LAUREN NEW TOP

LAUREN AND LIESE ARE IN THE CAFÉ AREA OF A SPORTS CENTRE.

LAUREN	I got a new top for tonight.
LIESE	Is it?
LAUREN	I got a well good price for it.
LIESE	Did ya?
LAUREN	It was £15.99, right.
LIESE	Yeah.
LAUREN	But I didn't pay that.
LIESE	Did you haggle though?
LAUREN	You should have seen me though. This is me, right. 'How much is that top?' And this is her, right. '£15.99.' And this is me, right. 'So what we saying?' And this is her, right. '£15.99.' And this is me, right. 'So what are we saying?' And this is her, right. '£15.99.' And this is me, right. 'So what're we really saying?' And this is her, right. '£15.99.' And this is me, right. 'I don't think so.' And this is her, right. 'What d'you mean?' And this is me, right. 'It's got a button missing.'
LIESE	What d'you pay for it, mate?
LAUREN	Fifteen pound.
LIESE	That is well good.
LAUREN	Innit though. I'm going to wear it for the gig tonight.
LIESE	What gig, mate?
LAUREN	Me and Ryan are going to a gig tonight.
LIESE	Is it?!
LAUREN	I'm gonna look well hip hop.
	RYAN ENTERS IN BOXING GEAR.
RYAN	Alright?
LIESE / LAUREN	Alright.
RYAN	I'm well worked out.
LAUREN	Did you win?
RYAN	I smashed him in the second with my dambuster.

LAUREN	Is it? Do you want some of my Snickers Bar?

RYAN SITS DOWN AT THE TABLE.

LAUREN	This gig's gonna be well alright. I can't wait to see Naughty.
RYAN	Who, mate?
LAUREN	Naughty Rascal.
RYAN	Naughty Rascal?
LAUREN	He's a well big shout out.
RYAN	It's Dizzee Rascal.
LAUREN	What?
LIESE	It's Dizzee Rascal, mate!
RYAN	Naughty Rascal! That is well bad.
LAUREN	Am I bovvered?
RYAN	Can you believe that?
LAUREN	Am I bovvered though?
LIESE	Take the shame.
LAUREN	No, 'cause I ain't bovvered.
LIESE	Take the shame though.
LAUREN	I ain't even bovvered though.
RYAN	You've well embarrassed yourself.
LAUREN	Do I look bovvered?
RYAN	You're an embarrassment though.
LAUREN	Do I look bovvered though?
RYAN	You're well shameful.
LAUREN	I don't care, 'cause I ain't bovvered.
RYAN	You've brought shame on your family
LAUREN	I don't care, 'cause I don't even like 'em.
RYAN	But you've shamed them though.
LAUREN	I don't even care, 'cause I don't even like 'em.
LIESE	But they're your parents though.
LAUREN	No they ain't though.
LIESE	Yes they are though.

LAUREN	No they ain't though.
LIESE	Well why do you live with them then?
LAUREN	Are you disrespecting my family?! Are you disrespecting my family though?
LIESE	No I ain't though.
LAUREN	You're disrespecting my family.
LIESE	I'm just saying!
LAUREN	Are you calling my mum a prostitute?
LIESE	No, I'm just ...
LAUREN	Are you calling my dad an alcoholic?
RYAN	But you said Naughty Rascal, mate.
LAUREN	But I ain't even bovvered though.
LIESE	But it's Dizzee though.
LAUREN	But I ain't even bothered though.
LIESE	Yeah, but ...
LAUREN	Do I look bovvered?
LIESE	Yeah, but ...
LAUREN	Is my face bovvered?
LIESE	No, but ...
LAUREN	Is my face bovvered though?
LIESE	Well ...
LAUREN	But is it bovvered though?
LIESE	I ...
LAUREN	Do I look bovvered?
LIESE	Just ...
LAUREN	Do you think I'm bovvered?
LIESE	What ...?
LAUREN	Aks me if I'm bovvered.
LIESE	You ...
LAUREN	Aks me if I'm bovvered.
LIESE	But that's ...
LAUREN	Aks me if I'm bovvered!

LIESE	Are you bovvered?
LAUREN	No, I ain't even bovvered.
LIESE	But you said that it's ...
LAUREN	Face.
LIESE	No ...
LAUREN	Look.
LIESE	But ...
LAUREN	Face.
LIESE	Just ...
LAUREN	Bovvered.
LIESE	Just ...
LAUREN	Look.
LIESE	Right ...
LAUREN	Face.
LIESE	Look ...
LAUREN	Bovvered.
LIESE	Come ...
LAUREN	Look.
LIESE	Wait ...
LAUREN	Face.
LIESE	Just ...
LAUREN	Bovvered.
	Face.
	Bovvered.
	Look.
LIESE	Just ...
LAUREN	Face.
	Bovvered.
	Look.
	Face.
	Bovvered.

LIESE	I've got ...
LAUREN	Naughty.
	Face.
	Rascal.
	What?
	Face.
	Bovvered.
	I AIN'T BOVVERED!!
RYAN	Have you got your autograph book?
LAUREN	Why?
RYAN	Naughty Rascal's right behind you, mate.

CUT TO A SMALL BOY BEHIND LAUREN POURING SUGAR ALL OVER THE TABLE.

MOO SHEPHERD / 1

MOO IS SHOWN AT WORK OUTDOORS, SEEMINGLY IN HER ELEMENT.

VOICE OVER	Moo Shepherd is thirty-six and lives in Studley, just outside Birmingham. She's been a professional dog trainer for more than ten years. Last year, after winning the Midlands six-part obedience championship, known locally as the 'Birmingham Six', her dog and lifelong companion, Mr Tibbs, died peacefully in his sleep.
	Now Moo has only eight weeks to train her new dog and retain her title of Dog Obedience Champion for the seventh year running.
	MOO IS LEADING A DOG TRAINING CLASS OUTDOORS, WITH A GROUP OF PUPILS, LEADS IN HAND.
MOO	So it's just a gentle trot and stay close. Stay close.
PUPILS	Stay close. Stay close. Stay close.
MOO	Come on, I can't hear you.
PUPILS	Stay close. Stay close.
MOO	What about the praise? Don't forget the praise, you'll get nowhere without the praise.
PUPILS	Good boy. Good boy.
MOO	Okay everyone, that's our ninety minutes. And as Will Young said in

2003, 'I think I'd better leave right now'.

A lot of you have done really well today, and if we keep up this standard, in a few weeks I can see myself letting some of you bring your dogs.

MOO IS WALKING ALONG A PATH TOWARDS THE CAMERA. CUT TO PUPILS RUNNING AROUND IN CIRCLES WITH LEADS BUT NO DOGS.

INTERVIEWER	(OUT OF VIEW) It's been said your teaching methods are somewhat unorthodox.
MOO	I've been called a maverick, and I'll be honest with you, it's not a title I shy away from.
INTERVIEWER	(OUT OF VIEW) Legend has it, during an obedience class in 2001 you made a woman eat a tin of dog food for arriving ten minutes late.
MOO	Is that what people are saying? (SHE LAUGHS)
INTERVIEWER	(OUT OF VIEW) Is it true?
MOO	Yes. You can't train the dog unless you've trained the owner. Fact.
INTERVIEWER	(OUT OF VIEW) Is it also true she tried to sue you for actual bodily harm?
MOO	Yes, she did try to sue, unsuccessfully I might add, but that rather unfortunate episode is behind me now. In the words of the king of pop, Michael Jackson: 'she's out of my life'.
INTERVIEWER	(OUT OF VIEW) And how about your new dog, Moo, how's he coming along?
MOO	She, it's a girl actually. Bit of a break from tradition, yeah. After ten years of competing with Mr Tibbs, I suddenly thought: come on, Moo, you can't knock what you've never tried, and next thing I know I've entered a bitch.

MOO ARRIVES AT HER CAR

Actually, could you cut that last bit out?

Oh I don't believe it! I think the keys have dropped out of me pocket again. I'm going to have to go back.

INTERVIEWER	(OUT OF VIEW) Will she be okay? It looks quite stuffy in there.
MOO	No, no, she'll be fine. The trick is to keep the window open about half an inch, that's all they need. Yeah.

MOO GOES TO THE WINDOW. IT'S CLOSED. MOO LOOKS CONFUSED.

She must have closed it. Won't be two ticks.

MOO RUNS OFF. THE DOG SLIDES DOWN THE WINDOW AND DISAPPEARS FROM VIEW.

BERNIE HYPNOSIS

BERNIE ENTERS A HOSPITAL SIDE WARD.

BERNIE   Sorry I'm late, Mr Hicks, but I've got a bit of a personal problem for which I was told to apply live yoghurt. Well I could only find a Muller Crunch Corner, so you can imagine the chafing I've had all morning.

So, Mr Hicks, I'll just ...

BERNIE NOTICES MR HICKS ISN'T IN HIS BED.

Mr Hicks? Mr Hicks?

SHE LOOKS UNDER THE BED.

Not here.

SHE SEES SOME CHOCOLATES ON THE BEDSIDE TABLE.

Oh my God, truffles! Oh my God, that's better than sex. Well almost. Oh God alive.

SHE TAKES THE REMOTE CONTROL AND TURNS THE TELEVISION ON.

HYPNOTIST   (ON TV) So basically ask yourself three questions: Are you stressed out at work? (BERNIE NODS) Do you feel undervalued? (BERNIE NODS) Do you want to change the pattern of failure in your life and enjoy the sweet smell of success? (BERNIE NODS)

Okay, don't think about this, just do it. Sit down and make yourself comfortable, or even better, lie down if you can. Okay. Are you feeling comfortable?

BERNIE   Hang on.

BERNIE LIES ON THE BED.

HYPNOTIST   (ON TV) First of all I need you to close your eyes and take a deep breath. In and out. In and out. You are feeling sleepy, very sleepy. Now repeat after me: My name is, and say your name.

BERNIE   My name is, and say your name.

HYPNOTIST   (ON TV) I'm a strong, independent woman and I will soon be smelling the sweet scent of success.

BERNIE   I'm a strong, independent woman and I will soon be smelling the sweet scent of success.

HYPNOTIST   (ON TV) My days of feeling undervalued are over.

BERNIE	My days of feeling undervalued are over.
HYPNOTIST	(ON TV) From now on, I'm going to fulfil my potential and walk the walk and talk the talk.
	BERNIE HAS GONE TO SLEEP ON MR HICKS' BED. SISTER WALKS INTO THE WARD WITH MR HICKS.
SISTER	Here we are Mr Hicks. Bernie!
	Bernie, wake up!
BERNIE	Oh my God.
SISTER	What on earth is going on?
HYPNOTIST	(ON TV) You're feeling sleepy, very sleepy.
BERNIE	Um ...
SISTER	What are you doing in a patient's bed? Come on, explain yourself.
BERNIE	I'm a strong smelling woman and I will soon be sucking independent sweets.
SISTER	I beg your pardon?
BERNIE	My days of feeling overvalued are under.
SISTER	Bernie, either you start making sense immediately or you will be out of this hospital so fast your feet won't touch the ground.
BERNIE	From now on I'm going to feel potentially full with a talkie walkie and a walkie talkie.
SISTER	Right, that's it! My office, now.
BERNIE	I'm sorry, Sister, I don't know what came over me.
SISTER	I've heard enough, just move yourself!
	I'm sorry, Mr Hicks, we'll soon get you settled.
MR HICKS	Thank you.
	BERNIE SPOTS THAT MR HICKS IS CARRYING A YOGHURT.
BERNIE	Excuse me, that's not a live yoghurt is it?
SISTER	Get out!

ANNOYING WAITRESS
BUSINESS LUNCH

A MAN AND A WOMAN ARE SITTING AT A RESTAURANT TABLE.

MAN	I'm sorry, I could have sworn I booked it last week.
WOMAN	It's not a problem, this will be fine, what is it? Burgers?
AMANDA	Hi guys!
WOMAN	Oh hello. Can we ...
AMANDA	Welcome to BBJ's. I'm your waitress for today. My name's Amanda, but my friends call me Zebedee. I'm a fiery Taurean with my moon in Uranus. Careful! I'll do the jokes. Any birthdays or anniversaries today for yourselves?
WOMAN	Look, we'd just like to eat, thank you. Do you know what you want?
AMANDA	All birthday cocktails are half price until seven o'clock, except 'A Poke in the Eye' and 'The Screaming Fadge', which are three for two until six thirty.
MAN	Thank you, but we just want to eat something quick.
AMANDA	I've also been asked to point out to our more generously proportioned customers that when we say the Hawaiian buffet is 'all you can eat', that is in fact an offer, not a challenge.
MAN	Can we just order, please?!
AMANDA	Thank you, sir, there's no need to take it out on your server.
WOMAN	Right. I'd like a Plain Jane burger, please.
AMANDA	Any Freaky Fries with that today for yourself?
WOMAN	It says it comes with Freaky Fries.
AMANDA	Yes, I know, but would you like them?
WOMAN	Yes.
MAN	Right, and I'd like a ...
AMANDA	Table four getting freaky with her fries!
	WE HEAR CHEERS FROM THE BAR.
MAN	And I'll have the Oops Upside Your Head burger ...
	MUSIC: 'OOPS UPSIDE YOUR HEAD'
	THE RESTAURANT LIGHTING CHANGES AND THE STAFF BEGIN A SYNCHRONISED DANCE. THE MYSTIFIED COUPLE LEAVE THE RESTAURANT.

HOW MANY HOW MUCH
LATIN DANCER

KATE AND ELLEN ARE WORKING AT THEIR DESKS.

KATE	(SINGS 'LA BAMBA' AT ELLEN)
ELLEN	Sorry, do you ...
KATE	(SINGS MORE)
ELLEN	Do you mind ...
KATE	(SINGS MORE)
ELLEN	Sorry, do you mind keeping it down, 'cause I'm ...
KATE	Sorry, was I doing that out loud?
	ELLEN NODS.
KATE	God, I did my Salsa class last night. I just can't get the music out of my head.
ELLEN	Can you not?
KATE	No. Never thought of myself as a dancer, but turns out I'm rather good.
ELLEN	Great.
KATE	Tonay says.
ELLEN	Who?
KATE	Tonay. My instructor.
ELLEN	Tony?
KATE	Yeah, but he's from Rio.
ELLEN	Oh, right.
KATE	He's always praising me.
ELLEN	Look, I've really got to get this finished.
KATE	Yeah. He said I moved like a gazelle.
ELLEN	Did he?
KATE	He said I'm ready to do the workshops in Barcelona.
	NO RESPONSE.
	He said I'm ready to do the workshops in Barcelona.
ELLEN	Did he?

KATE	He's been really complimentary about everything actually.
	Guess how old he thought I was? How old did Tonay think I looked?
ELLEN	Well I really wouldn't like to say.
KATE	Why not? Have a guess!
ELLEN	I have no idea.
KATE	Well that's the point of guessing, come on!
ELLEN	Please don't make me do this.
KATE	It's just a bit of fun, have a guess!
ELLEN	But I don't want to.
KATE	It doesn't matter, just guess.
ELLEN	Well ...
KATE	Come on. How old did he say I was?
ELLEN	I can't think.
KATE	Yes you can, just guess!
ELLEN	Sixteen.
KATE	Sixteen? Sixteen?!
ELLEN	Twenty.
KATE	He's not blind!
ELLEN	Twenty-five.
KATE	Right, have you ever looked at me?
ELLEN	Forty-two?
KATE	What?
ELLEN	Forty-eight?
KATE	Forty-eight?! Vanessa Feltz is forty-three!
ELLEN	Thirty-seven?
KATE	Right, do you think I look thirty-seven?
ELLEN	No.
KATE	No, neither does Tonay.
ELLEN	Twenty-eight?
KATE	Older than that.
ELLEN	Thirty-five?

KATE	Not that old.
ELLEN	Thirty-three?
KATE	I don't think so.
ELLEN	Thirty-one?
KATE	Right, forget it.
ELLEN	Twenty-nine?
KATE	Thirty! He thought I looked thirty.
ELLEN	Wow. That is flattering.
KATE	Yes, it is.
ELLEN	I used to tap.
KATE	Right, do you ever stop talking?!

MOO SHEPHERD / 2

MOO IS OUTSIDE A HOUSE, HER DOG LYING STILL ON THE FLOOR WHILST SHE TRIES TO ENCOURAGE IT TO RESPOND TO HER COMMANDS.

VOICE OVER Champion dog trainer Moo Shepherd has now been preparing her new protégé for seven weeks. It's not looking good. So far Moo has only managed to stop Lady Penelope urinating on her clothes. Apart from this, despite being sure she had a future champion on her hands, they have achieved absolutely nothing. And with the Birmingham Obedience Championships only one week away, it looks like Moo's reputation of being able to train any dog to do anything is very much on the line.

THE DOG FINALLY RUNS OFF, THEN RUNS BACK AND JUMPS UP AT MOO. SHE SCREAMS.

MOO I don't understand it, we can't even get past the basics. I can honestly say I have never known a dog like it.

Desperate situations call for desperate measures. Now, I've never been a big fan of these, but at this stage we've got nothing to lose, however. Lady Penelope is wearing a collar that when I press this remote gives off a small electric charge. Now, it's nothing to worry about, it's completely harmless, it's just guaranteed to give an unruly canine a nudge in the right direction.

Now, watch this. Lady Penelope, sit. (THE DOG REMAINS STANDING) Lady

Penelope, sit. (THE DOG REMAINS STANDING) Now, with the gentle electronic pulse, Lady Penelope, sit.

THE DOG IS GIVEN AN ELECTRIC SHOCK. SHE KEELS OVER.

INTERVIEWER	(OUT OF VIEW) Is she okay?
MOO	Who?
INTERVIEWER	(OUT OF VIEW) Lady Penelope?
MOO	Oh yeah. Yeah, no, she's, she's had a busy day. She's just having a lie down. Actually shall we, shall we um, shall we turn that off now, shall we?

SHE INDICATES THE CAMERA.

IRENE & VERN DESMOND TUTU

NEVILLE WALKS UP TO A ROADSIDE BURGER VAN. IRENE AND VERN ARE BEHIND THE COUNTER.

IRENE	Morning, Nev.
NEVILLE	Morning, Irene.
IRENE	What did I say, Vern? As soon as something happens, you can guarantee, ten minutes later, Neville arrives. Double cheese?
NEVILLE	Yes please.
IRENE	Double cheese for Neville.
NEVILLE	So what happened then, Vern?
IRENE	Oh it's been non-stop. You'll never believe who was here about an hour ago.
NEVILLE	Go on.
IRENE	Vernon, what's the name of that man with the Calor Gas bottle?

VERNON SAYS NOTHING.

IRENE	Black fella, always on the telly laughing.
NEVILLE	Always on the telly laughing? Um ...
IRENE	Oh. Desmond Tutu!
NEVILLE	What, the Bishop?
IRENE	Yeah. Calor Gas bottle had gone in his caravan and he was trying to find a Halfords.

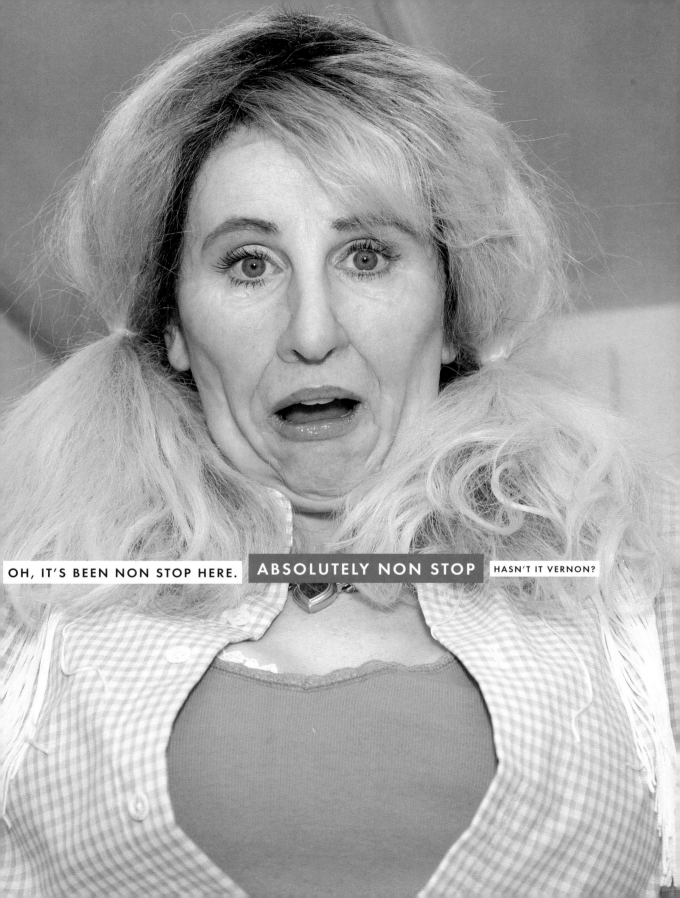

OH, IT'S BEEN NON STOP HERE.   ABSOLUTELY NON STOP   HASN'T IT VERNON?

NEVILLE	Well he's not going to change a Calor Gas bottle at Halfords, he wants a Homebase.
IRENE	Well that's what Vern said.
NEVILLE	So where's he got a caravan?
IRENE	Well that's it, he hasn't. He's done one of these holiday swaps with the Archbishop of Canterbury. Well he's absolutely livid. Archbishop of Canterbury is sunning himself on a fifty-acre South African farmhouse, while Des arrives to find he's swapped for a two-berth caravan on Canvey Island with no heating.
NEVILLE	Did he not think to ask what he was swapping for?
IRENE	Well obviously not, judging by his language. I said to Vern, they'll be taking that Nobel Peace Prize off him when they hear where he's going to stick that Calor Gas bottle.
	Any sauce?
NEVILLE	No, this is smashing. Right, see you tomorrow.
IRENE	All right, Neville, take care.

OLD WOMAN
DOCTOR'S SURGERY

PATIENTS ARE SEATED IN A SURGERY WAITING ROOM. A MALE DOCTOR WALKS IN.

MALE DOCTOR	Kate Moorcroft?
	A PATIENT FOLLOWS THE DOCTOR. THE OLD WOMAN AND HER GRANDSON WALK IN.
OLD WOMAN	Here we go. Oh here we go. Oh have a look who it is! Hello, sweetheart, you're Lizzy Jackson's granddaughter, aren't you, yeah? I used to go to school with your grandmother. Oh isn't it lovely to see you? I haven't seen you since you were that big. Oh, I've heard your grandmother ain't too well, she's had her hip done again, ain't she? Will you give her my regards? Tell her I've missed seeing her about. It's beautiful to see you, sweetheart. Give me regards to your grandmother. Oh, be lucky darling.
GRANDSON	Who's that?
OLD WOMAN	Gawd knows. There you are look, what did I tell you, it's packed out.

GRANDSON	It's not that bad.
OLD WOMAN	Oh there's nothing wrong with half these people, have a look.
GRANDSON	Come on, Nan.
OLD WOMAN	(POINTS TO A BLACK MAN IN A TRACK SUIT) And look at this one in a running suit! Years ago you had to be spewing up your guts to see a doctor and now they turn up in running suits. Oh they've got a cheek.
GRANDSON	Nan, come on.
RECEPTIONIST	Have you got an appointment?
OLD WOMAN	Eh?
RECEPTIONIST	Do you have an appointment?
OLD WOMAN	No, dear, I'm here to see Doctor Bailey.
RECEPTIONIST	Is it an emergency?
OLD WOMAN	Who is it?
RECEPTIONIST	Is it an emergency?
OLD WOMAN	What's she talking about?
RECEPTIONIST	What is it that's wrong with you?
OLD WOMAN	What's it got to do with you?!
RECEPTIONIST	What is it that's wrong with her?
OLD WOMAN	Oi oi oi, I'll thank you to talk to the organ grinder, not the monkey.
RECEPTIONIST	If it's not an emergency, you won't see a doctor today. The next appointment is Thursday at ten o'clock.
GRANDSON	We rang this morning and the lady we spoke to said ...
OLD WOMAN	Excuse me, I'm talking. Yes it is.
RECEPTIONIST	Yes it is what?
OLD WOMAN	Yes it is an emergency.
RECEPTIONIST	What is it that's wrong with you?
OLD WOMAN	Me head's hanging off!
GRANDSON	We rang this morning and the lady we spoke to said we could see a doctor if we came in before eleven.
OLD WOMAN	'Is it an emergency', she says. I ain't never seen a room full of such healthy looking people.
RECEPTIONIST	What name is it?

GRANDSON	Mrs Taylor.
RECEPTIONIST	If you'd like to take a seat.
OLD WOMAN	Oh well, only if you're sure. I mean I don't want to be pushing in front of Daley Thompson here.
GRANDSON	Come on, sit down, I'll get you a magazine.

ANOTHER MALE DOCTOR WALKS IN.

MALE DOCTOR	(QUIETLY) Keith Merryweather. Keith Merryweather. Keith Merryweather? Keith ...
OLD WOMAN	(SHOUTING) Keith Merryweather!! Come on, let's be having you, next cab off the rank. We're not all here for a free day out.
TIRED WOMAN	(TURNING TO OLD WOMAN) I'm really sorry, but would you mind keeping the noise down, I suffer from migraines.
OLD WOMAN	You do what, darling?
TIRED WOMAN	I'm really sorry, but I have terrible migraines.
OLD WOMAN	Oh I am sorry, sweetheart. I feel terrible for you, truly I do.
TIRED WOMAN	I've had them for years, but they've just really started ...
OLD WOMAN	No no, my darling, don't feel you've got to explain anything to me. I feel dreadful, really I do. I wish there was something I could do to help you. Would you like a mint?
TIRED WOMAN	No, honestly, I'll be fine, thanks. I just need to see the doctor.
MALE DOCTOR	Julie Hedges.
TIRED WOMAN	Oh that's me.
OLD WOMAN	Is that you, darling? Go on then, go and see the doctor, sweetheart, he'll sort you out. Oh. Aah.

THE TIRED WOMAN LEAVES THE ROOM.

	What a fucking liberty! She's got headache! The woman's sat in a doctor's surgery 'cause she's got headache! Oh they want shooting, they really do.
GRANDSON	Nan.
RECEPTIONIST	Excuse me, would you mind being quiet. You're upsetting the other patients.
OLD WOMAN	Oh take a fucking chill pill, you! Come on, you, I've had enough of all this.

A FEMALE DOCTOR COMES OUT.

DOCTOR   Mrs Taylor?

OLD WOMAN   Oh, have you found a window in your diary? Well it's too late now, love.
                It's too fucking late dot co dot uk! (CACKLES)

                Emergencies only? What a load of old shit!

HOW MANY HOW MUCH
PIZZA QUICKIE

KATE AND ELLEN ARE WORKING AT THEIR DESKS.

KATE   I went to Pizza Express for lunch.

ELLEN   Four Seasons, no onions, no anchovies, mixed salad and a Diet Coke.

KATE   Yeah.

                KATE GETS UP AND PUSHES ELLEN'S FILING TRAYS ONTO THE FLOOR.

MOO SHEPHERD / 3

MOO IS ONE OF FOUR CONTESTANTS LINED UP READY TO TAKE PART IN THE
OBEDIENCE CHAMPIONSHIPS.

VOICE OVER   It's the day of the Birmingham Six-Part Dog Obedience Championships
                and Moo Shepherd is with Lady Penelope. No progress has been made,
                and against all the advice of friends and family, Moo, as one of
                Birmingham's leading dog trainers, is risking professional suicide.

ANNOUNCER   Please welcome into the arena our penultimate finalist, Robert Freeman
                and Sinatra.

INTERVIEWER   (OUT OF VIEW) So, despite no improvement in Lady Penelope's abilities,
                you're going ahead?

MOO   Yes. As last year's winner I get an automatic place in the final, so I'd be a
                fool to waste that.

INTERVIEWER   (OUT OF VIEW) Of course, last year you had Mr Tibbs. Tell us about him.

                MOO FLASHES BACK TO IMAGES OF HER PREVIOUS DOG. 'SHE'S LIKE THE
                WIND' PLAYS IN THE BACKGROUND.

MOO   (OUT OF VIEW) Mr Tibbs, he was a one-off. He was to training and

201

obedience what Patrick Swayze was to the power ballad: sublime.

There were times when I wondered if I'd known Mr Tibbs in a previous life. I'm a strong believer in reincarnation and there were some uncanny similarities between him and my late father. The smell, mainly, but also an uncanny ability to carry an egg between his teeth without breaking it.

But more than that, it was a look in his eyes, a look that said: don't worry, kid, I'll always be here for you.

BACK TO MOO AND LADY PENELOPE WAITING TO GO INTO THE ARENA.

INTERVIEWER   (OUT OF VIEW) But now, with Lady Penelope, aren't you worried that you're going to lose your crown?

MOO   Moo Shepherd does not understand the concept of losing. Whatever you might think, this dog is a champion and I'm about to prove it.

ANNOUNCER   Please welcome into the arena our last competitor, Moo Shepherd with Lady Penelope.

MOO   Right, here we go.

LADY PENELOPE RUNS OFF, MOO RUNS AFTER HER. FADE TO BLACK AND UP AGAIN.

MOO   (COMING BACK OUT) Well, we came to do our best and that's exactly what we did.

INTERVIEWER   (OUT OF VIEW) How did she do?

MOO   She was rubbish, absolutely shocking. Basically ignored me all the way through the six categories.

INTERVIEWER   (OUT OF VIEW) You don't seem very bothered by that, Moo?

MOO   No, and I'm not. And I'll tell you for why. This dog has taught me the greatest lesson I'm ever likely to learn. Enjoy life! I told her to sit, she ran around. I asked her to fetch, she peed on a judge. This dog has the personality to do the one thing Wham!, the greatest pop duo of all time, told us to do way back in 1984 ... Choose life! (MOO IS PULLED OUT OF SHOT BY LADY PENELOPE.)

SHOTS OF MOO AND LADY PENELOPE RUNNING AROUND TOGETHER IN MOO'S GARDEN – LADY PENELOPE NOT DOING AS SHE'S ASKED AS USUAL – TO THE TUNE OF 'WAKE ME UP BEFORE YOU GO GO'.

FREEZE FRAME 'PHOTO' OF MOO AND LADY PENELOPE.

END CREDITS

SERIES 2   EPISODE 3

OPENING TITLES / THEME MUSIC

ANGIE BARKER   DEAD LADY

A POLICE CAR SIREN SOUNDS AS IT ARRIVES AT A CRIME SCENE. A WOMAN'S BODY IS LYING IN THE ROAD.

CONSTABLE 1	This must be her.
	HE INDICATES TOWARDS THE CAR IN WHICH ANGIE HAS JUST ARRIVED.
ANGIE	Afternoon. Angie Barker, the new DI. This is DS Harris.
CONSTABLE 1	Ma'am, Sir. (THREE KIDS GET OUT OF THE CAR) And these are?
ANGIE	Never seen a working mother before, Constable? Right, what have we got?
	A COLLEAGUE HANDS ANGIE HER BABY.
CONSTABLE 1	Er, body of a woman, late thirties, we think she might be a local ... (HE PAUSES, AWARE THERE ARE CHILDREN PRESENT) ... prostitute.
ANGIE	Okay, let's take a look. Come on. (TO KIDS) Come on, let's see the dead lady with mummy. (TO CONSTABLE) Right, do we know how she died?
CONSTABLE 1	Er, several wounds to the torso, looks like a knife.
ANGIE	Multiple entry wounds, looks like quite a frenzied attack.
	ONE OF THE CHILDREN JUMPS ON THE BODY.
ANGIE	Jessica, no jumping on the body, please. Any sign of a murder weapon?
CONSTABLE 1	We've not found anything yet, Ma'am.
HARRIS	Do we know how long she's been dead?
CONSTABLE 1	Police surgeon reckons no more than a couple of hours.
	THE BOY HAS FOUND A STICK AND IS POKING THE BODY WITH IT.
ANGIE	Give me that stick. So we may have some witnesses?
CONSTABLE 1	A local lady says she might have seen a white saloon car driving away at speed some time after midday.
	JESSICA IS SWINGING FROM THE PC'S COAT.
ANGIE	Problem, Constable?

CONSTABLE 1	Your little girl's hanging off my jacket, Ma'am.
ANGIE	Really. You want to try taking an oral swab from a seventy-five-year-old rape victim whilst changing a dirty nappy, checking two sets of homework and looking for Barbie's cocktail handbag. Now that's a tough shift.
CONSTABLE 1	Ma'am ...
ANGIE	Right, Harris, I want a complete house-to-house within a one-mile radius, a cross-reference check on every convicted sex attacker in this area in the last five years and a flask of boiling water.
HARRIS	Ma'am?
ANGIE	Heat up the milk, she's due a feed. (SHE GIVES HIM THE BABY.)

JESSICA HAS BEEN PLAYING 'MAKE-OVER' WITH THE VICTIM.

| ANGIE | Unplait the victim's hair, would you. Put it back the way it was. And wipe off those cat's whiskers. |

TACTLESS WOMAN BIRTHMARK

A PARTY IS TAKING PLACE.

NIKY	Congratulations on your new job.
MATT	Oh thanks. I know, I'm really excited.
NIKY	Well done.
MATT	Ally!
ALLY	Hello. I've just heard about your good news.
MATT	Yeah.

A MAN JOINS THEM WEARING A BASEBALL CAP.

STEVE	It's Ally, isn't it?
ALLY	Yeah, hello.
STEVE	Steve, Carole's brother.
ALLY	Hello, how nice to meet you.
STEVE	At last.
ALLY	Oh, have you just got here?
STEVE	Yeah, I had a nightmare waiting for a taxi.

HE TAKES HIS CAP OFF, REVEALING A BIRTHMARK.

ALLY	Ooh. Oh, that's left a horrible mark.
STEVE	Sorry?
ALLY	Your hat, it's left a dreadful mark on your head, give it a rub, that looks dreadful.
STEVE	It's a birthmark.

ALLY INSPECTS STEVE'S HEAD.

ALLY	Right. Yeah, no no, God, no, not that long thing, It's not even long, is it. It's just, no I meant, no I meant on this side. Oh no, oh hold on a minute, it's gone. There, no, it's gone, it was just the light. Yeah. It's just, oh no, I'm sure it was a shadow, just a shadow. Fucking shadows! I hate shadows. (TURNS TO MATT AS IF HE'S JUST SAID SOMETHING) Hmm?
	So, do you know where the people are?
STEVE	There are some people in the other room.
ALLY	I'm just ... got to see the people. I'm gonna see da people. See, haaa!

SHE RUNS OFF EMBARRASSED.

IVAN & TRUDY GET KNOTTED
A DAY IN THE LIFE / 1

IVAN AND TRUDY ARE WALKING DOWN THE STREET, ARGUING. THEY SPOT THE CAMERA AND SMILE.

VOICE OVER	Married couple Trudy and Ivan Dodd work together at their highly successful theatrical wig emporium in the West End of London. They have a hectic schedule, fitting wigs for film stars, television personalities and personal clients. It's hard work, but for the Dodds, it's a labour of love.

IVAN AND TRUDY ARE IN THEIR STUDIO. IVAN IS SITTING ON THE DESK.

IVAN	I suppose to many people we have what must seem a very glamorous life, making wigs for international film stars and television personalities, but what you'll be seeing, however glamorous it may appear, is for my wife, Trudy, and I just another working day.
TRUDY	Of course our lives could be very glamorous indeed, film premieres,

showbiz parties, but we're always so incredibly busy here at Get Knotted, it's often just not possible to find the time.

Yesterday, for example, Ivan had to personally hand finish six wigs for the new Harry Potter in the morning, and then he had Stephen Gately in the afternoon.

IVAN LOOKS AWKWARD.

TRUDY	And that was a quiet day.
IVAN	I'm sorry, I'm going to have to get off here, my arse has gone to sleep.

IVAN AND TRUDY ARRIVE AT THEIR OFFICE.

TRUDY	Morning, Carole-Anne.
CAROLE-ANNE	Morning, Trudy, morning, Ivan. What a day! (SHE LAUGHS)
IVAN	This is Carole-Anne, she's been with us since day one. Obviously she's not just a receptionist; in this business you often have to see everything and say nothing. Luckily discretion is Carole-Anne's middle name.
TRUDY	Any messages, Carole-Anne?
CAROLE-ANNE	Yes, Terry Wogan's people called, he's having problems with his new ...
TRUDY	Carole-Anne!

TRUDY POINTS OUT THE CAMERA.

CAROLE-ANNE	Apparently it's ...
TRUDY	Ah ah ah ah ah.
CAROLE-ANNE	No, no messages.
IVAN	Carole-Anne, this afternoon Trudy has a private client and I'll be fitting Sir Michael West for his new play at the National. So neither of us are to be disturbed, okay?
CAROLE-ANNE	Understood, yes.
IVAN	Is Bruno here yet?
TRUDY	Take a wild guess!
IVAN	Bruno is our assistant.
TRUDY	Your assistant.
IVAN	He's from Argentina. Not that much experience, but very enthusiastic.
TRUDY	Not as enthusiastic as you.

TRUDY LEAVES AND BRUNO ENTERS.

... AND THEN HE HAD STEPHEN GATELY IN THE AFTERNOON

IVAN	Ah, morning Bruno.
	BRUNO WALKS THROUGH THE OFFICE WITHOUT A WORD.
	Very temperamental, these Latin types.
CAROLE-ANNE	Terry Wogan ...
IVAN	Oh shut up!

LAUREN GYM

LAUREN IS WALKING EXTREMELY SLOWLY ON A TREADMILL.

INSTRUCTOR	Everything okay over there?
LAUREN	Are you talking to me?
INSTRUCTOR	I was just seeing if everything's all right.
LAUREN	It's rubbish here.
INSTRUCTOR	You know you might enjoy it a bit more if you speeded up a bit.
LAUREN	Are you talking to me again?
INSTRUCTOR	You're going at a snail's pace.
LAUREN	What?
INSTRUCTOR	I'm just saying, you're going at a snail's pace.
LAUREN	I ain't got a snail's face!
INSTRUCTOR	Why don't you just try running?
LAUREN	Are you Kelly Holmes?
INSTRUCTOR	What I mean is ...
LAUREN	But are you Kelly Holmes though?
INSTRUCTOR	Look, all I'm saying is ...
LAUREN	But is your name Kelly Holmes?
INSTRUCTOR	Look ...
LAUREN	But is your name Kelly Holmes though?
INSTRUCTOR	If you just ...
LAUREN	On your passport, right ...
INSTRUCTOR	What?
LAUREN	On the page marked name ...

209

INSTRUCTOR	Look ...
LAUREN	Does it say Kelly Holmes?
INSTRUCTOR	This is ...
LAUREN	But is your name Kelly Holmes though?
INSTRUCTOR	No my name is not Kelly Holmes.
LAUREN	Well shut up then.

LAUREN SPEEDS UP ON THE TREADMILL.

INSTRUCTOR	Well there you go, that's a lot better. Now why don't you try and maintain that speed for about ten minutes?
LAUREN	Don't tell me what to do.

LAUREN SPEEDS UP EVEN FURTHER.

INSTRUCTOR	I wouldn't go any quicker than that though if I were you.
LAUREN	You ain't me though.
INSTRUCTOR	No no, seriously.
LAUREN	But you ain't me though.
INSTRUCTOR	No no ...
LAUREN	Do you think you're me though?
INSTRUCTOR	No, you're going too fast now.
LAUREN	I ain't.
INSTRUCTOR	What?
LAUREN	I ain't bovvered though.
INSTRUCTOR	No, slow down.
LAUREN	I ain't bovvered though.
INSTRUCTOR	You're going to hurt yourself.
LAUREN	Do I look bovvered?
INSTRUCTOR	I'm not joking!
LAUREN	I ain't bovvered though.
INSTRUCTOR	Look, please, slow down.
LAUREN	I ain't bovvered.
INSTRUCTOR	Stop!
LAUREN	Face.

INSTRUCTOR	Please ...
LAUREN	Look.
INSTRUCTOR	No ...
LAUREN	Face.
INSTRUCTOR	You ...
LAUREN	Bovvered.
INSTRUCTOR	No ...
LAUREN	Snail's ...
INSTRUCTOR	No, please ...
LAUREN	Face.
INSTRUCTOR	You've got to ...
LAUREN	Bovvered.
INSTRUCTOR	Look ...
LAUREN	Kelly Holmes.
INSTRUCTOR	Please ...
LAUREN	Face.
INSTRUCTOR	No, you've got to ...
LAUREN	I ain't bovvered.
INSTRUCTOR	Please.
LAUREN	Face.
INSTRUCTOR	No, please ...
LAUREN	I ain't bovvered!!

SHE FALLS BACKWARDS OFF THE TREADMILL.

INSTRUCTOR	Are you all right?
LAUREN	Yeah, I'm fine. My laces came undone.

DEREK FAYE RECORD SHOP

DEREK IS AT THE CASH TILL OF A RECORD SHOP.

ASSISTANT	That's twenty pounds exactly, please.
DEREK	Twenty pound, twenty pound, twenty pound. Yes, dear, there you are. Twenty pound exactly, dear.
ASSISTANT	Thanks. Er, I don't know if you're interested, but we've just got tickets for Gay Pride on sale today.
DEREK	I beg pardon?
ASSISTANT	Tickets for Gay Pride. They're ten pounds cheaper if you get them in advance.
DEREK	How very dare you? I've never been so insulted!
ASSISTANT	What do you mean?
DEREK	Well, what exactly is it you are insinuating?
ASSISTANT	I'm just saying, we've got Gay Pride tickets on sale today.
DEREK	And how do you know I'm not married with a wife and kids?
ASSISTANT	Well, are you?
DEREK	Who, dear? Me, dear? Married, dear? No, dear. But whether I've found the right girl or not has got nothing to do with you, and to be quite honest, I find you impertinent.
ASSISTANT	No worries.

DEREK MOTIONS TOWARDS ANOTHER MAN IN THE SHOP.

DEREK	I mean, would you ask him if he wants tickets to this gay party?
ASSISTANT	It's Gay Pride, and no, probably not.
DEREK	And why's that?
ASSISTANT	He doesn't look gay.
DEREK	Right. That's it. Just because a man takes care of his appearance, you don't expect him to be accused of being a back-door Deirdre. My mother and I have been coming to this shop for twenty-five years, and I've never heard anything like it. Honestly, Gay Pride? How very dare you?!

DEREK MARCHES OFF, BUT HAS TO GO BACK FOR HIS SHOPPING BAG.

DEREK	My bag.

ASSISTANT	Right, it's the David Beckham calendar and the Best of Judy Garland, yeah?
DEREK	Thank you very much.

PAUL & SAM CHINESE

SAM IS LYING ON THE SOFA IN HYSTERICS. PAUL ENTERS THE ROOM.

SAM	Don't!
PAUL	What have you done? You've done something, haven't you?
SAM	Oh my God, you are not going to believe what I've just done!
PAUL	What have you done?
SAM	You are not going to believe it!
PAUL	What?
SAM	I can't even tell you.
PAUL	Why not?
SAM	'Cause you ain't gonna believe it.
PAUL	Here we go.
SAM	This is classic me.
PAUL	Tell me what you've done.
SAM	Last week, right, we went past that new Chinese and you said to me, do you remember, you said 'we should try that,' and I said, 'how about Saturday?' And you said, 'yeah, all right then,' do you remember? And I said, 'you know who loves Chinese, don't you, Shelley and Tony?' And you said, do you remember, 'ask them, see if they want to go Chinese Saturday.' And I said, 'all right then, I'll ask them.' So I'm ringing them to ask them ...
PAUL	Yeah?
SAM	So I'm on the phone and this voice at the other end says, 'Hello?'
PAUL	And what did you say?
SAM	I said, 'Hello?' And then I said, 'it's Sam, do you and Tony want to go Chinese Saturday?' And she said, 'me and Tony? Don't you mean me and Andy?'
PAUL	Me and Andy? But Shelley ain't married to Andy.

SAM	I know.
PAUL	It's Nicky that's married to Andy.
SAM	I said to her, 'Shelley, you ain't married to Andy, it's Nicky that's married to Andy,' and she said to me, 'Sam, you silly mare, this is Nicky.'
PAUL	No. What, it ain't Shelley?
SAM	It ain't Shelley! Well, we have collapsed. That's when I've realised, that's why she's speaking in a Scottish accent.
PAUL	So what's happened?
SAM	You know what I've done, don't you? I've rang Nicky by mistake!
PAUL	You've rang Nicky by mistake?
SAM	She said to me, 'you're a lunatic, you've rang me by mistake, what are you like?' I said, 'you know what I'm like.' She said, 'I know what you're like,' she knows what I'm like.
	I've looked at the phone like that. (FACE) That's when it's dawned on me what's happened.
PAUL	What's happened?
SAM	I've pressed the wrong number.
PAUL	No!
SAM	Straight. It's all on the memory, innit? Shelley's number four and Nicky's number five.
PAUL	And you've pressed number five?
SAM	I have pressed number five instead of number four like a nutter.
	So now I'm speaking to Nicky and I've asked her and Andy to go Chinese Saturday instead of Shelley and Tony.
PAUL	So what did Nicky say?
SAM	Well she said they can't go Chinese Saturday, 'cause her and Andy have got to go up his mum's Saturday, 'cause his mum's just got a satellite TV, and anyway they go Chinese Fridays.
PAUL	So what are we going to do now?
	THEY BOTH THINK HARD.
SAM	Why don't I ring Shelley, see if her and Tony want to go Chinese Saturday?
PAUL	Genius.

SAM	Wait till I tell Shelley what I've done.
PAUL	She will collapse.
SAM	She is gonna die.
PAUL	What am I gonna do with you?
SAM	I dunno. (ON PHONE) Hello Shelley? Lisa?! No! Lisa, you are not going to believe what I've just done!

JANICE & RAY SANDWICH

JANICE AND RAY ARE SITTING ON THE SOFA.

JANICE	We haven't told you about Harrogate, have we?
RAY	Listen to this.
JANICE	Where do you start? Last week we went up to Harrogate for a half day out.
RAY	Only a half day.
JANICE	Anyway, we went into this café.
RAY	Listen to this.
JANICE	And every one of the sandwiches they had was in French bread.
RAY	This is in Harrogate.
JANICE	So anyway, we're starving hungry by this point, so we says we'll have a cheese sandwich, you know, in the French bread.
RAY	French bread, that's all they had.
JANICE	So we gets these two cheese sandwiches, what sort of cheese did they say it was?
RAY	Brie. Don't ask.
JANICE	So they bring us these sandwiches and we bite into them.
RAY	This is unreal.
JANICE	And you'll never guess what they've put in a cheese sandwich.
RAY	Have a guess. Grapes.
JANICE	They've put grapes in't cheese sandwich.
RAY	In French bread. The dirty bastards.

JANICE	I mean, not that he's got anything against the French, you know, 'cause he loves that Inspector Clouseau.
RAY	Very funny man. Hey, but that's not it. Listen to this.
JANICE	So we pick the grapes out and we eat the sandwiches and we get the bill.
RAY	This is unbelievable.
JANICE	Two cheese sandwiches, we didn't have a brew, did we?
RAY	We had a flask in the van, didn't we?
JANICE	Two cheese sandwiches, in French bread, £5.60.
RAY	£5.60!
JANICE	£5.60, and we had to pick the grapes out ourselves. Honestly, they greed it off you.
RAY	Dirty robbing bastards!

IVAN & TRUDY GET KNOTTED
A DAY IN THE LIFE / 2

SECRETARY CAROLE-ANNE IS BEING INTERVIEWED WHILST SITTING AT HER DESK.

INTERVIEWER	(OUT OF VIEW) So you've been with Ivan and Trudy for over twenty years?
CAROLE-ANNE	Yes, since the Berwick Street days. It seems like yesterday, but we're all a bit older, even if we're no wiser! (SHE LAUGHS A LOT)
INTERVIEWER	(OUT OF VIEW) With many celebrities being private clients, I suppose it's up to you to keep matters as discreet as possible.
CAROLE-ANNE	Oh indeed, I mean I could write a pretty explosive exposé of some of the more, shall we say, follically challenged stars of today. Of course, I'd never dream of doing such a thing.
INTERVIEWER	(OUT OF VIEW) So there are more bald celebrities than we'd think?
CAROLE-ANNE	Well, where do we start? Um, Trevor McDonald, Lesley Garrett, Delia Smith, all completely bald. Pierce Brosnan's got his own hair, but no eyebrows. And poor Helen Mirren, bless her, she looks like a snooker ball with ears. Of course there's absolutely no way I can say any of this when the camera's on.

SHE GIVES THE CAMERA A WORRIED LOOK.

INTERVIEWER	(OUT OF VIEW) Cut there.
CAROLE-ANNE	Oh.

OUTSIDE A FITTING ROOM.

TRUDY	Unfortunately you can't come into this room with me as it's a personal fitting.
INTERVIEWER	(OUT OF VIEW) Oh right. So it's not all films stars then?
TRUDY	Well, as it happens, this is a celebrity client who wears a wig in his or her day-to-day life, and as all our wigs, of course, are totally undetectable, we have to keep their identities completely secret.
INTERVIEWER	(OUT OF VIEW) You can't give us a clue?
TRUDY	I'm sorry, confidentiality has been the foundation on which we've built our business. I couldn't even drop a hint ... All I can say is this particular actor or actress has been very shrewd indeed, no Dolly Parton or Shirley Bassey creations here. The wig he or she wears is very understated, you'd never guess that she, or he, was actually bald as a coot.

SHE POPS INTO THE FITTING ROOM. CAROLE-ANNE ARRIVES WITH A MUG OF COFFEE. SHE KNOCKS ON THE FITTING ROOM DOOR.

TRUDY	Yes?
CAROLE-ANNE	Dame Judi's coffee.

TACTLESS WOMAN CLEFT PALATE

A PARTY IS TAKING PLACE.

SUSAN	Oh I'm so excited.
ASH	Why is that?
SUSAN	Because it's Christmas! You know, we've got Secret Santa, mince pies, mistletoe. I've brought me own, watch out, boys!
JON	Oh, look out, she's off already.
ASH	Ally!
ALLY	Hello. You're all full of festive fun, aren't you? Hello, we've not met, I'm Ally.
SUSAN	Oh hi, I'm Susan. I'm in a really silly mood.
ALLY	(COPYING SUSAN'S VOICE) Hello, Susan, so am I.

(STILL COPYING SUSAN'S VOICE) Are you two in silly moods too?

THEY'RE ALL SILENT.

ASH	She's got a cleft palate.
ALLY	Hmm? Yeah, yeah, God, yeah, no, yeah, I mean, right, I mean I've got a, you know that, I didn't mean. I didn't, I mean, I didn't ... Pardon?
	So, oooh.
	(SINGS) 'Ding dong merrily on high, in heaven the bells are ringing.' Aaaaah ...

SHE RUNS OFF VERY EMBARRASSED.

ANNOYING WAITRESS
DISCO DOGS

JAMES AND RACHEL ARE SITTING AT A RESTAURANT TABLE.

JAMES	Of course I'm going to leave her.
RACHEL	You've been saying that for months.
JAMES	It's just difficult at the moment.
AMANDA	Hi guys! Welcome to BBJ's. I'm your waitress for today, my name's Amanda, but my friends call me Zebedee. I'm a fiery Taurean with my moon in Uranus. Careful, I'll do the jokes!
JAMES	Can we have some menus, please?
AMANDA	Okay guys, here's the story on the menus. Due to a non-human-based error at head office, we only have Braille menus for yourselves today. But I'm delighted to inform you that table six have a blind person in their party and I'd be happy to ask if you could borrow him.
RACHEL	Burger and fries will do me. We haven't got a lot of time ...
AMANDA	One potato, two potato, three potato four, five potato, six potato, seven potato more, hey!
	What kind of burgers can I get you guys for yourselves today?
JAMES	Well, we don't know what kind you've got.
AMANDA	Okay guys, here's the story on the menus. Due to a non-human-based error at head office ...

JAMES	Yeah, yeah, we know about the menus. Um, we just want regular burgers, I guess.
AMANDA	Just burgers for yourselves today then, nothing else with that for yourselves today?
RACHEL	And fries.
AMANDA	One potato, two potato, three potato four, five potato, six potato, seven potato more, hey!
JAMES	Do you have to do that song every time someone mentions fries?
AMANDA	One potato, two potato, three potato four, five potato, six potato, seven potato more, hey!
	We're not forced to, but most servers find it helps to create a feeling of fun.
	Okay guys, here's the story on the regular burgers. I'm afraid we're out of regular burgers today. The only burgers we have is the Belly Buster, three seventy-two-ounce steak burgers in a twelve-inch dusted sesame seed bap with fried onion, corrugated gherkin and various home-made sauces and pickles.
JAMES	Look, I'm really sorry, but we're running out of time, can we just have some fries and a drink ...
AMANDA	One potato, two potato, three potato four, five potato, six potato, seven potato more, hey!
	RACHEL PICKS UP A RESTAURANT ADVERTISING CARD FROM THE TABLE.
RACHEL	Okay, um, let's have this. Boogie Dogs, frankfurter hot dogs with onions and ranch sauce?
AMANDA	Table three going for Boogie Dogs!
	MUSIC: 'I'M IN THE MOOD FOR DANCING'
	THE RESTAURANT LIGHTING CHANGES AND THE STAFF BEGIN A SYNCHRONISED DANCE. THE COUPLE GET UP AND LEAVE.

IVAN & TRUDY GET KNOTTED
A DAY IN THE LIFE / 3

TRUDY AND IVAN ARE IN THEIR OFFICE.

TRUDY	Sir Michael! Are you leaving us already?
SIR MICHAEL	Trudy. Ivan said you were with a private client.
TRUDY	Yes, she, or he, left through the back door. How was your fitting for the new play?
CAROLE-ANNE	Trudy ...
TRUDY	I'm talking, Carole-Anne.
SIR MICHAEL	Wonderful. I know you're going to be away in June, but I'm counting on Ivan to be there on press night.
TRUDY	Oh I'm sure you can count on him. When has Ivan ever missed one of your openings?
CAROLE-ANNE	Trudy, it's quite important.
SIR MICHAEL	*Bonne chance!*
	SIR MICHAEL LEAVES.
CAROLE-ANNE	Ivan!
IVAN	What is it?
CAROLE-ANNE	Hmm hmm hmm's people are on the phone. His ... (MIMES WIG) ... was supposed to be with them by five o'clock.
IVAN	Who are you talking about?
CAROLE-ANNE	Well I didn't think I could say because of the camera.
TRUDY	Just say his first name.
CAROLE-ANNE	Well his first name is more of a giveaway than his surname.
IVAN	Just write it down, you idiot!
	CAROLE-ANNE WRITES THE NAME ON A POST-IT NOTE AND PASSES IT TO TRUDY.
TRUDY	Give me that phone.
	SHE PASSES THE NOTE TO IVAN.
IVAN	Jesus Christ! Bruno!
TRUDY	Hello, Trudy Redfearn here, how can I help you? I'm sure he's literally minutes away.

IVAN HAS FOUND BRUNO AND IS FOLLOWING HIM AROUND THE OFFICE.

IVAN   Look, what part of the message didn't you understand?! It's very straightforward: 'Important, Bruno, deliver by hand before 4pm'.

CAROLE-ANNE   Do you want me to pop it round? I've never met ... hmm hmm hmm before.

TRUDY   Oh for God's sake, one of them's a deaf Brazilian mute, the other one speaks in Morse code, what chance do we have?

IVAN   Carole-Anne, call Showtime couriers and get that on a bike now! (TO BRUNO) You, come with me! Oh, come on!

INTERVIEWER   (OUT OF VIEW) Is it a big name client?

TRUDY   Look, there is absolutely no way I can divulge the name of any client. We went through all this a dozen times before you started filming. I cannot compromise our confidentiality, it is as simple as that.

But, suffice to say, if that Jiffy bag doesn't get to Wembley Arena by seven o'clock, it'll be the first time anyone's ever heard 'Candle In The Wind' sung in a crash helmet.

OLD WOMAN HOSPITAL

THE OLD WOMAN IS SITTING UP IN A HOSPITAL BED. HER GRANDSON ENTERS THE WARD.

OLD WOMAN   Here he is.

GRANDSON   Hello, Nan.

OLD WOMAN   You come up and see me?

GRANDSON   Yeah.

OLD WOMAN   You come up and see me, ain't ya?

GRANDSON   Here I am.

OLD WOMAN   Oh you are a good boy. Did you bring me up me bits?

GRANDSON   Course I did.

OLD WOMAN   That's it, lovely.

GRANDSON   How are you feeling?

OLD WOMAN   Yeah, not too bad thank you, sweetheart. Now, did you remember me nightgown?

GRANDSON   Yeah, it's all in there.

OLD WOMAN	Oh, I can't be wearing this one much longer. The collar's too high. I feel very educated. I'll be able to go home soon, won't I, love?
GRANDSON	Not yet, Nan, you had a nasty fall. They're going to keep you in for a few more days.
OLD WOMAN	Oh I can't be in here much longer, love, I'll go off my nut.
GRANDSON	Come on, it's not that bad.
OLD WOMAN	Not much! Glory be, it's like a fucking circus in here! May God forgive me for swearing, I ain't never seen a mob like it.
GRANDSON	All right, Nan, don't be rude.
OLD WOMAN	I mean, have you had it here, have a look.

SHE INDICATES TOWARDS THE WOMAN IN THE NEXT BED WHO IS EATING A BISCUIT AND DRINKING A CUP OF TEA.

	Have a look. I'm not ending up like that!
GRANDSON	Nan ...
OLD WOMAN	Oh, wait for it, here you are, wait till she tries putting it in her mouth. Oh it is choice, all smothered round her face.
GRANDSON	Keep your voice down.
OLD WOMAN	She can't hear me. She's got more hair in her ears than she has on her chin. (CACKLES). Now, did you bring me tomatoes?
GRANDSON	Everything you asked for is in the bag, Nan.
OLD WOMAN	Oh that's it. Ah yeah, I'll have a couple of them tonight, that'll be lovely. I've still got a slice of tongue under there, so I'll have that an' all. I'm not eating that muck they bring round here. Phwoar, no fear. Have you seen it? Oh, oh it is rough. Here you are, have a look, a menu if you don't mind.
GRANDSON	Well you should try it, Nan, it all looks really nice.
OLD WOMAN	Oh what, tray of slop? No thanks.
GRANDSON	It's sweet and sour chicken.
OLD WOMAN	Who is it?
GRANDSON	It's Chinese, it's nice, just try a little bit.
OLD WOMAN	Oh no, I couldn't eat Chinese food, son, their faces make me feel sick.
GRANDSON	Nan!

A NURSE ENTERS THE WARD.

OLD WOMAN	(CACKLES) Here she is, here's me lovely Anita. Here you are, what did I tell you, Anita? Here's me grandson. He's at a university.
ANITA	Nice to meet you.
GRANDSON	You too. Thanks for everything you're doing, Nurse.
OLD WOMAN	Her name's Anita.
GRANDSON	All right, Nan.
OLD WOMAN	Yeah, don't take no notice of him, sweetheart, he ain't got a job. I'm very much obliged to you for all your kindness, darling. I'm going to give you a nice drink when I leave here, you can buy yourself a new pair of tights, that's it.
ANITA	Well that's very kind of you.
OLD WOMAN	Yeah.
ANITA	You have a comfortable night, Mrs Taylor, and I'll see you in the morning. (TO GRANDSON) Nice meeting you.
OLD WOMAN	Oh ta da, sweetheart. Take care, I'll see you tomorrow.
	ANITA LEAVES.
OLD WOMAN	Thieving bastard!
GRANDSON	Oh no.
OLD WOMAN	She only comes over here so she can take tights.
GRANDSON	Come on, Nan, she's a nurse.
OLD WOMAN	Waiting for me to turn me back so she can have a rough dive down me handbag.
GRANDSON	Don't talk rubbish.
OLD WOMAN	As God is my judge, she's had the lot. She's had the lot. She's had the pension book, the gift vouchers, all me loose change, not to mention eighty pound in cash. Gone, finished, done, in cold blood, that's your lot.
GRANDSON	If this is true, Nan, we'll have to report it to the police.
OLD WOMAN	Ah, well, now, that's where she's cunning, see.
GRANDSON	What do you mean?
OLD WOMAN	She put it all back.
GRANDSON	Did she now?
OLD WOMAN	Well she knew I was on to her, didn't she, so she's returned it all before I

can do anything about it. It's a criminal mind, see. And you know me, I don't like to say nothing. Anyway, I've got to keep her sweet in case she gives me a sly dig when no one's looking.

AN OLD MAN IS BEING WHEELED BACK ONTO THE WARD.

OLD WOMAN   Oh, here we go. That's all I need!

GRANDSON   Nan that's Alf, you know him.

OLD WOMAN   Oh, he's back, is he? Walks around with his underclothes all undone, oh it is pretty having to watch his Ni's walloping around. No wonder I ain't been able to keep anything down since I've been here.

GRANDSON   He's got senile dementia.

OLD WOMAN   Senile dementia? (CACKLES). Don't make me laugh!

GRANDSON   Nan, that's enough. Look around you. This ward is full of vulnerable people suffering with dignity. It's about time you started to have a little consideration for those less fortunate than yourself.

OLD WOMAN   Oh fucking chill out! (CACKLES).

ANNOYING WAITRESS
PENSIONER

MUSIC: 'ROCKAFELLER SKANK'

AMANDA AND THE WAITERS ARE DANCING TOGETHER TO FATBOY SLIM. AN OLD LADY IS SITTING AT THE TABLE DRINKING A CUP OF TEA, TAKING NO NOTICE.

END CREDITS

SERIES 2 EPISODE 4

OPENING TITLES / THEME MUSIC

OLD WOMAN CHERYL

THE OLD WOMAN IS IN HOSPITAL AFTER A BAD FALL. SHE IS SITTING UP IN BED. HER GRANDSON COMES TO SEE HER.

OLD WOMAN	Here he is.
GRANDSON	Hi, Nan.
OLD WOMAN	You come up and see me?
GRANDSON	Yeah.
OLD WOMAN	You come up and see me, ain't ya?
GRANDSON	Yeah.
OLD WOMAN	Ha ha, I noticed that.
GRANDSON	Are you all right?
OLD WOMAN	Not bad, son.
GRANDSON	Here you are, I'll do your pillows.
OLD WOMAN	Oh you are a good boy coming all this way to see me.
GRANDSON	Well I've got to make sure you're keeping out of trouble, haven't I?
OLD WOMAN	Oh, I don't know what I'd do without you, sweetheart, really I don't. I mean, I'd be dead on me fucking back if I had to rely on these sorry bastards.
GRANDSON	Nan, that's not fair.
OLD WOMAN	And that fat woman was here again yesterday. Her with her library books. Oh she does look well, you seen her? She comes waddling in here pushing that trolley. Oh!
GRANDSON	Nan, don't be like that, she's a volunteer.
OLD WOMAN	Who is it?
GRANDSON	She's a volunteer, she don't get paid to bring the library books round.
OLD WOMAN	She don't get paid?
GRANDSON	No.

OLD WOMAN	Fucking busybody!
GRANDSON	Nan!
OLD WOMAN	She said to me, she said to me, 'you look bored, Mrs Taylor, I've got three words for you: Barbara Taylor Bradford.' I said, 'yeah, I've got three words for you, love: calorie controlled diet!' (CACKLES)
	No, but you mustn't be so wicked. She don't get nothing for coming up here, that woman, she don't get a penny. She does that all out of the goodness of her heart – her big, lard-coated, flaky pastry heart. (CACKLES)
GRANDSON	Nan, I've brought a friend of mine to see you, but if you're going to be like that, I'll tell her not to bother coming in.
OLD WOMAN	What do you mean, is it a girl?
GRANDSON	Yes.
OLD WOMAN	Oh thank God for that. Oh darling, what a relief! (TO THE WOMAN IN THE NEXT BED) Oh, 'ere Maud, Maud, do you hear that, he's got a girl coming up. Panic over. Oh! Oh you have made me happy, because you worry the fucking life out of me the way you titivate your hair sometimes.
GRANDSON	Nan, she'll be here in a minute and I don't want you being rude.
OLD WOMAN	No, me? What? I wouldn't say nothing. I'm only too pleased you ain't a theatrical.
GRANDSON	It's just there's something she's a little bit sensitive about.
OLD WOMAN	Oh, what, has she got spots?
GRANDSON	No she hasn't, but if you notice anything about her, I don't want you to mention it.
OLD WOMAN	Oh she ain't Welsh, is she?
GRANDSON	Now look, it doesn't matter what it is, she's lovely and I really like her, so please don't say anything.
OLD WOMAN	She's a dwarf. Oh well, I suppose it's better than nothing. (SHE LOOKS TOWARDS THE FLOOR) She ain't here already, is she? (CACKLES)
GRANDSON	No she isn't, and I won't bring her in unless you promise to behave yourself.
OLD WOMAN	May I never move, on my first Holy Communion, I welcome her with open arms, love. Whatever makes you happy, that's all I care about, sweetheart.
GRANDSON	Thanks, Nan. She's just outside, I'll bring her in.

HE LEAVES THE ROOM.

OLD WOMAN	Oh. 'Ere, Maud, she's outside, the girl. He's bringing her in now, innit lovely? Oh gawd, I'll have to give her a couple of fig rolls, I mean you've got to offer 'em something, ain't you?

HER GRANDSON AND CHERYL ARE BACK IN THE ROOM.

GRANDSON   Nan, this is Cheryl.

THE OLD WOMAN LOOKS UP.

OLD WOMAN   Glory be to God!

GRANDSON   Nan!

CHERYL   Are you okay, Mrs Taylor?

OLD WOMAN   Fuck that!

SHE STARES AT CHERYL'S NOSE. IT IS ENORMOUS.

CHERYL   Can she see me all right?

OLD WOMAN   I can hardly fucking miss you, love!

GRANDSON   She gets a bit disorientated.

CHERYL   Oh I know, it's horrible when you're not feeling well. I'm just getting over a really bad cold.

OLD WOMAN   That must have nearly killed you!

GRANDSON   All right, Nan.

OLD WOMAN   What do you do for tissues, love?

GRANDSON   Oh God!

OLD WOMAN   I mean, them little pocket-sized ones, they ain't going to be any good to you, are they?

GRANDSON   Nan, please.

OLD WOMAN   'Ere, I've got a couple of old sheets in me airing cupboard. You're welcome to them if you want 'em. (CACKLES) Have a look. 'Ere, I tell you what, she don't mind me, do you, Cheryl? Course not. I'm full of admiration for you, sweetheart, I mean that.

GRANDSON   Come on, we'll go.

OLD WOMAN   I mean, fair's fair. It takes a lot of character to wake up every morning, look in the mirror and still walk outside your door with a great big walloping snout like that! I couldn't do it. (CACKLES)

GRANDSON	I'll see you tomorrow.

THEY STAND UP.

OLD WOMAN	Are you going? Cheryl ain't had no fig rolls yet.
GRANDSON	I'll be up in the morning.
OLD WOMAN	Oh right, go on then, be like that, won't you. Ta ta.

THEY LEAVE.

OLD WOMAN	'Ere, Maud, what a beautiful girl.

DEREK FAYE TRAVEL AGENT

DEREK IS BOOKING HIS ANNUAL HOLIDAY AT THE TRAVEL AGENT'S.

JASMINE	Right, that's all booked for you. There's your card.
DEREK	Thank you, dear.
JASMINE	Let me just go over the main details of the holiday.
DEREK	Details, dear? Yes, dear.
JASMINE	So that's two weeks in Ibiza, half board at the Adonis Apartments. Your price includes flights, airport tax and all transfers. Passengers flying are Mr Derek Lesley Faye and Mr Leonard Mincing.

WE SEE HIS FRIEND, LEONARD MINCING, SITTING NEXT TO HIM.

DEREK	That's right, dear.
JASMINE	Now, as the holiday is for two men, the computer has automatically given you a twin room with two beds. I'm afraid our booking system is still a bit archaic in that respect. Would you like me to change it to a double bed for you?
DEREK	I beg pardon?
JASMINE	Your apartment has two single beds. Would you like a double instead?
DEREK	What on earth are you insinuating?
JASMINE	Sorry, I just assumed ...
DEREK	How very dare you? What has the world come to when two men can't enjoy a simple holiday together without being accused of sexual perversion?
JASMINE	But I never said anything about sexual perversion.

DEREK	My mother and I have been coming to this travel agent for twenty-five years, and in all that time I've never been accused of taking deliveries up the back passage.
JASMINE	I'm very sorry, Mr Faye, I seem to have misjudged the situation.
DEREK	Who, dear? You, dear? Misjudged, dear? Yes, dear. I'll thank you for my tickets and bid you good day, dear. Come on, Leonard. Double bed? How very dare you?!
	THEY START TO LEAVE. DEREK COMES BACK.
DEREK	Can I just make sure – we have got a four-man Jacuzzi on the balcony, haven't we?
JASMINE	Yes, that's booked for you.
DEREK	Thank you, dear.
	HE MINCES OFF.

DRUNK BRIDE / 1

A WEDDING RECEPTION IS IN FULL FLOW. THE BRIDEGROOM STANDS UP TO MAKE HIS SPEECH.

GROOM	Right, well, I'd, er, just like to thank you all for coming here today on this, the happiest day of my life. And I won't stay long because I know everyone wants to crack on with the dancing, but just before we do, I thought I'd tell you about the second happiest day of my life. Um, the day that Victoria agreed to marry me.
	Now it was going to be a holiday for us both on this lovely Greek island, and ...
BRIDE	(HECKLING) Get off!
GROOM	... and, um, we went to this lovely little restaurant overlooking the sea, and, um, I ordered a seafood platter. Now unbeknown to Victoria, I took the waiter aside and gave him the engagement ring and asked him to put it on the claw of the lobster.
BRIDE	Come on!
GROOM	Now, when the moment arrived, he brought the platter over to the table, put it down in the middle, lifted up the lid and there ...

BRIDE	John asked me to marry him and I said yes! In a nutshell.
GROOM	Yeah.
BRIDE	Great. Is that it?
GROOM	Yes.
BRIDE	Great! Is it my turn now? (SHE STANDS; HER HUSBAND TRIES TO MAKE HER SIT DOWN) Don't touch me. Well. I should first of all like to start by apologising for my husband's fucking dull story. He gets a bit carried away sometimes.

John proposed to me seven times. Seven! A lesser man would probably have given up by around the fourth, but not my John. Not my little Johnny. He just kept banging away, wearing me down, until finally, to save him any more humiliation, I said yes. There comes a time in every woman's life when she says, 'oh all right, for God's sake, I'll marry you.' If only for a bit of peace and quiet.

When John first got up to speak, I wasn't sure which one of the seven proposal stories he was going to tell, and I thought, Christ, I hope he doesn't go through them all, because although the ring on the end of a lobster claw is probably the best, it's still shit! But you know what they say, darling, seven times lucky. Do, do they say that?

I know what you're thinking: she's had a few too many. Well I'm here to tell you I've had a few, a few too many, I don't know, I shall let you be the judge of that, because I know how much you all enjoy judging. To date I have had thirty-nine − all men. Thirty-nine sexual liaisons in fifteen active years. I just wish I could remember what number John was.

SHE SLUMPS INTO HER SEAT.

CRAP CROUPIER ROULETTE / 1

PEOPLE ARE GATHERED AROUND A ROULETTE TABLE.

RONNIE	Five thousand pounds on red.
HAYLEY	No more bets, please.

SHE SPINS THE WHEEL. AS THE BALL STARTS TO SETTLE ...

It's red!

RONNIE et al	Yes! Yes!
HAYLEY	Oh no, I'm sorry, I'm sorry, it's not red, it's black. Isn't it funny how all the colours sort of merge when they go round.

SHE COLLECTS THE CHIPS FROM THE TABLE.

ANNOYING WAITRESS
JUNGLE PIZZA

TWO WOMEN ARE SITTING AT A RESTAURANT TABLE.

AMANDA	Hi guys, welcome to BBJ's. I'm your waitress for today, my name is Amanda but my friends call me Zebedee. I'm a fiery Taurean with my moon in Uranus. Careful! I'll do the jokes. I've worked here for three years and hold the current BBJ's record for taking only forty-five seconds to eat a full can of squirty cream without being sick.
SARAH	I think we're just going to share a pizza, thank you.
AMANDA	If we're talking pizzas, I'm going to have to go and get Pedro, the pizza waiter.
SARAH	Well we know what we want.

AMANDA PRODUCES A WOODEN SPOON PUPPET – 'PEDRO' – FROM HER APRON POCKET.

AMANDA	(IN COD ITALIAN ACCENT) 'Mama Mia, whadda you want-a? I was having a nice-a little sleep-a in there-a.'
	Oh, hi Pedro, we were just wondering if you knew what pizzas we had today?
SARAH	Sorry, I don't mean to be rude, but do we really need to go through all this? Only we know what pizza we want.
AMANDA	Oh, did you hear that, Pedro? These people haven't got time to listen to you, so you're going to have to go straight back into my apron.
	'Mama Mia, not-a back into the apron, not-a that, please-a, izza so lonely in there-a.'
SARAH	Can we just have a Jungle Pizza with two Diet Cokes, please?
AMANDA	'Mama Mia, izza gonna take more-a than a Diet Coke to make you thin!'
	Now, Pedro, that's really rude. I want you to apologise to these ladies.

235

| SARAH | Please, can we just order one large Jungle Pizza? |
| AMANDA | 'Table-a seven a-going for-a the Jungle-a Pizza!' |

MUSIC: 'THE LION SLEEPS TONIGHT'

THE RESTAURANT LIGHTING CHANGES AND THE STAFF BEGIN A SYNCHRONISED DANCE. THE TWO WOMEN LEAVE THE RESTAURANT.

HOW MANY HOW MUCH HAIRDRESSER

KATE AND ELLEN ARE WORKING AT THEIR DESKS.

KATE	I'd never go and work on a kibbutz.
ELLEN	Right. Sorry, do you mind if I just get on with this?
KATE	Imagine what it would do to your hair.
ELLEN	Look, I really need to get this done.
KATE	My hairdresser was saying, about my hair, that going to a hot country would be really damaging for it.
ELLEN	Hmm.
KATE	And he should know.
ELLEN	Should he?
KATE	He's very well travelled.
ELLEN	Sorry?
KATE	My hairdresser, he's seen a lot of things.
ELLEN	Has he?
KATE	Lovely complexion.
ELLEN	Great.
KATE	Beautiful accent.
ELLEN	Really?
KATE	Guess where he comes from?
ELLEN	Oh.
KATE	Go on, have a guess where my hairdresser is from.
ELLEN	Well I really have no idea.

KATE	You'll never guess.
ELLEN	So what's the point?
KATE	Because it's fun! Have a guess.
ELLEN	I have no idea.
KATE	From whence does he hail?
ELLEN	I really don't have time for this.
KATE	Make time, it's fun!
ELLEN	Not for me.
KATE	You love it! Come on, just guess.
ELLEN	I can't!
KATE	You can.
ELLEN	I can't.
KATE	You can.
ELLEN	Norfolk.
KATE	Norfolk?! Norfolk?! They don't have hairdressers in Norfolk!
ELLEN	Birmingham.
KATE	Beautiful accent?
ELLEN	Scotland?
KATE	Lovely complexion? I don't think so.
ELLEN	Liverpool.
KATE	Is this a perm?
ELLEN	Denmark.
KATE	Denmark? It's not a mullet!
ELLEN	Hastings?
KATE	He's not a murderer or a transvestite.
ELLEN	Er, Eastbourne?
KATE	He's not incontinent! Come on!
ELLEN	Is he from the North?
KATE	He doesn't smell!
ELLEN	Um ...
KATE	Come on, use your imagination, just guess!

ELLEN	Bolivia?
KATE	Where?
ELLEN	Prague.
KATE	No!
ELLEN	Africa.
KATE	Cardiff! My hairdresser is from Cardiff.
ELLEN	Wow! So he's Welsh?
KATE	Yes, he is.
ELLEN	I need a haircut.
KATE	You need more than a haircut, you scab-faced old trout!

CRAP CROUPIER ROULETTE / 2

HAYLEY SPINS THE ROULETTE WHEEL.

HAYLEY	No more bets, please.

THE BALL DOESN'T STOP, SO HAYLEY PUTS HER HAND ON THE WHEEL TO STOP IT AND PICKS UP THE BALL.

HAYLEY	This is really annoying me.

SHE GATHERS THE CHIPS OFF THE TABLE.

DRUNK BRIDE / 2

THE DRUNK BRIDE IS CONTINUING HER SPEECH.

BRIDE	It's funny ... isn't it funny, when you start to think of how many different men you've slept with. Because it makes you wonder: do I have a type? Well I realise I don't have a type, unless you can count 'they all wore shoes'.

No, but seriously, they all did have one big thing in common, and it's not what you're thinking because I'm including John in this. No, everyone I've ever slept with has always been very, very conscientious about contraception. Even though I'm on the pill, they always insisted that we should also use a condom. Now I thought, that's amazing, isn't it, because subconsciously I've always been attracted to sort of sensitive, caring, new age kind of men. You know – 'I care about my body, you care about my body.' And it turns out they just didn't want to have ginger kids.

I don't know if there are any other ginger people out there today, are there? Hmm? Hmm? Do you know any ginger people? Yes you do, but they're not here, are they, because they've got no friends. They're all at home gnawing on a turnip. I know there's a few liberal people out there going, no no no no, let the ginger babies be born, just don't let them grow up and live next door to me. We don't want them bringing down our house prices, cluttering up our nice tree-lined streets with their empty bottles of sun block. Oh ... anything.

I remember when we met, me and him. He said to me – presumably it was some sort of a compliment – he said, 'I really like your colouring, I think it's very Elizabethan.' Oh, Elizabethan? Hmm? Hmm? What's that? Oh yes, bad teeth and syphilis. Still, a shag's a shag, I thought. You've got to take it where you can get it when you look like Mick Hucknall.

SHEILA CARTER CONFESSIONAL

A PRIEST IS IN THE CONFESSIONAL BOOTH. SHEILA ENTERS THE OTHER SIDE AND SITS DOWN.

SHEILA   Bless me, Father, for I have sinned. It's been over two months since my last confession.

PRIEST   Speak my child. Take your time, there's no rush. Whatever it is inside that's troubling you, just let it go.

Just let it go.

SHEILA GIVES OUT A LONG, NOISY FART. THE PRIEST IS SHOCKED.

SHEILA   I'm sorry, it's very stuffy in here, I'm going to come back later.

THE PRIEST IS LEFT HOLDING HIS NOSE.

LAUREN TATTOO

LAUREN AND LIESE ARE IN A CLASSROOM, LOOKING AT A MAGAZINE.

LIESE	Oh my God, what does she look like with them boobs?
LAUREN	They're well fake, innit.
LIESE	They're too big for her head though.
LAUREN	Look at the nasty shape though.
LIESE	They're not even the same size, innit.
LAUREN	Maybe the left one was cheaper, is it?
LIESE	You know they explode when you go on the London Eye.
LAUREN	I'm definitely getting them when I'm older.

LIESE SEES LAUREN HAS A TATTOO ON HER ARM.

LIESE	Oh my God, what is that?
LAUREN	What?
LIESE	When d'you get that?
LAUREN	Get what?
LIESE	The tattoo.
LAUREN	Oh right, yeah, I got that yesterday. Ain't you got any?
LIESE	No I haven't.
LAUREN	You are so dry.
LIESE	A tattoo though. What's it say? 'Ryan and Lauren'.
LAUREN	You got beef with that?
LIESE	No, I just didn't know you was doing it.
LAUREN	What's your beef?
LIESE	I ain't got beef.
LAUREN	Is it that you got beef with that?
LIESE	I ain't got no beef.
LAUREN	You have got beef.
LIESE	Did it hurt?
LAUREN	About three hours of it, but love is pain, innit?
LIESE	I can't believe it.
LAUREN	That's nothing. Look at that.

RYAN'S FACE IS TATTOOED ON HER OTHER ARM.

LIESE	Bloody hell, what are you thinking?!
LAUREN	I don't need your opinion, is it?
LIESE	Does Ryan know you done that?
LAUREN	He's getting one of my face on his chest and 'Ryan and Lauren' on his wrist. We're like Bonnie and Clive.
LIESE	It's Clyde.
LAUREN	Whatever.
	Right, shut up, he's coming, he's coming, he's coming.

RYAN ENTERS.

RYAN	Alright?
LIESE & LAUREN	Alright.
RYAN	Listen, I was thinking that we shouldn't see each other no more. I need to concentrate on my MC'ing and stuff.
LAUREN	Yeah, that's fine.
LIESE	Did you get your tattoo though?
RYAN	What tattoo?
LIESE	She got a tattoo.
LAUREN	No I ain't.
LIESE	She got a tattoo of your face though.
LAUREN	No I ain't though.
LIESE	But yes you have though.
LAUREN	No I ain't though.
LIESE	But yes you have though.
LAUREN	Lies.
LIESE	But it's there though.
LAUREN	Why don't you shut up though.
RYAN	That is well bad.

RYAN LEAVES.

LIESE	Oh my God! You have got tattoos of him all over your body and he's just chucked you!

LAUREN	Am I bovvered?
LIESE	But he's chucked you though.
LAUREN	Am I bovvered though?
LIESE	But you got his tattoos on your body.
LAUREN	I ain't bovvered.
LIESE	But ...
LAUREN	Do I look bovvered?
LIESE	You ...
LAUREN	Do I look bovvered though?
LIESE	Why ...
LAUREN	Look at my face.
LIESE	Yeah, but ...
LAUREN	Look at my face.
LIESE	Right.
LAUREN	Is any part of it bovvered?
LIESE	But what you gonna do?
LAUREN	Nothing, 'cause I ain't bovvered.
LIESE	Take the shame though.
LAUREN	No, 'cause I ain't bovvered.
LIESE	But you got his name and his face on your body though.
LAUREN	Are you deaf?
LIESE	But ...
LAUREN	Are you a deaf?
LIESE	No, but ...
LAUREN	Do you speak like a deaf though?
LIESE	No, I ...
LAUREN	What's sign language for 'am I bovvered?'?
LIESE	I'm not ...
LAUREN	Deaf?
LIESE	No, but ...
LAUREN	Look.

LIESE	I know ...
LAUREN	Face.
LIESE	Just ...
LAUREN	Bovvered.
LIESE	I can't ...
LAUREN	Deaf.
LIESE	Yeah, but ...
LAUREN	Look.
LIESE	But ...
LAUREN	Face.
LIESE	I just ...
LAUREN	Look.
LIESE	It's just ...
LAUREN	Bovvered. I ain't bovvered!
	Do you know anyone else called Ryan?

CRAP CROUPIER ROULETTE / 3

HAYLEY SPINS THE WHEEL.

HAYLEY	No more bets, please.

THE BALL FLIES OUT AND FALLS ON THE FLOOR.

HAYLEY	Oh! It would have probably been red.

SHE GATHERS UP THE CHIPS.

IRENE & VERN GORBACHEV

NEVILLE WALKS UP TO A ROADSIDE BURGER VAN. IRENE AND VERN ARE BEHIND THE COUNTER.

IRENE	Morning, Neville, you're early. Have you had a slow morning?
NEVILLE	Oh, shocking. I've not had a job since half past nine.
IRENE	Oh, it's been non-stop here. Absolutely non-stop, hasn't it, Vernon?

VERNON SAYS NOTHING.

IRENE	Yeah, you're lucky you just missed the rush. Double cheeseburger?
NEVILLE	Yes please.
IRENE	Double cheese for Neville.
NEVILLE	Thanks, Vern.
IRENE	Yeah, you missed all the action. You'll never believe who was here.
NEVILLE	Go on.
IRENE	What was his name? Russian fella. Vernon, what was the name of that man who asked if we had a toilet? Oh, what's his name? Funny little red mark on his head.
NEVILLE	Not Gorbachev?
IRENE	That was it, Gorbachev. I didn't recognise him at first, 'cause he got off a minibus.
NEVILLE	Yeah, he was Soviet President '85 to '91.
IRENE	Oh yes, I know that now! Anyway, I said, 'you've only got a couple of miles to go before you get to Wigan Services', but he said they were on their way to watch the rugby, he's had a few cans and he's busting.
NEVILLE	Who was he going to see?
IRENE	Doncaster. Anyhow, he goes round the back of the van and he has a wee there.
NEVILLE	Who are they playing?
IRENE	West Hull. So Vern goes round to drain the fat, you'll never guess what: he's weed over Vern's onions.
NEVILLE	Mikhail Gorbachev peed over your onions?
IRENE	I know. We had to throw half of them away. Any sauce?
NEVILLE	Er, no, this is fine. Can I settle up with you on Friday?
IRENE	Course you can. See you tomorrow, Neville.

DRUNK BRIDE / 3

BRIDE	It's, you know, it's funny actually, when I, when I sit here and I, I listen to John say how happy he is that we're married and how much he loves me, because like most of us in this room, I've got a sneaking suspicion that John is gay. Something that both he and his family are very, very quick to deny.

I must say how wonderful it is to see so many of my husband's family here today. You know, it's ... I'm very touched. My father-in-law, James. Hello, sir. Who I know is very, very proud that his baby boy has married such a free-loading ginger gyppo. I believe those were your words, James.

My mother-in-law, Janice. (TAPPING MICROPHONE) 'One two, one two, my mother-in-law's so fat!' But she is.

And by contrast, my sister-in-law, Susan, who's a very thin woman. She's so thin. In fact, she's so thin, we weren't actually sure whether or not she was here today. Well I know that she's out there, because I can smell the sick. (SUSAN WALKS OUT) No no no no, don't talk about the bulimics, it's a disease.

I should also like to thank our Best Man, Jason, who flew in all the way from Sydney to be here today, and in true Antipodean style said to me just before the ceremony, 'How are you, love? You look great in white. Have I got any chance of shagging you?' And I said, 'Well you didn't have, but you do now, you smooth-talking bastard.'

I should like to thank you all for coming and finally propose a toast – to me and all who sail in me.

SHE FALLS OVER.

HOW MANY HOW MUCH
PHANTOM OF THE OPERA QUICKIE

KATE AND ELLEN ARE WORKING AT THEIR DESKS.

KATE	I went to the theatre last night.
ELLEN	Phantom of the Opera.
KATE	Yeah.

KATE GETS UP, GOES OVER TO ELLEN AND SINGS VERY LOUDLY INTO ELLEN'S EAR.

KATE	'The Phantom of the Opera is there inside my mind.'

SHE SPITS ON ELLEN'S HEAD AND GOES TO SIT DOWN AGAIN.

DRUNK BRIDE CODA

ALL THE GUESTS HAVE LEFT THE WEDDING RECEPTION.

THE DRUNK BRIDE IS SLUMPED ASLEEP AT THE TOP TABLE, HOLDING ONTO A CHAMPAGNE BOTTLE.

A YOUNG BRIDESMAID WAKES HER UP TRYING TO PRISE THE BOTTLE AWAY FROM HER.

DRUNK BRIDE NOTICES THAT THE RECEPTION ROOM IS DARK AND EMPTY. SHE TAKES A FINAL SWIG FROM THE BOTTLE.

END CREDITS

SERIES 2 EPISODE 5

OPENING TITLES / THEME MUSIC

PAUL & SAM FANCY DRESS

PAUL IS READING THE PAPER IN THE LOUNGE. SAM IS STANDING AT THE DOOR.

SAM	Have I told you about the fancy dress?
PAUL	No.
SAM	I've not told you about the fancy dress?!
PAUL	No you ain't, babe.
SAM	The fancy dress party when I was living at me mum's?
PAUL	No.
SAM	I have told you!
PAUL	You ain't told me.
SAM	(CALLING OUT) Mum, he said I ain't told him about the fancy dress party!

MUM ENTERS.

MUM	She must have told you about the fancy dress party.
PAUL	No, she ain't.
MUM	He says you ain't.
SAM	I have told him.
MUM	She says she has told you.
PAUL	She ain't told me.

DAD ENTERS.

DAD	She ain't told you?
PAUL	No! What happened?
DAD	A fancy dress party, that's what happened.
MUM	We had a fancy dress party.
PAUL	No!
SAM	Can you imagine?

PAUL	Don't make me laugh!
DAD	Don't start me off.
MUM	Don't start him off.
SAM	You started him off!
MUM	Here we go.
DAD	I nearly died, it was so funny.
SAM	I was in agony, I laughed so much.
MUM	Are you ready for this?
PAUL	I don't know if I am.
SAM	Go on, Dad!
DAD	Melanie has come as Shirley Temple licking a big lollipop and tap dancing all over the gaff.
PAUL	Who's Melanie?
SAM	Melanie Baker, Mum's friend from aerobics.
MUM	Works in the multiplex. Got a cat with double paws.
DAD	She done that fun run dressed as a bottle of Cinzano ...
SAM	And forgot to get sponsored.

THEY LAUGH SILENTLY.

MUM	Pauline, with the big hands, she's come as Posh Spice. Which is a bit much, because she must be eleven stone. Halfway through the day she says she ain't Posh Spice, she's Carol Vorderman, before she went on the detox. I nearly died.
DAD	She's walloping herself round the kitchen saying, 'consonant or vowel?'. It was lethal.
SAM	Lisa Jackson, she's gutted she ain't got a costume and wants to know if she puts some ink toner on her face, can she come as Ainsley Harriott?
PAUL	She can't say that.
DAD	She don't mean nothing by it, she's deaf in one ear.
SAM	Shut up, will ya! We ain't got to the funny bit yet.
PAUL	Don't tell me there's more.
MUM	This is a classic.

I MIGHT AS WELL RING THE AMBULANCE NO

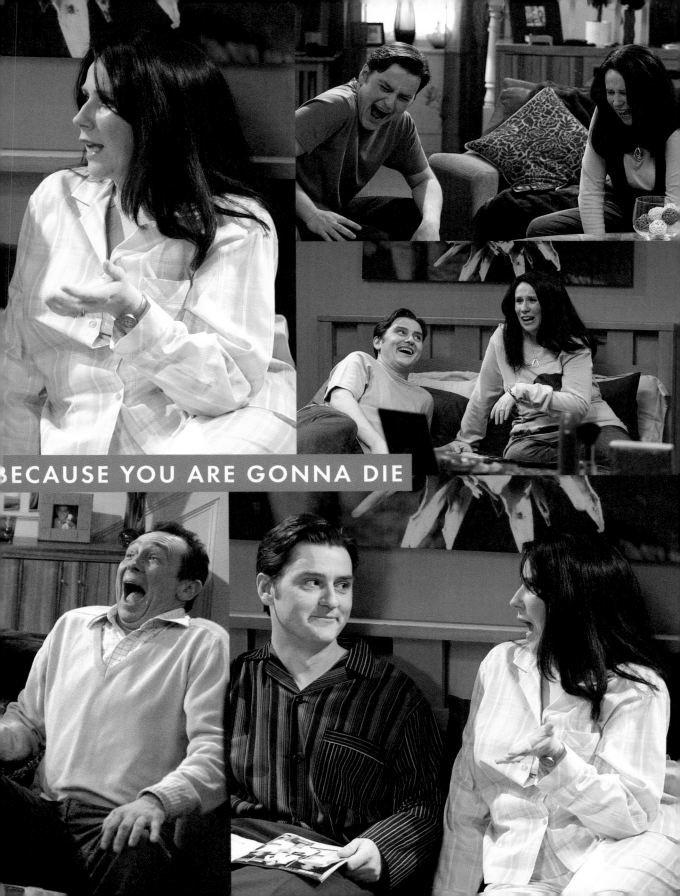

BECAUSE YOU ARE GONNA DIE

SAM	Lunchtime, right, I've sent me mum down Sainsbury's to get the food. I'd have gone meself, but I promised Shelley I'd do her highlights before the party because she wanted to come as Kylie, and I said I'd do what I could but I couldn't promise nothing 'cause she's got hair like cotton wool.
MUM	So, I've gone armed with a list. I've got specific instructions to get ...
MUM/DAD/SAM	Four packs of sausage rolls, eight bags of chicken drumsticks and an unwaxed lemon.
PAUL	Stop it!
DAD	Well you know what she's like when she gets in the shops. Guaranteed she's gonna bump into someone she knows, and when she starts yapping, that's it, list or no list, game over, it is out of control.
PAUL	What are you like?
SAM	You know what she's like.
DAD	What are you like?
MUM	You know what I'm like.
DAD	She's come back from the shops, she's put the bag on the table, we've opened the bag, we've looked in the bag ...
PAUL	What's in the bag?
MUM/DAD/SAM	A tray of vegetarian chipolatas and a strawberry cheesecake.
SAM	Well, I've looked at her like that. (FACE)
MUM	She's looked at me like that. (FACE)
DAD	I've looked at both of them like this. (FACE)
MUM/DAD/SAM	We're all looking at each other like this. (FACES)
DAD	You know what she's done, don't you?
PAUL	What's she done?
SAM	She's bought the wrong thing.
PAUL	Oh my God!
SAM	I know!
MUM	I know!
PAUL	You are mental!
SAM	Stop it, I'm gonna wet meself!
MUM	I'm gonna wet meself as well!

DAD	I have wet meself.
	THEY LAUGH SILENTLY.
PAUL	What's an unwaxed lemon?
MUM/DAD/SAM	We dunno!

ELAINE FIGGIS, WOMAN OF COURAGE GUMMIDGE / 1

ELAINE IS WALKING ALONG A LEAFY SUBURBAN STREET.

VOICE OVER	Elaine Figgis is one of a growing number of women prepared to go to extraordinary lengths to find love. Sadly, however, last year she suffered a set-back, when her husband of nine days was electrocuted on Death Row in his Texan penitentiary. But Elaine hasn't given up.
	ELAINE IS SITTING AT HER COMPUTER.
ELAINE	This is Gummidge, he's my computer. Although don't call him a computer, he'll take offence. My friend Tex at line dancing class, that's his country name, his real name's Rowland ... he says that Gummidge is my global pimp. I'm not exactly sure what a pimp is, to be honest, but ... although I know Gladys Knight had three of them.
	Oh hang on, Paulo's just signed on. I'd better just tell him I'm busy, otherwise I'll never hear the last of it. (SHE TYPES)
	There. Do you know, I've met people from all over the world, all from this little chair. America, Brazil, Australia, Africa even.
INTERVIEWER	(OUT OF VIEW) And where is Paulo from?
ELAINE	Reading. Hank's just signed on, he's from Wisconsin. He's a lovely man, but keeps sending me pictures of his penis.
INTERVIEWER	(OUT OF VIEW) Do you get a lot of that?
ELAINE	No, as I say, I don't get to meet many of them because of the distance involved. Oh, you mean pictures of them? Oh, yeah, I get tons of them. I don't encourage it, but I'm very broad-minded. Mind you, if it continues like this, I am going to have to get myself a bigger hard drive.

A NOISE FROM THE COMPUTER INDICATES ANOTHER MESSAGE.

Oh, hang on, who's this? Oh, oh that's Kyle. He's an actor, well at least he says he is.

INTERVIEWER   (OUT OF VIEW) Do you find a lot of people lie about themselves on internet chat rooms?

ELAINE   I think, at the end of the day, you have to take everything with a pinch of salt. I mean, for example, this is the picture I use on-line.

ELAINE PICKS UP A PHOTOGRAPH OF A BEAUTIFUL BLONDE.

Now, strictly speaking, that isn't actually me. It's my friend Cath's daughter, but we're both Sagittarius with Gemini rising, so you can't get much closer than that.

ANNOYING WAITRESS FAMILY

A COUPLE AND THEIR SON ARE SITTING AT A RESTAURANT TABLE.

DAD   Okay, what time does the film start?

MUM   Two o'clock.

DAD   Right, we've got enough time.

AMANDA   Hi guys! Welcome to BBJ's. I'm your waitress for today, my name's Amanda but my friends call me Zebedee. I'm a fiery Taurean with my moon in Uranus. Careful, I'll do the jokes!

MUM   Um, can we see the menus?

AMANDA   Okay guys, here's the deal. I can give you the menus, but we've got a special promotion on this week, where if you can tell us what we've got on the menus, you get entered into our special mind reader draw.

DAD   We'll just have some menus if that's okay, thank you.

AMANDA   Table nine ducking out of the mind reader draw. (SHE BLOWS A DUCK CALL WHISTLE)

Okay, guys, here's your menus, and here's your menu, you cheeky little munchkin. What's your name?

ROBBIE   Robbie.

AMANDA   And how old are you, Robbie?

ROBBIE	Eight.
AMANDA	Eight? I was eight when I was your age. Okalie dokalie. And what does little Robbie want?
ROBBIE	I want a Captain Octopus Fish Burger, please.
AMANDA	Aye aye, Captain, and would you like Soapy Fries with that today for yourself?
MUM	What are Soapy Fries?
AMANDA	They're like curly fries, except they're straight and they taste of soap.
MUM	Just normal fries.
DAD	I'll have a Hot Hot Hot Burger ...
AMANDA	Table nine going for Hot Hot Hot Burgers!

MUSIC: 'HOT, HOT, HOT'

THE RESTAURANT LIGHTING CHANGES AND THE STAFF BEGIN A SYNCHRONISED DANCE. THE BEMUSED FAMILY LEAVE THE RESTAURANT.

NEW PARENTS ALPHABET GAME

AN EXHAUSTED MUM IS SITTING ON THE FLOOR WITH HER BABY. SHE PICKS UP ALPHABET BRICKS.

MUMMY	Oh look, A. A is for Apple. Yum yum. And Aeroplane. (MAKES AEROPLANE NOISES) T is for Train. (MAKES TRAIN NOISES) And also for Tired. Oh, H is for Haven't slept in weeks and House. Hmm, that's right, darling, because Mummy doesn't sleep any more, does she, Molly? Hmm? N is for No sleep for Mummy. R, what's R for, sweetheart, do you know what R's for? It's for Rabbit, floppy floppy bunny rabbit, and Really need to go to bed.
	P is for Parents, F is for Forever. K, well K can be loud like Kayak, or silent, as in Knackered. I is for Igloo, that's where the Eskimos live, and also for I need to sleep so much I could vomit. B is for Bags under the eyes. E is for Exhaustion and Eternal suffering evermore and Elephant.

HER EYES CLOSE AND HER HEAD DROPS WITH EXHAUSTION.

BERNIE SURGEON

A SMART MAN IS SITTING IN THE HOSPITAL WAITING AREA, READING HIS NEWSPAPER. BERNIE SITS DOWN NEAR TO HIM, A PACKET OF SWEETS IN HER HAND. SHE SMILES AT HIM.

MAN	Good morning.
BERNIE	Oh hi, how's it going?
MAN	Very well, thank you.
BERNIE	Been here long?
MAN	Five or ten minutes.
BERNIE	Oh you may as well bed yourself down for the night then.
MAN	I beg your pardon?
BERNIE	Oh I didn't mean with me. God, I'm not that easy. (SNORTS) I can see I'm going to have to keep me eye on you, aren't I?

SHE MOVES TO SIT NEXT TO HIM.

	No, I just mean we're really understaffed at the moment.
MAN	Really?
BERNIE	Sorry, where are my manners? Would you like a rhubarb and custard?
MAN	Not for me, thank you.
BERNIE	No, I'm not a big fan of boiled sweets meself, but it's nice to have something to suck on in between blanket baths, you know what I mean?

BERNIE'S PHONE BUZZES. THE MAN CHECKS HIS OWN PHONE.

MAN	Oh, it's you.

BERNIE LETS THE PHONE VIBRATE. SHE IS OBVIOUSLY ENJOYING IT.

MAN	Aren't you going to answer that?
BERNIE	No. It's on vibrate.
MAN	It must be a relief ... er to, to find time for a break.
BERNIE	Oh God no, we're too busy for breaks, no. I've just been sent here to meet a new member of staff.
MAN	Oh, any luck finding him?
BERNIE	Her. She's a her, a female doctor, more trouble than they're worth if you ask me.

MAN	I take it you get on better with the male doctors then?
BERNIE	Well, how can I put it, they don't allow pets in here, but I've had a cockatoo, you know what I'm saying? (LAUGHS) Oh, I've just thought, you're not a doctor, are you?
MAN	No, I'm not a doctor. Why?
BERNIE	No, it's just that you have that look about you, you know, the look of authority. Can be very attractive in a man, if you know what I mean? (SNORTS)
MAN	You're very kind. Um, you must have a continual supply of admirers.
BERNIE	Well, I am seeing someone here at the moment, but it's not common knowledge. I don't kiss and tell.
MAN	Good for you.
BERNIE	I shag and shout! So you'd better be careful. (SNORTS) No no, but seriously, it's rare to see an attractive man around the place without a wedding ring.
MAN	Oh I'm married, I just don't wear a ring.
BERNIE	Oh, I see what you're saying. You like to keep your options open. No point in being in a stable if you can't ride a few of the horses, you know what I mean though?
MAN	Do you do much riding?
BERNIE	Sorry, I was talking about sex.
MAN	Yes, I know.
BERNIE	Oh nice one. Well, you know, you're only young once. Mind you, you can play many a good tune on an old fiddle, if you know what I mean? (SNORTS) I was talking about sex again.
MAN	Yes, I know.
BERNIE	Great. Well, how about me and you have a bit of a fiddle tonight then, say seven o'clock? You could pick me up outside A&E.
	A DOCTOR FINDS THEM.
DR WALKER	Ah, Bernie, I see you've found each other.
BERNIE	Doctor Walker, I got your memo about the new doctor, but I'm very sorry, she's not here yet.
DR WALKER	What do you mean 'she'?

BERNIE	(LOOKING AT MEMO) Um, Doctor Hilary Donovan.
DR WALKER	Bernie, this is Sir Hilary Donovan.
BERNIE	What?! Sir Hil, Hilary, you said you weren't a doctor.
MAN	And I'm not, I'm a surgeon.
DR WALKER	I do hope Nurse Bernadette hasn't been bothering you, Sir Hilary.
MAN	On the contrary, she's been more than friendly.
BERNIE	Thank you, your majesty.

BERNIE CURTSEYS.

DR WALKER	Shall we?
MAN	Yes, let's.
BERNIE	Excuse me your highness, are we still on for that fiddle at seven o'clock?
MAN	Oh, please!
BERNIE	Nice one!

ELAINE FIGGIS, WOMAN OF COURAGE MOHAMMED / 2

ELAINE IS SITTING AT HER COMPUTER.

INTERVIEWER	(OUT OF VIEW) Have any of your on-line relationships turned into anything more serious, Elaine?
ELAINE	Well, as you know, Tanya, I had met my Prince Charming ...
	... But he was cruelly taken away from me. Jerry, God rest his soul, was a one off. I was convinced no one could ever take his place, until I met Mohammed.
INTERVIEWER	(OUT OF VIEW) Where is Mohammed?
ELAINE	He's in Egypt. He's twenty-four and he sells spices outside Luxor Temple. I mean, it's so romantic. I sometimes think I'm living in a Barbara Cartland novel.
INTERVIEWER	(OUT OF VIEW) How are you finding the cultural differences?
ELAINE	We've both had to make our sacrifices. Mohammed's had to buy a six-month pass for his local internet café and I've had to change my religion.

INTERVIEWER	(OUT OF VIEW) That must have been a very big decision.
ELAINE	Not really. I've had to change to halal meat, I pray to the east five times a day, and a couple of weeks ago Mohammed told me I'm not allowed to do the lottery. I still do the odd scratch card; I mean, he's not a fundamentalist.
INTERVIEWER	(OUT OF VIEW) So has a date been set for the marriage?
ELAINE	Not yet, no. We've not been without our set-backs. I keep sending him money to keep him going till he sells his spice stall, but apparently Mohammed thinks that the man who delivers his post is a bit light-fingered.
INTERVIEWER	(OUT OF VIEW) Are you sure it's safe to be sending large amounts of money to someone you've only been chatting to for a few weeks?
ELAINE	Tanya, you've got to understand something about being a Muslim. The word 'Islam' actually means 'love'. I send him money and he loves that.

OLD WOMAN FUNERAL

THE OLD WOMAN'S GRANDSON IS SITTING IN HER LIVING ROOM. HE STANDS UP AS HE HEARS HER RETURN HOME.

GRANDSON	All right, Nan?
OLD WOMAN	Oh hello, darling, there's a nice surprise to find you here.
GRANDSON	I didn't want you coming home to an empty flat. How are you?
OLD WOMAN	Not bad, thank you, darling. It was very emotional, but yeah, I'm all right.
GRANDSON	Was it a big funeral?
OLD WOMAN	Oh it was beautiful. Church was packed. She had seven cars follow her, seven. I didn't think she knew that many people. And you want to see the food they laid on, oh it was out of this world.
GRANDSON	Here you are, sit down, I'll make you a cup of tea.
OLD WOMAN	Yeah, I'm all right for the minute, thanks, love. I had a couple of Guinness when we came back from the grounds. I didn't want 'em really, but young Charlie Ford got 'em for me and I didn't want to be rude.
GRANDSON	No, course not.
OLD WOMAN	Oh it don't seem real, does it? I only see her last week, she was out there mopping that landing. Poor old Lena. Still, it's a happy release for her though, I suppose.

GRANDSON	Yeah.
OLD WOMAN	She weren't never the same after her Jackie died. She only went out once a week, got her pension, knocked it out on Babycham, came back … came back, sang at the top of her voice till three o'clock in the morning. Oh I will miss her!
GRANDSON	Did you manage to eat anything, or shall I make you something now?
OLD WOMAN	No, I had a little something while I was there, love, a nice plate of boiled bacon and potato salad, bowl of jellied eels, nice bit of crusty bread, couple of sausage rolls, you don't like to be rude.
	I can't believe she's gone.
GRANDSON	Come on, Nan, it'll be all right.
OLD WOMAN	I suppose it'll be me next.
GRANDSON	Now don't talk like that.
OLD WOMAN	She didn't have anyone, did she, poor old Lena? She went from week to week without a living soul come up and see her. God help us, that ain't no way to go, is it? Oh well, rest in peace, Lena, love.
	A THOUGHT DAWNS.
OLD WOMAN	She owed me money!
GRANDSON	What?
OLD WOMAN	She owed me money, the woman!
GRANDSON	What are you talking about?
OLD WOMAN	I gave her fifteen quid beginning of last week, she never give it back.
GRANDSON	Nan, it hardly matters now.
OLD WOMAN	What a fucking liberty! That's typical of her, that is.
GRANDSON	She hardly knew she was going to have a heart attack and die before she could pay you back!
OLD WOMAN	Not fucking much she didn't! I bet she felt the first twinge go down her arm and thought, that's it, I'll go and tap her across the road. She was an artful cow! Fifteen quid. I sent a wreath worth twenty-five pound and all, oh it gets worse.
GRANDSON	Nan, just leave it, I'll give you the money.
OLD WOMAN	I don't want your money! Don't you dare, don't you dare, I've got more money than the lot of you put together.

GRANDSON	Great, well you won't miss that fifteen quid then.
OLD WOMAN	'Ere, any more talk like that and I shall leave it all to the cats' home. (CACKLES) What about them old gels who leave all their money to the cats' home? Oh that do make me laugh. What do the cats want with it? What do they care? They're fucking cats! What are they going to do, go on a cruise? All the little cats sailing around the world on a cat yacht, sipping champagne, getting all dressed up to have dinner with the captain. They're fucking cats!
GRANDSON	Great, well that's all sorted then. Would you like a cup of tea now?
OLD WOMAN	Yeah, lovely. Oh there's a good boy, go and put the kettle on, that's it. Here you are, we can have a couple of these with it an' all.

SHE UNWRAPS SOME CHOCOLATE ECLAIRS FROM A SERVIETTE IN HER HANDBAG.

GRANDSON	You've not brought those back from the wake?
OLD WOMAN	Course I did. Didn't fancy 'em while I was there, but I knew I'd want some later. Always the same whenever I have a drink, always fancy a nice bit of cake a couple of hours after.
	(SHE TAKES A BITE) Oh that's beautiful.
GRANDSON	God, I hope no one saw you.
OLD WOMAN	Oh get in there and put the kettle on, you, or I won't let you have any of this quiche.

SHE PULLS A WHOLE QUICHE FROM HER HANDBAG.

CACKLES.

SHEILA CARTER CINEMA

SHEILA IS IN THE CINEMA, WATCHING A FILM. SOME PEOPLE NEXT TO HER ARE EATING POPCORN.

| SHEILA | Do you mind? Very noisy, terribly distracting. |

SOMEONE ELSE OPENS A PACK OF SWEETS.

| SHEILA | For goodness sake! We're trying to watch the film back here. Honestly, I've never known such rudeness. |

A MAN BEHIND HER OPENS A CAN OF COKE. SHE STARES AT HIM.

265

SHEILA	Unbelievable.
	SHEILA LETS OUT A LONG FART. THE OTHERS LOOK AT HER, HORRIFIED. SHEILA TURNS TO THE WOMAN SITTING NEXT TO HER.
SHEILA	Have you been eating garlic?!

IRENE & VERN MADONNA

NEVILLE WALKS UP TO A ROADSIDE BURGER VAN. IRENE AND VERN ARE BEHIND THE COUNTER.

IRENE	You're late.
NEVILLE	Yeah, I had to take a woman up to Uxbridge. Only just got back.
IRENE	Oh, it has been chocka here. Absolutely chocka, hasn't it, Vernon?
	VERNON SAYS NOTHING.
IRENE	Yeah, you're lucky you just missed the rush. Double cheeseburger?
NEVILLE	Yes please.
IRENE	Double cheese for Neville.
NEVILLE	Thanks, Vern.
IRENE	Yeah, you missed it all go off earlier. You'll never believe who was here.
NEVILLE	Go on.
IRENE	Oh, what's her name? American woman. Vernon, what's the name of that woman who was here earlier?
	You know, that big blonde woman off the telly.
NEVILLE	Off the telly you say?
IRENE	Married to a funny looking little bloke with ginger hair. Madonna!
NEVILLE	Oh right, right. So what was she doing up here then?
IRENE	They were on their way to the garden centre. She bought one of them bolt-together barbecues last Saturday and they've not given her enough nuts.
NEVILLE	Well couldn't she have just got some nuts from B&Q?
IRENE	Well that's what I said, but she said they're a funny size. Anyhow, they have a burger each, get back in their car and it wouldn't start. They'd run out of petrol.
NEVILLE	Oh dear.

IRENE	Apparently she knew they needed to fill up, but she wouldn't because they'd been passing Esso garages and she only uses BP.
NEVILLE	Oh, right. Is that a political thing?
IRENE	No, apparently she's collecting the Nectar points. So anyway, Vernon gives the little ginger bloke a lift up to Sainsbury's garage. Meanwhile, I'm left here with her for twenty minutes and she starts banging on about Iraq.
NEVILLE	Oh dear.
IRENE	I said, 'don't talk to me about Middle Eastern policies, I met Geoff Hoon in the cash and carry last Thursday, I'm up to here with it.' And what with him wittering on all day, me head's banging. Any sauce?
NEVILLE	No, that's smashing. Right, see you tomorrow.
IRENE	See you later, take care.

ELAINE FIGGIS, WOMAN OF COURAGE WEDDING / 3

ELAINE IS BRINGING IN THE WASHING.

INTERVIEWER	(OUT OF VIEW) I believe, Elaine, that some of your friends are worried about you marrying a man who lives two thousand miles away and who you've only spoken to via the internet.
ELAINE	Tanya, this is the twenty-first century, people should realise anything is possible. We've got cordless phones, compact discs. I mean, just last night I was watching Sky Travel and they've got a chimpanzee in Las Vegas who can ride a bike while smoking a cigar. We're not living in the dark ages any more.
INTERVIEWER	(OUT OF VIEW) So what's the plan?
ELAINE	Well, plan is I meet Mohammed at Heathrow and then we go straight to the registry office and get married.
	ELAINE'S MOBILE PHONE BEEPS.
ELAINE	Oh, it's from Mohammed.
INTERVIEWER	(OUT OF VIEW) No last minute nerves, I hope.
ELAINE	(READING THE TEXT) Hmm? No, no, I just asked him to let me know if the

money I sent him yesterday went into his bank account.

INTERVIEWER	(OUT OF VIEW) How much did you send him, Elaine?
ELAINE	Well, what with tomorrow's air fare and various bits and bobs, it did come to a couple of thousand this time.
INTERVIEWER	(OUT OF VIEW) What did the text say?
ELAINE	Hmm? 'Yes'. He's a man of very few words, and not all of those are in English. I must be mad! (SHE LAUGHS)

Right, well, I'm off. I've got to go and pick up my outfit, and yes, it is very special, and no, you can't get a sneak preview. Right, I shall see you lot tomorrow. Once more into the bridge, dear friends.

SHE STANDS STILL, STARING NERVOUSLY INTO THE CAMERA.

Is it alright if I go? Yes, right.

LAUREN TEACHER

LAUREN IS SITTING IN HER CLASSROOM, IN DETENTION. HER TEACHER IS AT HER DESK.

TEACHER	Lauren, I'm sure you don't like staying behind any more than I do, but until you learn to focus more when you're in class and do the work set for the lesson, you're going to stay behind and do it in your own time.
LAUREN	Are you a northerner, Miss?
TEACHER	Excuse me?
LAUREN	You're from the North, innit?
TEACHER	Do your work, Lauren.
LAUREN	Are you a northerner though?
TEACHER	Why do you ask, Lauren?
LAUREN	'Cause you speak funny, is it.
TEACHER	That's enough.
LAUREN	I'm only aksing a question. Can't I aks a question? I'm only aksing a question though.
TEACHER	I'm from Bristol, Lauren. Does that answer your question?
LAUREN	Yeah.

TEACHER	Good.
LAUREN	Are you a farmer, Miss?
TEACHER	Lauren.
LAUREN	Are you a farmer though?
TEACHER	Don't be ridiculous!
LAUREN	You talk like a farmer.
TEACHER	Carry on with your work.
LAUREN	Why do you talk like a farmer though?
TEACHER	Lauren, I'm not going to tell you again.
LAUREN	Do you live on a farm, Miss?
TEACHER	Lauren, be quiet.
LAUREN	Miss, are you the farmer's wife?
TEACHER	If you don't be ...
LAUREN	Are you the farmer's wife though?
TEACHER	No I'm not!
LAUREN	Are you Old MacDonald, Miss?
TEACHER	Don't be ...
LAUREN	Do you know Old MacDonald, Miss?
TEACHER	Stop this.
LAUREN	Ee eye ee eye oh, Miss.
TEACHER	Stop this nonsense! You know perfectly well I'm not a farmer, now get back to your work immediately.
LAUREN	I'm not being funny or nothing, Miss, but you do smell like a farmer.
TEACHER	Now that's enough!
LAUREN	Is it the pig swill?
TEACHER	Right.
LAUREN	Miss, do you eat pig swill?
TEACHER	Be quiet. I am not from the North and I am not a farmer, now let that be the end of it. No doubt you think yourself very amusing, but look around, Lauren, no one's here to see your little show. Now I suggest you pick up that book and start reading, because you are well on your way to coming bottom of your whole year.

LAUREN	Am I bovvered? Am I bovvered though?
TEACHER	Lauren ...
LAUREN	I ain't bovvered.
TEACHER	Lauren ...
LAUREN	I ain't bovvered though.
TEACHER	Can you ...
LAUREN	Look at my face. Look at my face.
TEACHER	Just ...
LAUREN	Is my face bovvered?
TEACHER	You ...
LAUREN	Is my face bovvered?
TEACHER	You sound ridiculous.
LAUREN	You sound like a farmer.
TEACHER	You're making a fool of yourself.
LAUREN	Don't care, 'cause I ain't bovvered.
TEACHER	Lauren ...
LAUREN	I ain't bovvered.
TEACHER	Stop this.
LAUREN	I ain't bovvered though.
TEACHER	Right now!
LAUREN	I ain't bovvered.
TEACHER	Come on.
LAUREN	Look ...
TEACHER	Just ...
LAUREN	Farmer.
TEACHER	I'm ...
LAUREN	Face.
TEACHER	Just stop it!
LAUREN	Look.
TEACHER	Please ...
LAUREN	Farmer.

TEACHER	Stop it!
LAUREN	Face.
TEACHER	Lauren ...
LAUREN	Farmer.
TEACHER	Please ...
LAUREN	I ain't bovvered!
TEACHER	No, Lauren, you're not bovvered, you're fifteen years old and you don't even know where Bristol is!
LAUREN	I don't need to know, I ain't a farmer.
TEACHER	Right, that's it. I'm washing my hands of you. I've had just about enough of this. Read the book, don't read the book, it's not my problem any more.
	THE TEACHER TURNS TO LEAVE.
LAUREN	Miss? Have you got to go and milk the cows, Miss?

ELAINE FIGGIS, WOMAN OF COURAGE
AIRPORT / 4

ELAINE IS WAITING IN INTERNATIONAL ARRIVALS WITH A SIGN SAYING 'MOHAMMED'. SHE IS IN FULL MUSLIM DRESS.

MUSIC: 'SHE'

TIME PASSES AND THE LAST PERSON COMES THROUGH THE ARRIVALS GATE. MOHAMMED DOESN'T SHOW AND EVENTUALLY ELAINE SITS DOWN, DEFEATED.

END CREDITS

SERIES 2 EPISODE 6

OPENING TITLES / THEME MUSIC

TACTLESS WOMAN
AGE DIFFERENCE

A PARTY IS TAKING PLACE.

ANGELA	Ally!
ALLY	Hello!
ANGELA	I didn't know you were back. How was your holiday?
ALLY	Oh it was fantastic.
ANGELA	Ally's just come back from Greece.
POLLY	Oh, we were there at the beginning of June.
ALLY	No! Oh it's gorgeous, isn't it?
POLLY	Yeah, I've been loads, but it's the first time I'd taken Nick.
ALLY	Oh God, you went together?
POLLY	Yeah.
ALLY	Do you know, I think that is fantastic.

NICK AND POLLY ARE SLIGHTLY PUZZLED.

ALLY	I'd never go on holiday with my mum.
NICK	Polly's not my mum, she's my girlfriend.
ALLY	Hmm? Right. Yeah, God, 'cause I didn't mean you looked older than him, no no, I didn't, you look ... You look taller than him. Just, you just seem a bit taller than him ... Which is odd, isn't it, given that you're shorter than him. Odd in a good way. Hmm? (LOOKS AS IF SOMEONE HAS JUST ASKED HER SOMETHING)

Hmm? So, you've got beautiful eyes. God ...

ALLY IS EXTREMELY EMBARRASSED. SHE STARTS SINGING.

'Bright eyes, burning like fire.'

SHE RUNS OFF.

JANICE & RAY
VEGETABLE TEMPURA

JANICE AND RAY ARE SITTING ON THE SOFA.

JANICE	Well, you won't believe this one.
RAY	This one is unbelievable.
JANICE	About three weeks ago we was in Leeds.
RAY	We'd been to see her brother. Don't ask.
JANICE	Anyhow, we're on our way back and we thought we'd stop for a pub lunch. What was that pub called?
RAY	No idea.
JANICE	Anyhow, we gets in ...
RAY	Listen to this.
JANICE	And they were all from Thailand, weren't they?
RAY	Not the customers, the people doing the food.
JANICE	All of them, from Thailand.
RAY	Chinese, basically.
JANICE	You went mad, didn't you?
RAY	All I wanted, right, was fish and chips, maybe a pie.
JANICE	But all they did was this Thai food. Food from Thailand.
RAY	This is in Leeds.
JANICE	So you asked if they did chips, didn't you?
RAY	Now you tell me somewhere that don't do chips.
JANICE	No chips. Well, you went mad, didn't you?
RAY	I'm only flesh and blood.
JANICE	So the woman says, 'why don't you try vegetable ...' what were it called?
RAY	Tempura.
JANICE	So we've ordered two of 'em and two lager shandies, didn't we?
RAY	Just half each.
JANICE	Well, this tempura stuff arrived, didn't it?
RAY	This is unbelievable.
JANICE	Well, he went absolutely mad, didn't you?

RAY	Do you know what it is, eh? This, this tempura, right, shall I tell you? Battered veg.
JANICE	We couldn't believe it, could we?
RAY	Battered veg.
JANICE	Nowt with it.
RAY	Veg, battered.
JANICE	Well actually there was summat with it, weren't there?
RAY	Oh, listen to this.
JANICE	Spicy jam.
RAY	Seriously. Little blob of jam, jam, like that, but spicy.
JANICE	Battered veg with spicy jam.
RAY	The dirty bastards.
JANICE	But that's not the best bit.
RAY	Oh, two plates of battered veg, right, blob of spicy jam like that, two lager shandies.
JANICE	Halves.
RAY	Eleven pound forty.
JANICE	Not even pints.
RAY	Eleven pound forty for battered veg.
JANICE	The dirty, evil, robbing bastards.

DEREK FAYE NEWSAGENT

VIVIENNE (NEWSAGENT)	(TO OTHER CUSTOMER) Five pounds and another five makes ten. Thank you.
DEREK	Morning. How are we today?
VIVIENNE	Morning, Derek. Oh yeah, can't complain. Do you want to pay for your papers?
DEREK	Yes please, Vivienne.
VIVIENNE	And where were you yesterday?
DEREK	Mother and I had a little day out.

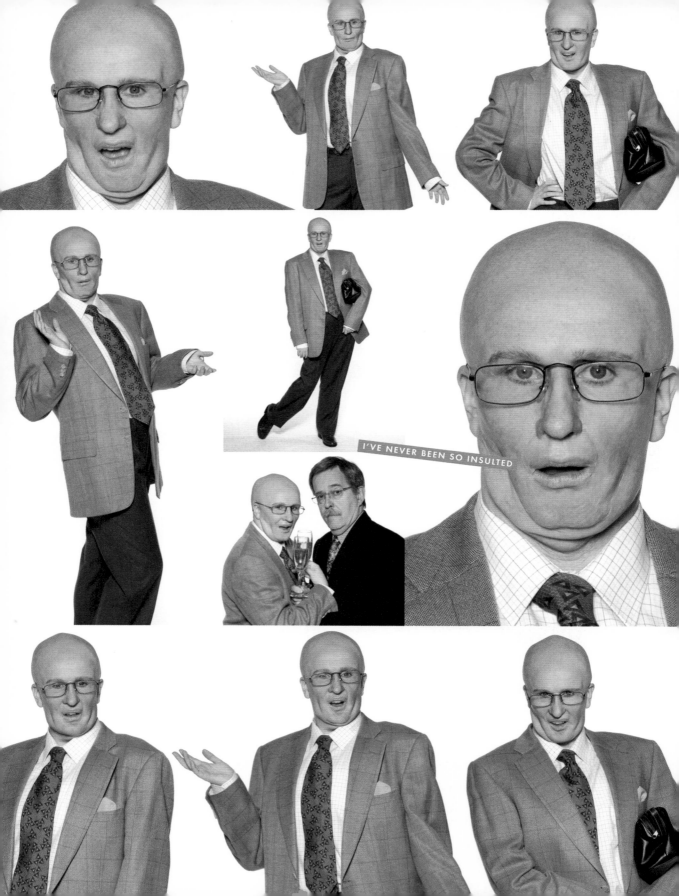

I'VE NEVER BEEN SO INSULTED

IT'S A GENTLEMAN'S SPONGE BAG. COME ON LEONARD, WE'RE OFF!

VIVIENNE	Oh lovely. That's six pounds please, Derek.
	And these as well?
DEREK	Er, yes. Er, £2.50 and £1.50.
VIVIENNE	Right, that's ten pounds exactly please, Derek. Thank you.
	Derek, can I ask your advice on something?
DEREK	Who, dear? Me, dear? Advice, dear? Yes, dear.
VIVIENNE	It's something delicate.
DEREK	Well you know me, dear, I'm discretion personified.
VIVIENNE	It's Paul, our eldest. Well he's ... well, we think he might be gay.
DEREK	Oh, I see.
VIVIENNE	In your experience, do you think we should ask him, or do you think we should wait for him to tell us?
DEREK	What do you mean, 'in my experience'?
VIVIENNE	Well, did you tell your mother you were gay, or did she know already?
DEREK	I beg pardon?
VIVIENNE	Oh I'm sorry, I didn't mean to be rude.
DEREK	How very dare you?! How very dare you? Mother and I have been coming in this shop for twenty-five years and I have never been so insulted.
VIVIENNE	Derek, I'm sorry, I've just always assumed ...
DEREK	Just because a man wears a little bit of foundation and takes care of his appearance, you automatically accuse him of hiding the sausage? Well I find you impertinent.
VIVIENNE	I don't know what to say.
DEREK	'Just always assumed'? How very dare you?!
	HE MARCHES OUT, BUT COMES BACK FOR THE MAGAZINES.
DEREK	I forgot Mother's magazines.
VIVIENNE	They're here. *Wildlife Countryside* and *Hot Muscle*?
DEREK	She's been very ill.

HOW MANY HOW MUCH
SWEARING

KATE AND ELLEN ARE WORKING AT THEIR DESKS.

KATE	You've been to China, haven't you?
ELLEN	No.
KATE	I thought you had.
ELLEN	No, not me.
KATE	I could have sworn it was you that went to China.
ELLEN	No, I've never been to China.
KATE	Incredible language, Chinese.
ELLEN	Hmm.
KATE	'Chee pok at chow. Chee pok at chow.' Sounds a bit like that, doesn't it?
ELLEN	Yeah. Listen, I've really got to get on with this, so ...
KATE	Do you know, there are no swear words in the Chinese language.
ELLEN	Right.
KATE	We were having a conversation about swearing in the workplace at lunch.
ELLEN	Were you?
KATE	Yeah, a really good conversation actually.
ELLEN	I'm sure. Look, I'm not being rude, but I've really got to finish this.
KATE	Guess which swear word people find most offensive?
ELLEN	Oh.
KATE	Go on, guess which swear word people in this office find the most offensive?
ELLEN	Well I really wouldn't know.
KATE	Of course you wouldn't, that's what makes guessing such a brilliant game.
ELLEN	Um ...
KATE	Come on.
ELLEN	Well I don't swear very much.
KATE	It doesn't matter, join in the game.
ELLEN	I suppose it depends on the individual.
KATE	Come on, which swear word did everyone in this office collectively find the most offensive?

ELLEN	I haven't a clue.
KATE	Just take a bloody guess! Look, there's one already.
ELLEN	I'm really no good at this sort of thing.
KATE	It's just a bit of fun, guess!
ELLEN	Um ...
KATE	Come on!
ELLEN	Tit wank.
KATE	Tit wank? Tit wank? When have you ever heard anyone in this office say tit wank?
ELLEN	I said I didn't know.
KATE	Anyway, tit wank is two swear words, not one, so try again.
ELLEN	I think it might be hyphenated.
KATE	Come on!
ELLEN	Willy?
KATE	Willy? Willy?! I said the most offensive swear word in the office, not the playground.
ELLEN	Twat?
KATE	No, come on.
ELLEN	Tosser.
KATE	No.
ELLEN	Tosspot.
KATE	No.
ELLEN	Tossed off.
KATE	Stop tossing! Come on.
ELLEN	Phallus.
KATE	What?
ELLEN	Minge?
KATE	Right, forget it.
ELLEN	Frig. It's frig, isn't it?
KATE	No.
ELLEN	Jizz?

KATE	(BEHIND HER HAND) Cunt.
	The most offensive swear word to people in this office is (BEHIND HER HAND) cunt.
ELLEN	That word is so offensive!
KATE	Yes, it is.
ELLEN	Are you sure people in this office use that word? I've never heard them.
KATE	That's because they're usually talking about you, not to you.

BOOB JOB BABE

WE'RE ON THE SET OF AN AMERICAN HOSPITAL DRAMA.

DR SCOTT	Thank you for coming, Annie, take a seat.
ANNIE	So, what's the problem this time?
DR SCOTT	Annie, I think you know. Your methods of late have become somewhat unorthodox.
ANNIE	I get results, Robert, and I save lives.
DR SCOTT	You overruled the decisions of two senior doctors.
ANNIE	I saved the lives of three people who would otherwise have died had I been too polite to intervene.
DR SCOTT	You're making enemies around here, Annie. I'd be careful if I were you.
ANNIE	Funny, I thought I was making a difference.
DR SCOTT	For what it's worth, I think you're one of the most talented doctors to come to this hospital in a long time, but my advice: don't be a maverick.
ANNIE	Of course, I know what all this is really about. It's because I'm a woman!
DIRECTOR	(OUT OF VIEW) Cut! Okay, guys, that's a wrap. We'll pick it up on Monday.
	FILM LEADER FLASHES. THE ACTION RESUMES ON MONDAY.
DIRECTOR	(OUT OF VIEW) Mark it. Action.
DR SCOTT	For what it's worth, I think you're one of the most talented doctors to come to this hospital in a long time, but my advice: don't be a maverick.
ANNIE	Of course, I know what all this is really about ...
	ANNIE TURNS TO CAMERA. SINCE THE LAST SHOOT SHE HAS OBVIOUSLY HAD A BOOB JOB AND NOW HAS A HUGE CLEAVAGE.

281

ANNIE   ... It's because I'm a woman!

DR SCOTT   Don't be ridiculous.

ANNIE   Oh come on, Robert, if Jack Morgan had done this, or any other junior doctor for that matter, they'd have been applauded. This isn't about hospital policy or protocol, this is plain old-fashioned double standards.

HE IS HAVING DIFFICULTY CONCENTRATING.

DR SCOTT   For God's sakes, get a hold of yourself. There's no such thing.

ANNIE   Open your eyes, Robert, it happens all the time.

DR SCOTT   You're not seriously going to file a complaint on the grounds of sexism?

DIRECTOR   (OUT OF VIEW) Okay, let's hold it there. George, George, we're losing your eyeline. Okay, let's pick it up. Action.

DR SCOTT   For God's sakes, get a hold of yourself, it's no such thing.

ANNIE   Oh open your eyes, Robert, it happens all the time.

HE IS STILL TRANSFIXED BY HER BUST.

DR SCOTT   You're not seriously going to file a complaint on the grounds of sexism?

ANNIE   You try and stop me. I'm going to drag this hospital into the twenty-first century if it's the last thing I do.

DOCTOR SCOTT'S HANDS APPEAR IN ANNIE'S SHOT, REACHING TOWARDS HER CHEST.

ANNIE   (NOT IN CHARACTER) What are you doing?

DIRECTOR   (OUT OF VIEW) Hold it there. George, George, are you okay?

DR SCOTT   (NOT IN CHARACTER) Yeah, I'm sorry.

FILM LEADER FLASHES BETWEEN TAKES.

DIRECTOR   (OUT OF VIEW) Okay, mark it. Action.

DR SCOTT   Frankly, the way you behaved, I think you're getting off lightly with a warning. Annie, Annie, a minute, I...

UNABLE TO CONTROL HIMSELF ANY LONGER, HE BURIES HIS FACE IN HER CHEST AND MAKES NUZZLING NOISES.

ANNIE   (NOT IN CHARACTER) Gross.

DIRECTOR   (OUT OF VIEW) Cut!

ANNIE   Gross.

FILM LEADER FLASHES

LAUREN GAY

LAUREN AND LIESE ARE SITTING IN THE CLASSROOM, EATING THEIR LUNCH.

LIESE	Did you see that thing on last night about plastic surgery?
LAUREN	Did you see it though? Oh my God, that was well bad, I thought I was going to be sick or something.
LIESE	Did you see that woman having liposuction though?
LAUREN	Did you see it though? Did you see when they ripped open her stomach though? Did you see what her fat looked like though?
LIESE	I nearly puked up, man. All that white stuff mixed up with blood.
LAUREN	Innit though?
LIESE	Did you see how they get it out though?
LAUREN	Oh my God, did you see it though? That big metal contraption thing, they stuck it in her bum innit, sucking out the blubber. I can't eat no more.

SHE PUTS HER YOGHURT DOWN.

LIESE	Did you see how much it cost though?
LAUREN	Did you see it though? Three thousand pound, can you believe it? I'm definitely getting that when I'm older.
LIESE	You better start saving now then, innit?

A MALE TEACHER ENTERS.

TEACHER	Hello, girls.
LAUREN/LIESE	Alright.
TEACHER	Why aren't you outside? It's a nice day, you know.
LIESE	It's boring outside, sir.
TEACHER	Well if you don't mind me joining you, I need to prep for my next lesson.
LAUREN	That's fine.

THE GIRLS STARE AT THE TEACHER.

LAUREN	I like your trainers, sir.
TEACHER	Thank you.
LAUREN	Where did you get them?
TEACHER	I bought them in New York.
LAUREN	Is it? Have you got a lot of shoes, sir?

TEACHER	A few pairs.
LAUREN	Are you gay, sir?
TEACHER	What?
LAUREN	Are you gay, sir?
TEACHER	Lauren, please.
LAUREN	Are you gay though, sir?
TEACHER	No of course I'm not gay.
LAUREN	Are you homophobic, sir?
TEACHER	Am I what?
LAUREN	Are you homophobic, sir?
TEACHER	No of course not.
LAUREN	So you're gay then?
TEACHER	No I'm not.
LAUREN	Do your friends know you're gay?
TEACHER	Oh for goodness sake ...
LAUREN	Are you their funny gay friend, sir?
TEACHER	All right, that's enough.
LAUREN	Do you know Graham Norton, sir?
TEACHER	Oh ...
LAUREN	Are you Graham Norton's bitch, sir? Do you love him, sir?
TEACHER	No, Lauren, I don't love Graham Norton.
LAUREN	Did Graham Norton break your heart, sir?
TEACHER	Lauren, I'm actually married with two children.
LAUREN	Are you in the closet, sir?
TEACHER	Oh for goodness sake.
LAUREN	Come out of the closet, sir.
TEACHER	Lauren ...
LAUREN	You should come out of the closet though.
TEACHER	Lauren, please.
LAUREN	It's only fair on your wife.
TEACHER	I'm warning you.

LAUREN	Is your wife a lesbian, sir?
TEACHER	Right, I'm getting angry now.
LAUREN	Are you a militant gay, sir?
TEACHER	What?
LAUREN	Do you go on marches?
TEACHER	Lauren, for goodness sake, how many times, I'm not gay.
LAUREN	Are you homophobic, sir?
TEACHER	You don't even know what homophobic means.
LAUREN	I don't need to, I ain't gay.
TEACHER	All right, now that's enough. You two should be ashamed of yourselves. This sort of behaviour is totally unacceptable and you, you young lady, you are skating on very thin ice, and believe you me, you are this far away from being expelled.
LAUREN	Am I bovvered?
TEACHER	Lauren ...
LAUREN	Am I bovvered though?
TEACHER	Lauren, please.
LAUREN	I ain't bovvered though.
TEACHER	Oh for goodness sake.
LAUREN	Is my face bovvered?
TEACHER	Lauren ...
LAUREN	Is my face bovvered?
TEACHER	Listen to me.
LAUREN	Look at my face.
TEACHER	Lauren ...
LAUREN	Look at my face.
TEACHER	Lauren ...
LAUREN	Look at my face.
TEACHER	Lauren ...
LAUREN	Are you looking at my face?
TEACHER	Yes.
LAUREN	Is any part of it bovvered?

TEACHER	Oh, you sound ridiculous.
LAUREN	You sound gay.
TEACHER	What do you think your friends really think of you?
LAUREN	I don't care, 'cause I ain't bovvered.
TEACHER	Oh for goodness sake.
LAUREN	Face.
TEACHER	Lauren ...
LAUREN	Look.
TEACHER	I don't ...
LAUREN	Face.
TEACHER	Please ...
LAUREN	Bovvered.
TEACHER	Can't you ...
LAUREN	Face.
TEACHER	Look ...
LAUREN	Bovvered.
TEACHER	Can we ...
LAUREN	Look.
TEACHER	Will you just ...
LAUREN	Face.
TEACHER	Can ...
LAUREN	Bovvered.
TEACHER	Look ...
LAUREN	'Shut that door. Shut that door.'
TEACHER	Look!
LAUREN	Face.
TEACHER	Look ....
LAUREN	Look.
TEACHER	Can you just ...
LAUREN	Bovvered.
TEACHER	You've got ...

LAUREN	Face.
TEACHER	No don't ...
LAUREN	Bovvered.
TEACHER	No ...
LAUREN	'I'm free! I'm free!'
TEACHER	What?
LAUREN	'Shut that door, shut that door.'
TEACHER	Look, Lauren!
LAUREN	'Ooh Betty, Ooh Betty!'
TEACHER	Can you ...
LAUREN	Face.
TEACHER	Look ...
LAUREN	Look.
TEACHER	Can you not ...
LAUREN	Bovvered.
TEACHER	Just ...
LAUREN	Face. I ain't bovvered!
TEACHER	Lauren! I am so disappointed in you. God, when everyone else in this school had given up hope on you, I was the only one prepared to give you another chance. Unlike you, I am bovvered. I feel let down, and, well, to be honest, I'm a little bit hurt.
LAUREN	You are gay, sir.

PAUL & SAM REVERSAL

PAUL IS IN THE BEDROOM, READING A NEWSPAPER. SAM ENTERS.

SAM	You are not going to believe what's happened to me today.
PAUL	What have you done?
SAM	I'm not joking, you are gonna die when you hear what I did.
PAUL	What's happened?
SAM	I can't tell you.
PAUL	Why not?

SAM	'Cause you're gonna die.
PAUL	Tell me what you've done.
SAM	This morning, right, I've gone down the shop by the bus stop to get some milk, you know like I do sometimes when we run out of milk, and the man behind the counter says, 'that's three twenty-five, please.' And I thought, hold on, three twenty-five for two pints of milk, that's a bit steep, innit? Then I've looked down. I'm only holding a Marie Claire, Hair & Beauty and a Caramel Wispa.
PAUL	What are you like?
SAM	I know. But that ain't it.
PAUL	That ain't it?
SAM	So, I give him a fiver, he looks at me and he says ...
PAUL	What's he say?
SAM	He says, 'I can't take this, love.'
PAUL	He can't take it?
SAM	He says, 'this ain't a fiver.'
PAUL	It ain't a fiver?
SAM	It weren't a fiver!
PAUL	It weren't a fiver?
SAM	It weren't a fiver. You know what I've done, don't ya?
PAUL	What you done?
SAM	I've opened me purse to give him the money, I've pulled out a note, I've give him the note, he's taken the note, I'm standing waiting for me change, he's give me one look, he's staring at the note, he said, 'I can't take this.' I said, 'what do you mean, you can't take this?' He said, 'this ain't a fiver, this is five euros.'
PAUL	What, you've given him five euros?
SAM	I've give him five euros.
	SHE LAUGHS SILENTLY.
PAUL	Yeah, well, it's an easy mistake to make.
	PAUL GOES BACK TO HIS NEWSPAPER. SAM STARES AT HIM BECAUSE HE ISN'T LAUGHING WITH HER. SHE MOVES AWAY FROM HIM, CONFUSED.

SAM	I ain't told you what else happened to me today.
PAUL	What happened?
SAM	You are gonna wet yourself when I tell you this.
PAUL	What did you do?
SAM	Lunchtime, right, I've gone down Gino's with Shelley and that new girl who sits by the machine, don't really like her but she brought in panettone cake on her first day and everyone deserves a chance. So we get to the counter and Shelley says, 'I think I'm gonna have one of them buffalo mozzarella sandwiches'. And I said, 'I think I will too as it goes'. The new girl couldn't make up her mind, so we just left her there. I mean, I'm not Nelson Mandela. I get back to me desk ...
PAUL	Yeah?
SAM	I sit down, I open me bag ...
PAUL	Yeah?
SAM	You'll never guess what's in my sandwich.
PAUL	What?
SAM	Egg and cress!
PAUL	No!
SAM	My life, I've picked up an egg and cress instead of buffalo mozzarella!
	SHE LAUGHS SILENTLY.
PAUL	Yeah, well you picked up the wrong one, it can happen.
	HE RETURNS TO THE PAPER, AGAIN WITHOUT LAUGHING. SAM LOOKS DESPERATE. SHE MOVES AWAY FROM HIM AGAIN, STILL CONFUSED.
PAUL	'Ere, Sam.
	PAUL STARTS TO LAUGH.
SAM	You've been having me on!
PAUL	I've been having you on!
SAM	You've been having me on since I walked through that door!
PAUL	Since you walked through that door!
SAM	I thought you thought it weren't funny!
PAUL	Not funny? 'I've only given him five euros!'
SAM	I've give him five euros!

PAUL	You thought it was a fiver.
SAM	I know!
PAUL	And then the sandwich shop ...
SAM	Don't!
PAUL	Egg and cress. You thought you was getting buffalo mozzarella!
SAM	I know!
	THEY LAUGH SILENTLY.
PAUL	What is buffalo mozzarella?
SAM	I don't know!
	THEY COLLAPSE LAUGHING.

JANICE & RAY ESCARGOT

JANICE AND RAY ARE SITTING ON THE SOFA.

RAY	One word – 'escargot'.
JANICE	This is in Paris.
JANICE & RAY	The dirty bastards!

TACTLESS WOMAN CHARADES

A PARTY IS TAKING PLACE.

DAVID	(SIGNS TO TOM) 'I like your jacket.'
TOM	Oh thank you. I bought it last week.
	Ally!
ALLY	Hello, I heard you were here.
TOM	Yeah, do you know David?
ALLY	No, hello, I'm Ally.
DAVID	(SIGNS TO TOM) 'I'm sure I met her at Jane's wedding.'
ALLY	Film. How many words?
TOM	No ...

ALLY	Oh. Book?
DAVID	(SIGNS TO TOM) 'Why don't you tell her I'm deaf.'
TOM	No, no ...
ALLY	Slow down! Do the whole thing.
DAVID	(ANGRILY SIGNS TO TOM) 'Just tell her I'm deaf.'
TOM	Yeah, okay.
ALLY	Psycho!
TOM	He's deaf.
ALLY	My Left Foot.
TOM	No, he's deaf.
ALLY	Hmm? Right. Yeah, right, God, no, yeah, God, no, yeah, I didn't mean, can, sorry, can you tell him, I didn't mean ...
TOM	You can tell him yourself.
ALLY	(MIMING) Right. So. Hello. (WAVES) I'm sorry, I didn't mean to offend you. Hmm. (YAWNS) Are you tired? I'm, I'm tired. (RUBS EYES) I'm going to go to bed now. Downstairs. (MIMES GOING DOWNSTAIRS)

SHE LEAVES, VERY EMBARRASSED.

HOW MANY HOW MUCH
PAY RISE QUICKIE

KATE AND ELLEN ARE WORKING AT THEIR DESKS.

KATE	My boyfriend got a pay rise.
ELLEN	Thirty-seven thousand five hundred a year, plus perks, plus a company car.
KATE	Yeah.

KATE GETS UP AND GOES OVER TO ELLEN. SHE POURS A STRAWBERRY MILKSHAKE OVER ELLEN'S HEAD THEN GOES BACK TO HER DESK.

OLD WOMAN TOMMY UPSON

THE OLD WOMAN IS SITTING IN HER LIVING ROOM. HER GRANDSON
ENTERS.

OLD WOMAN	Is that you, sweetheart?
GRANDSON	Hello, Nan.
OLD WOMAN	Here he is. You come up and see me?
GRANDSON	You know I have.
OLD WOMAN	(CACKLES) Oh you are a good boy.
GRANDSON	You all right?
OLD WOMAN	Yeah, lovely. D'you bring me up me bits?
GRANDSON	Madeira cake.
OLD WOMAN	Oh, that's it, lovely. Oh, I just fancied a bit of madeira cake. You don't mind, do you, love?
GRANDSON	Course not.
OLD WOMAN	Oh that's it, look at that, I'll have a go at that later. (CACKLES)
GRANDSON	What are you laughing for?
OLD WOMAN	Oh God knows!
GRANDSON	Have you been drinking?
OLD WOMAN	I might have had a livener or three, what's it got to do with you? Ha ha ha ha. D'you want a nice bacon sandwich, son? I'll make you a nice bacon sandwich if you like.
GRANDSON	I'm all right thanks, Nan.
OLD WOMAN	I don't mind, throw a couple of rashers in the pan, bit of fat, crisp it up. Butter a few slices, you can have it with that nice red sauce you like.
GRANDSON	Nan, I don't want anything.
OLD WOMAN	What do you want then, a bit of coleslaw?
GRANDSON	Wouldn't mind a cup of tea.
OLD WOMAN	Oh I can't be messing about with cups of tea, love. It ain't an hotel. 'Ere, 'ere, I'll tell you who I saw, oh I'll tell you who I saw today. Coming out of the post office, bumped right into him, I ain't seen him in years, what a smashing fella.
GRANDSON	Who's that?

OLD WOMAN	Who's what?
GRANDSON	In the post office?
OLD WOMAN	I was in there this morning.
GRANDSON	Yeah, you said. Who did you see in there?
OLD WOMAN	Here, I'll tell you who I saw in there, young Tommy Upson.
GRANDSON	Who's Tommy Upson?
OLD WOMAN	Who?
GRANDSON	Tommy Upson?
OLD WOMAN	I saw him in the post office this morning. Yeah, used to live down Ormand Yard when we were kids. Oh, we have had a laugh.
	WE HEAR THE TOILET FLUSH.
GRANDSON	Who's that?
OLD WOMAN	I just told you who it is, Tommy fucking Upson! What's the matter with me? God forgive me for swearing, you'll make my nerves bad, you will.
	TOMMY ENTERS.
TOMMY	Aye aye.
OLD WOMAN	Here he is. Is that better, sweetheart?
TOMMY	Oh, I'm about a stone lighter now. Flushed itself.
OLD WOMAN	Oh yes.
TOMMY	I'll tell you something, it's good to see you've got plenty of loo rolls in there, thirty-six I counted.
OLD WOMAN	Yeah, well they don't eat nothing, do they?
TOMMY	I can't stand when you go to someone's house for a pony and you've got to ration your wipes.
OLD WOMAN	You never have to hold back up here, Tom, and I mean that sincerely.
TOMMY	Where are we?
OLD WOMAN	Here you are, go on, sweetheart, sit back down.
TOMMY	That's it, that's it.
OLD WOMAN	There's a drink there. Here you are, Tom. This is my Diane's boy, Jamie.
TOMMY	Hello, son.
GRANDSON	Nice to meet you.
TOMMY	He's home early, ain't he got a job?

OLD WOMAN	No, he's tried everything, he ain't interested.
GRANDSON	I'm at university.
TOMMY	Oh that's right. Your Nan said something about you being gay.
GRANDSON	I'm not gay, I've got a girlfriend.
OLD WOMAN	Very plain girl she is, but then again he is short.
TOMMY	My brother, he had a gay dog.
OLD WOMAN	Who, your Billy?
TOMMY	Yeah, that's right. Cost him a fortune in vet's bills.
GRANDSON	A gay dog?
TOMMY	No, not gay, um, diabetic. Some kind of disability.
GRANDSON	Being gay isn't a disability.
OLD WOMAN	Well it ain't exactly helped you in getting a job, has it!
TOMMY	You want to get out and push, son. When I was your age, I was up to my eyeballs in the shit. Three kids to feed and a Welsh dresser to pay for. I had no time for reading. My wife Lily … she was a grafter.
OLD WOMAN	Very hard working woman, she was.
TOMMY	Oh. I was blessed every day that I was with her. She used to model herself on Coco Chanel.
OLD WOMAN	That's right.
TOMMY	She always wore a matching hat, shoes, gloves, handbag. Not a lot of people can pull off a look like that in a motorised wheelchair.
OLD WOMAN	She had a lot of style, I'll say that about her.
TOMMY	I can't believe she's gone.
OLD WOMAN	She's with you, darling, she's always there, in your heart.
TOMMY	Oh I know. I know she is.
OLD WOMAN	Yeah. Now don't get upset, sweetheart, 'cause you'll start me off.
TOMMY	(SINGS) 'When you're weary, feeling small.'
OLD WOMAN	Go on, love.
TOMMY	'When tears are in your eyes … I will dry them all.'
OLD WOMAN	(JOINING IN) 'Dry them all.' That's it, sweetheart.
TOMMY	'I'm on your side.

Oh, when times get rough.'

OLD WOMAN	Go on, love.
BOTH	'And friends just can't be found.
	Like a bridge over ...'

TOMMY IS STRUGGLING TO STAND UP.

TOMMY	Help me! Help me!
BOTH	'Troubled water
	I will lay me down
	Like a bridge over troubled water
	I will lay me down.'

TOMMY THROWS HIS BEER GLASS BEHIND THE SOFA AND SUCKS ON HIS INHALER.

END CREDITS

OLD WOMAN	Oh, sweetheart, don't be upset, darling. She's looking down on you.
TOMMY	I know.
OLD WOMAN	She's looking down on you, sweetheart, don't you worry about that.
TOMMY	I know she is.
OLD WOMAN	She won't want to see you like this, will she?
TOMMY	No, she wouldn't want to see me upset though.
OLD WOMAN	That's it.
TOMMY	I'm gonna go. There's a feature length Taggart on tonight.

TOMMY HUGS OLD WOMAN AND SNORTS.

OLD WOMAN	Well you know where I am, sweetheart.
TOMMY	I know where you are. Ta ra.
OLD WOMAN	Ta ra darling.
TOMMY	Take care.
	Look after her, gay boy.
	Ta ta!
OLD WOMAN	Ta ta, Tommy, sweetheart, mind how you go, love.

THE OLD WOMAN SEES TOMMY OUT THEN COMES BACK INTO THE ROOM.

OLD WOMAN   What a fucking liberty! He's used all me fucking lavatory paper! What was he fucking doing in there?! Making fucking flags! And as for his old woman, Coco Chanel?! More like Coco the fucking Clown!

END OF SERIES 2

Written by CATHERINE TATE &
DERREN LITTEN

With ASCHLIN DITTA
MATHEW HORNE
ARTHUR MATHEWS
BRUCE MacKINNON

Starring CATHERINE TATE

With MATHEW HORNE
ELLA KENION
DERREN LITTEN
BRUCE MacKINNON
JONATHAN McGUINNESS
ANGELA McHALE
LEE ROSS
NIKY WARDLEY

And BUKI ARMSTRONG
JAMES HOLMES
JONATHAN BEE
ALAN DAVID
SEETA INDRANI
FRANCESCA ISHERWOOD

With special guest MICHAEL BRANDON

Documentary Narrator REBECCA FRONT

Title Music KIRSTY MacCOLL
Casting Director SARAH CROWE
Graphic Design TIM SEARLE
Stage Manager KATE HOLDSWORTH-JONES
Art Director CLAIRE JOHNSTON
Production Buyer KATRINA DUCE

THE CATHERINE TATE SHOW
SCRIPTS
SERIES 1

Properties Master	ANDY BEALES
1st Assistant Director	LEE TREVOR
2nd Assistant Director	BART BAILEY
Location Manager	JODI MOORE
Production Co-ordinator	HOLLY SAIT
Production Accountant	MIKE AMOS
Production Secretary	REBECCA CALLAS
Production Runner	ADAM CHALK
Script Supervisor	HAYLEY BOYD
Head of Production	TOBY WARD
Director of Photography	JOHN SORAPURE
Gaffer	MARTIN 'DAR' HEALEY
Camera Supervisor	PRAVIN SHETTY
Sound Supervisor	BOB NEWTON
Vision Mixer	BARBARA HICKS
Floor Manager	NICK KEENE
Make-up Designer	VANESSA WHITE
Costume Designer	LUCIA SANTA MARIA
Wardrobe Supervisor	CAT MORGAN-JONES
Dubbing	ROB BUTLER BIGGS
Lighting Director	CHRIS CLAYTON
Editor	CHRIS WADSWORTH
Production Designer	JO SUTHERLAND
Line Producer	JO HUNTER
Executive Producer for the BBC	LUCY LUMSDEN
Director	GORDON ANDERSON
Producer	GEOFFREY PERKINS

A TIGER ASPECT PRODUCTION FOR THE BBC

© BBC 2004

Written by DERREN LITTEN &
CATHERINE TATE

With GORDON ANDERSON
ASCHLIN DITTA
JENNY LECOAT
ELLA KENION
NIKY WARDLEY

Additional Material THE CAST

Starring CATHERINE TATE

With ASCHLIN DITTA
MATHEW HORNE
ELLA KENION
DERREN LITTEN
JONATHAN McGUINNESS
ANGELA McHALE
LEE ROSS
NIKY WARDLEY

And THOMAS BYRNE
JOHN CARLISLE
ANDY DENNEHY
SUE ELLIOTT-NICHOLLS
CHARLIE HICKS
FRANCESCA ISHERWOOD
SALLY ANN MATTHEWS
GEOFFREY PERKINS
ROBIN WEAVER
BEN WILLBOND
MAE WRIGHT
TAYLOR WRIGHT

With special guests ROGER ALLAM
MICHAEL BRANDON

THE
CATHERINE
TATE
SHOW
SCRIPTS

SERIES 2

JILL HALFPENNY
PETER KAY
GERALDINE MCNULTY
BRIAN MURPHY
SIOBHAN REDMOND
HUGH SACHS
UNA STUBBS
PAUL WHITEHOUSE

Documentary Narrator	REBECCA FRONT
Casting Director	KATE DAY
Title Music	HOWARD GOODALL
Graphic Design	TIM SEARLE
Stage Manager	LIZ SUMMERS
Art Director	NEIL BARNES
Production Buyer	KATRINA DUCE
Properties Master	ANDY BEALES
1st Assistant Director	JULIE SYKES
2nd Assistant Director	KIERAN BAINE
3rd Assistant Director	FINBARR HOPSON
Location Manager	JAMES LINDSAY
Production Co-ordinator	HOLLY BOWCOTT
Production Accountant	JACKIE SMITH
Production Secretary	HOLLY INGRAM
Script Supervisor	PAMELA WYLDE
Head of Production	TOBY WARD
Director of Photography	JOHN SORAPURE
Location Sound	BOB NEWTON
Gaffer	MARTIN 'DAR' HEALEY
Camera Supervisor	DUNCAN UNSWORTH
Sound Supervisor	ANDY TAPLEY
Vision Mixer	BARBARA HICKS
Prosthetics	NEILL GORTON

Make-up Designer	VANESSA WHITE
Costume Designer	LUCIA SANTA MARIA
Wardrobe Supervisors	EMMA ROSENTHAL
	CAT MORGAN-JONES
Dubbing Mixer	ROB BUTLER BIGGS
Editor	CHRIS WADSWORTH
Lighting Director	CHRIS CLAYTON
Production Designer	JO SUTHERLAND
Line Producer	PHILIPPA CATT
Executive Producer for the BBC	LUCY LUMSDEN
Director	GORDON ANDERSON
Producer	GEOFFREY PERKINS

A TIGER ASPECT PRODUCTION FOR THE BBC
© TIGER ASPECT PRODUCTIONS 2005